D1531356

From BOYCOTT *to* ANNIHILATION

From BOYCOTT *to* ANNIHILATION

The Economic Struggle of German Jews, 1933–1943

AVRAHAM BARKAI

Translated by William Templer

Published for Brandeis University Press by
University Press of New England
Hanover and London

University Press of New England
Brandeis University
Brown University
Clark University
University of Connecticut
Dartmouth College
University of New Hampshire
University of Rhode Island
Tufts University
University of Vermont

Printed in the United States of America

∞

Library of Congress Cataloging in Publication Data
Barkai, Avraham.
[Vom Boykott zur "Entjudung". English]
From boycott to annihilation : the economic struggle of German Jews, 1933–1943 / Avraham Barkai ; translated by William Templer.
p. cm.—(Tauber Institute for the Study of European Jewry series ; 11)
Translation of: Vom Boykott zur "Entjudung."
Includes bibliographical references.
ISBN 0-87451-490-8
1. Jew—Germany—Economic conditions. 2. Jews—Germany—History—1933–1945. 3. Germany—Ethnic relations. 4. Germany—Economic conditions—1933–1945. I. Title. II. Series.
DS135.G33B37313 1989
943'.004924—dc20 89-40228
CIP

1 2 3 4 5

Translated with the financial assistance of Inter Nationes.

The Tauber Institute for the Study of European Jewry, established by a gift to Brandeis University from Dr. Laszlo N. Tauber, is dedicated to the memory of the victims of Nazi persecutions between 1933 and 1945. The Institute seeks to study the history and culture of European Jewry in the modern period. The Institute has a special interest in studying the causes, nature, and consequences of the European Jewish catastrophe and seeks to explore them within the context of modern European diplomatic, intellectual, political, and social history. The Tauber Institute for the Study of European Jewry is organized on a multidisciplinary basis, with the participation of scholars in history, Judaic studies, political science, sociology, comparative literature, and other disciplines.

THE TAUBER INSTITUTE FOR THE STUDY OF EUROPEAN JEWRY SERIES

Jehuda Reinharz, General Editor

1
GERHARD L. WEINBERG, 1981
World in the Balance: Behind the Scenes of World War II

2
RICHARD COBB, 1983
French and Germans, Germans and French: A Personal Interpretation of France under Two Occupations, 1914–1918/1940–1944

3
EBERHARD JÄCKEL, 1984
Hitler in History

4
Edited by FRANCES MALINO *and* BERNARD WASSERSTEIN, 1985
The Jews in Modern France

5
JACOB KATZ, 1986
The Darker Side of Genius: Richard Wagner's Anti-Semitism

6
Edited by JEHUDA REINHARZ, 1987
Living with Antisemitism: Modern Jewish Responses

7
MICHAEL R. MARRUS, 1987
The Holocaust in History

8
Edited by PAUL MENDES-FLOHR, 1988
The Philosophy of Franz Rosenzweig

9
JOAN G. ROLAND, 1989
Jews in British India: Identity in a Colonial Era

10
Edited by YISRAEL GUTMAN, EZRA MENDELSOHN, JEHUDA REINHARZ, *and* CHONE SHMERUK, 1989
The Jews of Poland Between Two World Wars

11
AVRAHAM BARKAI, 1989
From Boycott to Annihilation: The Economic Struggle of German Jews, 1933–1943

To the memory of

ABRAHAM MARGALIOTH

CONTENTS

PREFACE TO THE ENGLISH EDITION

Economic arguments and motivations became increasingly dominant as secular, modern antisemitism replaced the medieval hatred of the Jews. In Germany, they became the central issues in antisemitic propaganda beginning in the 1870s and were ardently embraced and intensified, after Germany's defeat in World War I, by the numerous *völkisch* splinter groups that eventually constituted the Nazi party. When Hitler came to power in January 1933, this Old Guard looked forward impatiently to the immediate ousting of Jews (*Entjudung*) from the economy and their expropriation, as proclaimed in the NSDAP party program, hoping to gain individual lucrative benefits in the process. For this reason, and because more drastic methods were not yet feasible, the place of German Jews in the economy was the main target of the discriminatory policies pursued by the Nazi regime in its early years. The aim of this policy was to undermine and destroy the material basis of existence of the Jews, thus compelling them to emigrate.

The step-by-step ousting of the Jews from the economy has been the subject of several previous extensive scholarly investigations, to date available only in German. Most important among these is the work of the late Uwe D. Adam and, in particular, the excellent, still indispensable 1966 study by Helmuth Genschel. However, a new attempt to deal with this topic seemed necessary and desirable for two principal reasons: first, the large and growing body of new local and regional historical research has shed valuable light on many facets of the process, so a number of still widely held views among scholars regarding the basic trends of Nazi *Judenpolitik* need to be reevaluated. Second, and even more important, most earlier studies are marred by a skewed and one-sided perspective: The Jews tend to be viewed largely as mere objects of regime and party policy, passive victims of persecution. That is, very little information is presented on the Jewish responses to the barrage of harassments, the ways and means by which those who remained in Germany were able to survive and eke out a living before their ultimate deportation and extermination. Nor is much data given on the manner in which others managed to escape and/or salvage at least a part of their property and assets. The German Jews and their struggle for economic survival, rather than the Nazi policies, are thus the main subject and focus of the present study.

Accordingly, its sources differ significantly from earlier studies. Documentary materials on the anti-Jewish legislative, administrative, and propagandistic measures of the Nazi regime are, of course, a part of our story. Yet the main bulk of documentary evidence utilized here is contained in the still largely untapped reports and working papers of Jewish institutions, mainly the central Reichsvertretung—or, after 1939, the Reichsvereinigung der Juden in Deutschland—and the rarely preserved official files and other documents of the Jewish *Gemeinden* (incorporated local communities).

November 1988 marked the fiftieth anniversary of the wave of pogroms of November 9–10, 1938, in which hundreds of synagogues and thousands of Jewish shops and homes were devastated, one hundred Jews murdered, and many thousands interned in concentration camps, where they were manhandled and tortured. The date provided the occasion for a profuse number of commemorations, scholarly seminars, exhibitions, and religious services, extensively publicized by all German media. These efforts—impressive and in many cases undoubtedly honest and sincere—may mark the continuation and intensification of an ongoing process of historical self-confrontation, as Germans try to grapple and come to terms with their recent past. Alternatively, they may signal an attempt to finally "close past accounts," to put a premature end to these efforts at reorientation of historical memory.

The publication of the original German version of this book in close proximity to the anniversary was, however, not intended to be a part of the general 1988 *Kristallnacht* commemorations. The final version in German was finished in the summer of 1986, and its publication was delayed for technical reasons. I find it necessary to stress this because it is my conviction that the ongoing scholarly debates being given broad coverage in the German and foreign media, such as the recent *Historikerstreit,* should remain, as exclusively as possible, the domain of the Germans themselves. It is unavoidable that this process of trying to redefine their national identity and self-consciousness must take place under the heavy shadow of their recent past; and no one from outside, least of all the surviving victims, can free them from that burden.

In the course of my investigations, I was able to profit from the kind and interested assistance of many people in American, German, and Israeli archives and scientific institutions. My special thanks belong to the staff of the archives and library of Yad Vashem in Jerusalem, the Wiener Library at its new location at the Tel Aviv University, and the Leo Baeck Institutes in Jerusalem and New York. In Germany, the staffs of the Municipal Archives in Duisburg, the Federal Archives in Koblenz, and the State Archives in Düsseldorf, Münster, Berlin, and Berlin-Dahlem have been most helpful. Of the many friends and colleagues whose time I have often taxed, I wish to express my special thanks to Mrs. Danuta Dabrowska of Yad Vashem, Professor Jacob Toury, and Dr. Monika Richarz. The English edition has been made possible by the friendly interest of the Tauber Institute for the Study of European Jewry at Brandeis University and its director, Professor Jehuda Reinharz. I also wish to thank Dr. John Hose, the governor of Brandeis University Press, and the editors and staff of the University Press of New England. Last but not least, I wish to thank Mr. William Templer of the School of History, Tel Aviv University, for his perceptive and insightful translation.

My own scholarly involvement with the subject of this investigation began some ten years ago as part of an extensive research project of Yad Vashem in Jerusalem. It was my unforgettable friend Abraham Margalioth who, in his customarily amicable but persistent manner, persuaded me, after much hesitation on my part, to enter this depressing and often heart-rending field of research. Later, he patiently guided and advised me during all stages of my research. Without his constant support and learned and insightful comments, this book would never have been completed. After his untimely death in the spring of 1987, it is dedicated in sorrow to his memory.

Kibbutz Lehavot Habashan A.B.
January 1989

Introduction

The Social Profile of German Jewry in 1933

At the beginning of the Weimar Republic, the Jews were a declining minority in demographic and economic terms. The hundred years prior to World War I had been the most fortunate period in their long history in Germany. Despite substantial attrition due to emigration, the number of Jews in Germany had risen sharply over the century. The period of demographic and industrial growth since the middle of the nineteenth century had led to their concentration in branches of the economy that had been favored by the general structural changes.[1] Emancipation was also making slow progress, and by the time of the establishment of the Second Empire in 1871, formal legal equality had been achieved. By this time most Jews had also undergone considerable acculturation. However, toward the close of the nineteenth century, signs of demographic and economic crisis began to appear. These were indeed harbingers of later developments during Weimar.

The birth rate had been in decline among Jews since 1880, and their natural rate of growth lagged far behind that of the total population, in contrast with the previous period. The principal reasons underlying this trend lay in the intensified urbanization Jews were undergoing in Germany and the "almost grotesque" abnormality of age distribution patterns in the Jewish population.[2] That deviant pattern was a direct consequence of earlier waves of emigration and the increasingly middle-class character of the Jewish population. The 1910 Jewish population of the Reich—in its 1933 borders—numbered approximately 535,000. That number had climbed to 564,400 by the 1925 census but had fallen back to about 525,000 by January 1933.[3] More than two thirds of the Jewish population lived in urban areas—almost a third in Berlin alone. In contrast, there were still nearly one hundred thousand *Landjuden* (rural Jews) living in localities with populations of less than twenty thousand. That segment of the Jewish community has often been neglected within the general popular conception of German Jewry and has been slighted in research.[4] At the end of the Weimar Republic, the Jewish population was organized in some sixteen hundred *Gemeinden* (incorporated communities), not counting many towns and villages where individual Jewish families lived without setting up any communal organization. Even as late as 1937, there were still some fourteen hundred *Gemeinden* in existence.[5]

The demographic and economic structure of the Jewish population in the Weimar Republic was the consequence of a number of long-term developments.[6] The declining birth rate was the by-product of a wave of emigration among young Jews that had continued on down to the closing decades of the nineteenth century and led to a pattern of marked overaging in the population pyramid. That pattern had only partly been compensated for by the mounting influx of Jews from Eastern Europe. In 1925, 28 percent of all Jews living in Germany were over the age of forty; by 1933, that figure had risen to 33 percent.[7] The process of concentration in large metropolitan areas had begun in earlier decades but accelerated significantly in the twentieth century: in 1910, some 60 percent of all Jews were resident in cities numbering one hundred thousand or more inhabitants, contrasted with 24 percent for the total population. By 1933 the corresponding figures were 70.9 percent for the Jewish population, compared to 30.4 percent for the German population as a whole.[8]

In contrast to the nineteenth century, social and economic structural patterns in the Jewish population had undergone little change up to 1933. More than 60 percent of all gainfully employed Jews were concentrated in the commercial sector, the overwhelming majority of these in retail trade; that percentage had shown little change since 1925 or even since 1907.[9] Similarly, Jews in the sector of industry and crafts were active largely as proprietors of small businesses and shops or as artisans; some 40 percent of the latter also maintained open retail outlets.[10] Of the approximately eighteen thousand Jewish employees in industry, a significant number had positions in the sales departments of larger firms.[11]

Along with this enduring pattern in Jewish occupational structure, quite puzzling in the light of overall economic developments, the characteristic preference among Jews for independent economic pursuits also showed remarkable persistence. In 1925, 51 percent of all Jewish breadwinners were listed as self-employed; in 1933, that number stood at 46 percent. This should be contrasted with corresponding figures of 17 percent and 16 percent for the population as a whole.[12] In a period characterized by an increasing concentration in larger concerns, the Jewish population remained largely a part of the old commercial middle class. Then, as earlier, the Jewish population consisted principally of small entrepreneurs and proprietors of small and medium-size shops active in specific branches of consumer goods trade, along with the employees in these shops. In addition, there was a growing number of Jewish physicians and attorneys; for the most part, these professionals had individual independent practices. In a time of rapid large-scale industrialization and the concentration of capital, Jews adhered to their traditional occupations and social patterns, even though put at a comparative disadvantage as a result. "The gravitation among Jews into independent occupations in the economy, whether as a result of inner inclination or the product of external pressures of the environment, may have reduced their ability to adapt to the changing forms of economic life in industrial Germany."[13]

The statistical data do not point to the presence of any tendency among the Jewish population toward "productivization" or even "proletarianization," such as Jewish social scientists and functionaries at the time believed they could discern.[14] Yet it is important not to overlook a salient structural fact: more than half of all Jewish breadwinners in 1933 were over the age of forty and had therefore selected their chosen vocation before World War I. For this reason, the impact of war, inflation, the economic crisis of the 1920s, and the deteriorating political situation of the Jews was not yet fully reflected in the occupational statistics for 1925 or even for 1933.

Actually, there were a number of indications that a shift had occurred in occupational preferences among Jewish youth during the Weimar period. The commercial occupations of their fathers had lost much of their attraction. Whoever was able wished to go on to university and then choose one of the free professions, giving decided preference to those that facilitated economic independence. Young Jews in less favorable circumstances gravitated toward salaried white-collar professions, particularly in the commercial sector. Between 1907 and 1933, the total number of Jewish white-collar employees rose from 36,400 to 82,800. Of these, 22,900 were employed in the commercial sector in 1907; 50,600 in 1933. They constituted 10.8 percent of all gainfully employed Jews in 1907, a figure that rose to 21 percent by 1933. A large segment of this increase consisted of women; they accounted for approximately 34 percent of all Jewish employees in 1933, although they made up only 15 percent of the self-employed. There can be little doubt that this increase was attributable far more to the deteriorating economic situation among the Jewish population than to any consciously emancipatory change in the status of Jewish women.[15]

In addition, manual jobs in agriculture, artisan crafts, and industry exercised an increasing attraction for young Jews. The attractiveness of this sector derived in significant measure from the hopelessness and material pauperization that had beset the Jewish middle classes as a result of the inflation and Depression. However, it was also given impetus by intentional efforts of certain circles to bring about an "occupational restructuring" among the Jewish population.

The ideological premises that played a role here were highly diverse and often directly conflicting. Under the impact of the first generation of settlers in Palestine, Zionist youth wished to be prepared for life in Palestine, especially on the kibbutz, by participation in agricultural training farms and retraining courses, the so-called *hachshara* centers. In contrast, the agrarian-conservative pioneer ideology of the German right found its Jewish variant in the establishment in 1931 of a settlement of the Association of Jewish War Veterans (*Reichsbund jüdischer Frontsoldaten,* or RjF) in Gross-Gaglau near Kottbus. Most advocates of occupational restructuring, which was the subject of lively discussion at the time in the Jewish press and the public sphere, regarded it as a means to help combat the imminent threat of a "proletarianization" of Jewish youth. Only a small number of economic experts and social workers considered downward mobility into the industrial proletariat as the necessary way out of the critical economic situation besetting the Jewish population.[16]

It is impossible to say how this trend might have developed if it had been allowed to go its course undisturbed. However, when this process was abruptly interrupted in 1933 by the beginning of Nazi rule, no significant change in Jewish occupational structure was as yet in evidence. The only substantial increase in comparison with prewar figures was among the free and academic professions. In 1895, the percentage of Jews in the category Civil Service and Free Professions was only slightly above that for the population in Germany as a whole: 7.1 percent for Jews, contrasted with 6.4 percent for the entire gainfully employed population. By 1933, 12.5 percent of all employed Jews were in this category, versus 8.4 percent for the general population.[17] Two thirds of these were self-employed, principally as doctors and lawyers. In June 1933, after several thousand Jewish civil servants and those in the free professions had been dismissed—and in some cases had already emigrated from Germany—Jews still accounted for 10.9 percent of all practicing physicians in the Reich and 16.25 percent of all independent lawyers. Smaller in terms of percentages but not less conspicuous were the more than 870 Jewish writers and editors and the estimated 2,600 Jewish artists active in many fields of the arts, especially in the cinema and music.[18] This particular facet of Jewish occupational structure was seized on and emphasized in antisemitic propaganda, with singular bluntness and great effectiveness. Such propaganda was motivated by an unabashed and transparent competitive envy and was intensified by emphatic reference to the concentration of Jews active in the free professions in the large metropolitan centers.

It is especially difficult to make definite statements about the development of Jewish income and assets because the source materials do not permit a comparative computation of the turnover figures for the approximately one hundred thousand Jewish-owned enterprises.[19] Nonetheless, one can justifiably assume that Jews on average still constituted a comparatively prosperous group in the population. Based on various estimates, the Jewish contribution to tax revenues in several cities was three to four times larger than their percentage in the total population.[20] However, if one compares Jews with their true and proper reference group in the population—namely, the urban middle classes—that differential lead is cut considerably, even reversed in the case of certain occupational groups.

Like the entire "old middle class," Jews had been harder hit by the postwar economic crises than had other social strata. Individual large entrepreneurs of Jewish background, such as Paul Silverberg or Ottmar Strauss, may have numbered among the big "inflation profiteers," along with Christians of purely "Aryan" origin such as Stinnes and Thyssen.[21] Yet tycoons like Silverberg were a rare exception. The great mass of small-shop owners and tradesmen had lost their entire savings during the inflation, while rentiers and pensioners, whose numbers were relatively high in the Jewish population, suffered as a result of the real loss in the value of their incomes. As a concomitant of overaging in the demographic pattern, the percentage of Jewish recipients of social welfare was twice as high as that in the population as a whole. Even in Berlin, where the highest Jewish incomes were concentrated, Jewish income suffered a decline in real terms between 1912 and 1925.[22] Beginning in 1929, the Depression exacerbated these tendencies. This crisis also had a greater impact on the Jewish "new middle classes" than on the corresponding groups in the non-Jewish population, especially the broad ranks of Jewish white-collar employees. Jewish concentration in the garment industry, which had suffered more from declining demand than other branches of consumer goods manufacture, led to disastrous consequences for the Jewish entrepreneurs in this branch and for their many Jewish employees. The number of bankruptcies and liquidations of Jewish firms was especially high in provincial areas, where the impact of the antisemitic boycott was more direct and pronounced. The incitement stemming from antisemitic white-collar workers' associations also helped contribute to the above-average level of unemployment among Jewish white-collar groups.[23]

This deteriorating economic situation led to the formation of a number of aid organizations. A network of credit associations patterned along Eastern European lines was set up among the lower middle classes. These credit associations were maintained by the American Jewish welfare organization, the Joint Distribution Committee, known more popularly by its abbreviation: the "Joint." Job placement offices for unemployed Jews were opened in the larger Jewish *Gemeinden,* and these bureaus appealed openly to the feelings of solidarity among Jewish employers.[24] The scope and success of such organizations were initially limited. Their principal importance is that they laid the foundation for the various initiatives of economic self-help that were later to prove so crucial for Jewish survival under the Nazi regime.

The antisemitic boycott had already begun several years prior to the Nazi seizure of power and was intensified particularly during the 1929–1932 Depression. Both the appeal and the impact of this boycott were enhanced by the fact that Jewish economic activity was concentrated in a small number of especially prominent or crisis-prone branches of the economy. In the Weimar Republic, Jews "dominated" nothing but a few insignificant specialized branches: of the more than thirty thousand German cattle-trading firms, for example, upward of 50 percent were still in Jewish hands as late as 1930.[25] Jews were represented in overproportionately large numbers in the garment and shoe industry, certain branches of the metal trade, and department store companies. There were still a substantial number of Jewish directors and large shareholders in the private banking sector; however, those banking firms had been declining in importance since the later nineteenth century and had been increasingly taken over by the large commercial banks.[26] If one adds the already mentioned professions of medicine and law, this then constituted an exhaustive list of economic branches "dominated" by Jews.

Occupations like these were of little importance in terms of genuine economic or even political power. Yet in almost every locality, such pursuits and professions had high visibility. The great mining barons and industrial magnates operated exclusively within a circle of discreet contacts, hidden behind the closed doors of conference rooms from which the public was largely excluded. But anyone in the Weimar Republic who wanted to buy some new clothes was able to note the seemingly ubiquitous presence of Jewish-owned clothing stores in many towns and cities. Every farmer, at least in the southern and southwestern rural farming areas of Germany, had personal contact with Jewish cattle dealers, wine purchasers, and grain agents. The professional comportment of these tradesmen was certainly no better nor worse than that of their non-Jewish competitors. All of them tried to buy cheap and sell dear, in keeping with good business sense and capitalist reasoning. Yet by so doing, these Jewish tradesmen offered their customers and crisis-buffeted competitors a variety of real or imaginary reasons to believe they had been overcharged or underbid.

Jewish retail trade was the sector hardest hit by antisemitic boycott propaganda. Some 45 percent of all gainfully employed Jews were active in this branch, either as proprietors, family members helping out in the business, or salaried employees. Thus, the situation in Jewish retail trade determined to an appreciable degree the general economic fate of German Jews as a whole. According to reliable sources, there were more than fifty thousand Jewish retail trade outlets in Germany at the end of 1932. These made up only 6 percent of all retail firms yet employed a quarter of the entire labor force in this area, including family members assisting in the business. Moreover, the Jewish-owned stores accounted for approximately 26 percent of total retail sales. Generally, the larger and more profitable stores had Jewish proprietors. Numerous department stores were also in Jewish hands, yet they accounted in 1932 for only about 15 percent of the total volume of Jewish retail trade. Eighty-five percent of such trade was handled by medium-size specialist shops, particularly in the branches of clothing, shoes, and household goods. In 1932, Jewish merchants in Germany accounted for 62 percent of all sales in ready-to-wear clothing, 36 percent in household goods, and 18 percent in luxury articles![27]

This concentration in a small number of overcrowded areas that had been especially hard hit by the Depression created sources of potential conflict and tensions that proved readily exploitable for the purposes of antisemitic boycott propaganda. Since the end of the nineteenth century, retail trade in Germany had become an alternative source of livelihood for many craft artisans and sons of farmers, who had been uprooted in the course of the agrarian crisis and large-scale industrialization and had sought a new life in towns and cities. It was generally believed that a person had to have only limited previous knowledge and few business qualifications or savvy to open a small shop or establish a trade as peddler. In their attempt to earn a modest living, these persons found themselves confronting experienced, long-established Jewish competitors. For this reason, it is little surprise that the most primitive and violent variant of incitement to antisemitic boycott found an attentive and envious ear specifically in these strata as competition grew ever fiercer in the wake of the deepening Depression.

As strange as it may seem in view of the *völkisch* and National Socialist propaganda stereotypes of an "international Jewish finance oligarchy," this boycott had a far less severe impact on Jewish private bankers and large industrialists. Numerically, this was an elite group consisting of no more than a few hundred wealthy upper-class families. There is a widely held view in social-historical research that such exceptional strata are of importance for the economic fate of minority groups only if they provide gainful employment for a large number of the members of that group. If this is not the case—and it most certainly was not in respect to the German Jews in the period under consideration here—then a tiny number of successful large industrialists cannot be considered representative of the social structure of the entire minority group, and they remain of virtually no consequence for their economic development.[28] There is nothing unusual about this. The economic upper class in any society is only a diminutive fraction of the total population; its influence and significance are not dependent on its size. Even if this stratum was somewhat more heavily represented in the case of German Jews than its percentage in the population as a whole, it remained a statistically negligible minority. No one would think of considering a few dozen, several hundred, or even several thousand German large entrepreneurs as being *representative* of the situation of the German population as a whole.

However, when it came to the Jews, the perspective was skewed. In their case, German antisemites and Jewish apologists found themselves unintentionally united as partners in a disastrous overestimation of the influence and achievements of the so-called Jewish leaders in the economy. The antisemites, of course, wished to manipulate existing resentment and rancor for political aims, and the apologists wanted to underscore the contributions made by Jews to the economy of their "fatherland."[29] Both such tendencies led to generalizations and exaggerations—distortions that even today have not completely been expunged from historical writing, let alone from popular consciousness.

This overevaluation of Jewish entrepreneurial activity and prowess is based in part on the fact that Jewish businessmen were particularly concentrated in a small number of economic branches, such as private banking and textile and garment manufacture and wholesaling. Jewish firms constituted some 60 percent of those involved in the non-iron metal trades; there were approximately two thousand Jewish-owned firms involved in wholesale trade in agricultural products, about 20 percent of the total. It should be noted, however, that the number and proportion of Jewish enterprises had been on the decline in all of these branches of the economy.[30]

The Depression and the heightened competition from growing numbers of non-Jewish businessmen appear to have had an impact on the Jewish stratum of large entrepreneurs, even though belatedly. The "Jewish" department stores, which were locked in a fierce competitive struggle with both Jewish and non-Jewish retail traders, provided antisemitic propaganda with sinister images that were every bit as vicious and effective as the specters associated with the grain wholesale firms in the rural countryside. In this propaganda, private bankers and Jewish directors of large commercial banks represented "Jewish high finance," a target at which the Nazis skillfully deflected and redirected German social discontent and "anticapitalist longings." In this regard, it was inconsequential that a large proportion of these upper-class families had in fact been estranged from Judaism and Jewishness for decades and no longer were affiliated in even a formal religious sense with the community.

Antisemitism in the Ideology and Propaganda of the NSDAP

Neither the tenacity of the hatred for Jews nor its function in the ideology and propaganda of National Socialism can be *rationally* explained using economic motives alone. Antisemitism, after all, is essentially an irrational phenomenon, manifold and complex, appearing in repeatedly new guises and composed of deeply rooted, traditional stereotypes and prejudices. Given the present state of research, there can be little doubt about its centrality in Hitler's world view and thus in National Socialist ideology—this despite various attempts to accord antisemitism nothing but a basically instrumental function in the framework of general theoretical ideological constructs such as "fascism" or "totalitarianism." "The historian who is not hampered by ideological or theoretical blinders can easily recognize that it was National Socialist antisemitism and the anti-Jewish policies of the Third Reich which left their essential imprint on the special character of National Socialism."[31]

This is not the place for an in-depth analysis of modern racial antisemitism or its function within National Socialist ideology. No matter how one may choose to evaluate the differing roots of the phenomenon, socioeconomic arguments played a striking and dominant role in the formation of modern political antisemitism in Germany from the 1870s on. Deeply rooted popular prejudices about the "wealthy, usurious Jews" were effectively manipulated in antisemitic agitation and occupied a central position in such propaganda down into the Nazi period.

In Hitler's *Mein Kampf,* economic arguments are scattered and infrequent. At one point, he contends that Jews invented the institution of the modern stock market, which "destroyed the foundations of a true economy useful to the Volk."[32] Yet at another point, the same Jews turn up as the spiritual fathers of social democracy, whose "inner—and thus true—intentions" can be grasped only by "a knowledge of Jewry."[33] Hitler's obsessive hatred of the Jews apparently was derived only in small part from economic motives.

In contrast, the party program of the NSDAP, ratified in 1920 and declared by Hitler in May 1926 to be "unalterable," contained formulations for an anti-Jewish policy involving measures of economic discrimination. The decisive section in this 25-point program states: "4. Only a *Volksgenosse* [member of the folk community] can be a citizen. Only a person who has German blood, apart from any consideration of religion, can be a member of the community. Thus, no Jew can be a member of the folk community."

The concept of *Volksgemeinschaft* had central significance for the integrational capacity of Nazi ideology as a whole. The exclusion of the German Jews from this primary, all-inclusive organic folk community formed the basis for specific objectives in the economic sphere as well. Point 6 demanded the exclusion of Jews from all public offices in the Reich, at state and local level. Point 7 postulated the obligation of the state "to provide possibilities for employment and livelihood principally for citizens" and if necessary, "to deport the members of foreign nations (noncitizens)." Point 8 called for a halt to "any further immigration by non-Germans" and to deport any persons who had immigrated into Germany after August 2, 1914. Point 23, particularly detailed, proclaimed the necessity for barring Jews from journalism. Gottfried Feder, who functioned in the early years of the NSDAP as an authorized commentator on the party program, expressly emphasized that it was Jews who were intended by the expression "non-Germans," even if they were not specifically referred to in the relevant program points, "since they are, after all, the only foreign people residing among us in any substantial numbers."[34] Feder stressed that the ultimate basic aim of the program was to give preference to German interests above those of any residents who did not belong to the *Volk*—particularly the interests of the Jews, who had been excluded from the *Volksgemeinschaft*.[35]

Before 1933, Gottfried Feder was also regarded as the authoritative spokesman of the Munich party headquarters in matters of NSDAP economic policy, especially since Hitler had confirmed this status in *Mein Kampf*. It is clearly evident from Hitler's wording that he was less interested in Feder's theories on economic policy and more concerned about exploiting them for purposes of propaganda. Feder's totally abstruse distinction between "creative" and "rapacious" capital, the nucleus of Feder's theory about the "breaking of the yoke of bondage to interest," enabled Hitler to feign "anticapitalist" gestures while simultaneously wooing the support of large industrialist entrepreneurial circles.[36]

In its early years, National Socialist propaganda was targeted mainly at the middle classes, from which the greater proportion of early party members had been recruited. Especially in urban areas, small merchants, artisans, civil servants, and white-collar workers were heavily overrepresented in party membership ranks.[37] These occupational groups were particularly receptive to antisemitic arguments, whether because of competitive envy or because it proved possible here to skillfully mobilize and manipulate "the anti-modern sentiment which had accompanied antisemitism in Germany since the 1880s" against the Jews.[38] Before 1930, the "old" and "new" middle classes showed a relatively heavy representation in NSDAP party membership ranks in comparison with the total number of the gainfully employed.[39] According to recent research, the

NSDAP remained, at least until 1929, "an interest lobby for disgruntled members of the lower middle class," whose "purely economic motivation [was] traditionally heavily infused with antisemitic arguments."[40] However, starting in 1926, the number of members from the educated upper middle classes had begun to rise steadily. The Nazis gained influence among students and younger members of the free professions by the creation of special professional organizations, such as the League of National Socialist German Physicians (Nationalsozialistischer Deutscher Ärztebund) and the League of National Socialist German Lawyers (Bund Nationalsozialistischer Deutscher Juristen).

More recent analyses of the election results, especially for the years 1930 to 1933, prove that the NSDAP owed its successes to an improvement in its voter appeal, an attraction that extended far beyond the middle classes. Using only the data of historical electoral analysis, it is not possible to determine the exact role played by antisemitic propaganda in this connection.[41] However, an analysis of the propaganda literature, which was cleverly aimed at the various individual occupational groups, is quite revealing.[42] Abstract slogans like "international Jewish conspiracy" or the "gilded International of Jewish high finance" were not sufficiently concrete to serve as useful targets at which to direct the political aggressions of the impoverished middle classes or unemployed university graduates. Yet such aggressions could be effectively channeled against the "Jewish department store" or the more successful Jewish store owner across the street, or against Jewish doctors and lawyers and the young generation of Jewish law and medical students at the universities. The effect of such occupationally specific resentment, at least since the onset of the Depression and the deepening economic crisis, was to enable National Socialists to infiltrate numerous middle-class commercial interest associations. The Nazis were also able to achieve similar success in the interest associations of the medical and legal professions.

Recent research is increasingly of the opinion that by the early 1930s the NSDAP had already succeeded "in mobilizing members of all strata of the population . . . in such large numbers by means of its ideology of folk community and its exaggerated nationalism that . . . it had taken on the character of a popular people's party more than any other political grouping during those years."[43] Yet the segment of voters drawn from the middle classes—in the most extended sense of the notion, including the "new" middle classes—appears to have continued to predominate in the National Socialist constituency. Moreover, there is no doubt about the primarily middle-class origins of the older guard in the party membership.[44] In the context dealt with here, the expectations and desires of these "old stalwarts" (*alte Kämpfer*) played an important role. These veteran party activists wished to see the anti-Jewish slogans translated into action after the takeover of power. They wanted to reap personal benefits from the economic liquidation of the Jews as a well-earned reward for the "privations endured during the *Kampfzeit,*" the pre-1933 "struggle period" of the movement.

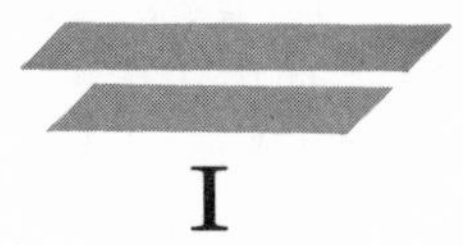

I

1933
Consolidation of Power and Boycott of the Jews

The torchlight parade of the jubilantly victorious Nazis streaming past the Reich Chancellery on January 30, 1933, was also a lurid signal to the German Jewish community that revolutionary changes were in the offing. Until that time, the instrument of the boycott had been applied against them only sporadically. It was a measure whose chief function in Nazi propaganda had been to mobilize their own supporters, and Jews had been able to defend themselves against its potential ravages. Now it was suddenly transformed into an essential component of the policy of the new regime, even if initially there was no official declaration to this effect. It was to take several more months before the National Socialist dictatorship consolidated its power. The burning of the Reichstag, the March 1933 elections, and the Enabling Act constituted stages, following in swift succession, of an astonishingly rapid process of *Gleichschaltung*—the bringing of all spheres of state and economy under Nazi domination. The illusion of a right-wing "coalition government" with a National Socialist minority soon crumbled. The Depression and foreign-policy considerations appeared initially to place limitations on the new rulers, checking their hand in the area of economic policy toward the Jews as well. In actual fact, however, precisely the opposite occurred: it was specifically these first early months of Nazi rule that were marked by pronounced antisemitic violence, directed primarily against targets of Jewish economic activity.

Violent Prelude

Even before January 30, 1933, violent acts against Jewish individuals had not been uncommon. In Jewish neighborhoods in the large metropolitan centers, such acts and incidents were as much a part of the everyday "street scene" as the brawls between members of the SA and the Communists. Yet the police had tried to maintain public law and order. Now the SA was itself part of the police force—sporting arm bands labeled Auxiliary Police and armed with carbine rifles, its men patrolled the streets. Terror against political opponents and against Jews had been legalized. In the "better" sections of town, such as along the fashionable Kurfürstendamm in Berlin, that terror remained low-key as long as there was a desire in the party leadership to avoid antagonizing the still-hesitant, solid middle-class burghers and foreign visitors to the city. In the poorer neighborhoods and in outlying regions, the SA was able, unencumbered, to give free rein to its passions.

The first victims of this violence were the *Ostjuden,* the Jews from Eastern Europe. The greater majority of these Jews had only recently come to Germany, in the period around World War I, and they adhered faithfully to their religious customs and traditions. Easily recognizable by their beards and forelocks, their distinct dress and headwear, they personified the image of "Jewry as a foreign race." It proved easy to mobilize the xenophobic animosity of broad sections of the population against such an "alien" group of Jews. For the most part, they were poor people of modest means: small merchants trading in low-price goods, workers who made inexpensive articles of clothing in tiny shops or, for example, cut and pasted rubber raincoats. Those Eastern Jews who were even poorer traveled as itinerant peddlers through the rural countryside, their case of samples in hand, earning the enmity of the local storeowners.[1]

There are numerous eyewitness accounts of the brutal terror to which Jewish tradesmen were exposed even before the organized boycott of April 1, 1933. Two will be cited here as representative examples. Along with Berlin, Munich, and several cities in Saxony, the Eastern Jewish population was concentrated in the industrial cities in western Germany. It was there that an especially rabid antisemitism festered and spread. On March 20, 1933 in Dortmund,

> members of the SA and SS dragged the butcher Julius Rosenfeld and his son from the Dortmund stockyards through the streets of the city to a brickyard at the Voss pit. Rosenfeld and his son were lined up against the wall several times and threatened with pistols. They were forced to sing the "Horst Wessel Song," and were greeted by a rain of blows when they arrived at the brickyard. The young Rosenfeld was forced to set fire to his father's beard with a burning newspaper. After this, father and son were compelled to jump into a clay-pit. After five hours, the elder Rosenfeld was released and sent home under the condition that within two hours he bring a slaughtered ox to his tormenters as a ransom for the release of his son.[2]

The second report comes from Duisburg:

> On March 24, a civilian accompanied by an armed member of the SS gained forced entry into the furniture store of the Polish Jew AAC, who apparently had antagonized his competitors by underselling them. The SS man accosted the Jew with his fists and left him covered with blood. AAC proceeded in this condition to the precinct station, where he was told that the police were powerless to act in such cases. On April 1, he was taken into protective custody, since there were fears of further acts of violence.[3]

The businesses owned by Eastern European Jews were not the only ones affected by reprisals. Especially during the month of March 1933, larger firms as well—mainly Jewish department stores and other retail shops—were singled out as targets for more or less violent demonstrations. Several newly installed mayors distinguished themselves in particular in this connection. Apparently, the National Socialist "revolution" was proceeding at too slow a pace for their taste; they felt it should be speeded up by so-called *Einzelaktionen,* "individual actions" against Jewish stores and businesses. The Kampfbund für den gewerblichen Mittelstand (League of Struggle for the Commercial Middle Class) appointed "commissars" everywhere to close stores or even to try to have them expropriated. This development took on such independent momentum that the government in Berlin found it necessary to intervene in order to maintain "peace and quiet in the economy" during those critical months marked by the consolidation of Nazi power and continuing massive unemployment. For this purpose, Hugenberg, the Deutschnational economy minister, appointed an experienced and proven National Socialist "expert on the economy"—Otto Wagener, former director of the Section on Economic Policy of the NSDAP—as special commissioner for economic affairs. Moreover, Hitler and his "deputy," Rudolf Hess, also issued urgent warnings against these autocratic and arbitrary *Einzelaktionen.*[4]

There were also excesses directed against Jewish doctors and lawyers. At its convention on March 14, 1933, the League of National Socialist Lawyers called for a purge of all courts as well as new elections to the bar associations in order to make sure these were "free of all Jews and Marxists." Earlier, there had been reports from various areas of the Reich of courthouses that had been occupied and scenes of "angry crowds" pushing their way into courtrooms. Subsequent to this and even before the official boycott and their "legal" barring from the profession by the Civil Service Law (*Berufsbeamtengesetz*) of April 7, 1933, Jewish judges and district attorneys had "been requested to take a short vacation."[5] The League of National Socialist German Physicians, which even before the takeover of power had engaged in an aggressive boycott directed against Jewish doctors, also distinguished itself now by a series of further measures. These were aimed in particular at doctors who had been members of the Association of Socialist Physicians. Many of them were arrested and manhandled. An accelerated boycott and a campaign of denunciations and repression was initiated against other doctors; these cost a number of lives.[6]

It was no accident that these first spontaneous antisemitic boycott actions were initiated specifically by the two professional groups. Even before 1933, the ranks of these professions had been marked by the presence of an especially virulent antisemitism.

> In small trade . . . the fear of superior competitors led to a particularly intensive animosity toward Jews. A similar situation prevailed among university graduates. . . . Antisemitism, which had become socially acceptable already in the late 19th century, especially through the influence of Heinrich von Treitschke, found more fervent adherents in the educated middle classes after 1918 than in any other social stratum. . . . A material cause suggests itself as an explanation for the antisemitic involvement of doctors and lawyers: they had dealings with an especially large number of Jewish colleagues, and figured that without that competition they would be better off.[7]

The intention to exclude Jewish competitors is certainly not the only explanation for the receptivity to antisemitic notions among these strata. An additional causal factor was a general aversion in such circles toward modern industrial society and the "system" of the Weimar Republic, which they saw embodied in the Jews. However, even if one attributes the antisemitic impulses of the Nazis primarily to their ideological "image of the enemy," one must consider the fact that "in the rank and file of the party, economically motivated antisemitism was virulent," and that "at the lower levels of local district leadership," the noisy rowdy antisemitism of the SA hordes was motivated by a desire for unobtrusive personal enrichment at the cost of Jewish retail trade.[8] The situation was probably not much different among antisemitic university students and graduates.

Although the struggle against the department stores, "against trusts and corporations," and against "Jewish high finance" were high on the list of priorities in the program and propaganda of the NSDAP as prime goals of economic antisemitism, it was the medium-size and small Jewish shops that were initially hardest hit by the measures after the Nazi takeover of power. The Jewish banks and large concerns and even the hated department stores were to remain largely unaffected for several years. It is true that in the early weeks following the Nazis' attaining power, as well as on the Boycott Day of April 1, the customary SA patrols were posted in front of several department stores. These SA troopers acted to prevent customers from entering the premises of stores; however, the proprietors and managers were generally able to find ways to utilize personal connections—as well as the concern of the new rulers regarding the continuing unemployment situation—to their advantage. In many instances, the employees of such large firms, for the most part non-Jewish, appealed to the government and to party officials not to endanger their jobs by boycott actions.[9] The example of the department store firm Hermann Tietz shows that such intervention by employees resulted in a certain success. As late as the middle of 1933, Tietz had obtained a large consolidation loan from the state treasury with Hitler's express consent, since the Tietz firm did, after all, employ fourteen thousand workers, mainly non-Jews. Consequently, the large Jewish concerns were able to profit temporarily from the general economic upswing and the rise in consumer demand that were already in evidence in 1933.[10]

Boycott Day, April 1, 1933

The organized boycott on April 1, 1933, ordered by the NSDAP party leadership on March 28, was the temporary high point of those "spontaneous" excesses, though by no means their end. The "Action Committees . . . for practical planned implementation of the boycott of Jewish businesses, Jewish products, Jewish doctors and Jewish lawyers," which were immediately formed everywhere, were to be "extended out to reach into the smallest farming village in order to strike a blow at Jewish tradesmen, especially in rural areas."[11]

Officially, the boycott was announced as a "purely defensive measure" against the "atrocity propaganda" being spread by Jewish organizations abroad. This was a threadbare pretext. The foreign press had indeed reported in detail on events in the Reich during the first three months of the Nazi regime and had published detailed stories on the persecution of political opponents and Jews, but the Jewish press and organizations had tended toward cautious moderation in their coverage and commentary. Voices had been raised in some countries calling for a boycott of German products, but the responsible Jewish organizations had warned against taking hasty action. Thus, for example, the united Jewish leadership in the United States had initially rejected an appeal by the European representative of the "Joint" to organize protest meetings against the persecution of Jews in Germany. There were fears that the situation could deteriorate as a result of such actions. Even before Goebbels's declaration, in a speech in May 1933, that the German people would take revenge against the Jews for any foreign boycott of German goods, it had become clear to Jewish organizations that the Nazis regarded the Jews in Germany as political pawns and hostages.

The decision for the boycott was probably made at a meeting of Nazi party chiefs in Berchtesgaden. Significantly, one of the most rabid antisemitic agitators, Julius Streicher, editor of the periodical *Der Stürmer* and *Gauleiter* (district party chief) in Franconia, was named head of the "Central Committee for Combatting Jewish Incitement to Boycott and Atrocity Propaganda." The boycott was supposed to begin on Saturday, April 1, at 10 A.M., "like a lightning bolt," everywhere throughout Germany. It was to continue "until terminated by order of the party leadership." This directive indicated not only the immediate and pressing targets of the boycott—namely, Jewish retail trade and Jewish physicians and lawyers—but also announced the "call for introduction of a relative quota for the number of Jews employed in all professions in keeping with their percentage in the total German population." Yet this demand would be initially limited to three areas only "in order to enhance the impact and power of the action."[12] Such formulations gave the lie even to the spurious pretext of a defensive action against Jewish "atrocity propaganda" contained in the official directive issued by the party leadership.

The true intention—namely, to force out the Jews for the benefit of their non-Jewish competitors—was revealed in even greater clarity in a renewed "Call to Action" made by Streicher on March 31. After the businesses to be boycotted had been named and the "budget-priced chain stores, department stores and branches of large firms in German hands," as well as "the American [and non-Jewish] Woolworth chain stores," had been expressly excluded, the local action committees were asked to organize collections of money among German businessmen "in order to finance this defensive movement."[13] Those who stood to profit from the boycott of the Jews were thus also asked to make some contribution toward defraying its expenses.

The fact that it was possible to organize such an extensive action nationwide in the brief span of less than three days is explicable only on the basis of experience that had already been gained in many towns with boycott actions. Once again, there were many who could not restrain their enthusiasm and wait for the "swift and sudden" onset of the boycott on April 1: In numerous localities, the demonstrations and the appearance of Nazi units posted in front of Jewish businesses had begun the day before. Thus, a report in the *Frankfurter Zeitung* of April 1 noted that, in Annaberg in Saxony, large SS contingents of "defensive guards" had already positioned themselves in front of Jewish businesses on the morning of March 31 and had rubber-stamped the face of every customer leaving the premises with abusive derogatory slogans.[14] The report mentioned similar incidents from the length and breadth of the Reich, mainly including verbatim quotes from the local press.

The Boycott Day itself went off in more or less "disciplined fashion," at least in the main streets of the large cities. Contingents of SA and Hitler Youth positioned themselves in front of Jewish businesses, carrying posters printed in advance, and attempted to stop those customers who nonetheless wished to try to enter the stores. Whoever persisted was photographed, and his picture was published in the following days in the local press. In the smaller towns and in more remote neighborhoods in the larger cities, the boycott proceeded in a less "civilized" manner: show windows were smeared with paint and obscene slogans in various instances, store windows were smashed and their contents plundered.

There were also a number of physical acts of violence. In the Scheunenviertel quarter in Berlin, in Dortmund, in Duisburg, and in Saxony, it was once again the Eastern European Jewish store owners who suffered most from the organized brutality of the "popular anger." This is clearly evident from a large number of documented complaints by foreign (particularly Polish) consulates; although the orders of the "Action Committee" had stipulated that businesses belonging to foreign Jews should be spared.[15]

The recollections of the boycott by Jewish eyewitnesses paint a diverse picture. Along with reports on candid and shamefaced expressions of sympathy from the German population, there are descriptions of enthusiastic and malicious participation by adults and youths. "There were plenty of non-Jews," wrote Jakob Ball-Kaduri, "who—specifically on this particular day—demonstratively went to Jewish stores or to their doctor, bringing him flowers and assuring him of their loyalty. Yet such were exceptions. The great mass of people remained indifferent or even expressed their elation, to the extent that they had already been processed and remolded along Nazi lines."[16] Edwin Landau described similarly contrasting behavior in a small town in rural West Prussia:

> Already during the early morning hours of that Friday [March 31] one could see the SA marching with its banners through town. "The Jews are our misfortune." . . . Later that morning, the Nazi guards began to take up position in front of Jewish businesses, and every customer was admonished not to shop at Jewish stores. Two young Nazis were also posted in front of our shop and prevented customers from entering. . . . And this was the people we young Jews had once stood in the trenches for, spilling our blood to protect the country from the enemy. Wasn't there any comrade-in-arms left from that period who felt disgusted by the spectacle he was now witnessing? You could watch them as they passed by in the street, and there were persons among them one had

Signs of the boycott: the show window of a Jewish shop in Berlin, summer 1933.

done a favor for. They had a smile on their face, a smile that betrayed their secret joy. . . .

I took my war medals, put them on, went out into the street and went to some Jewish stores, where at first I was also stopped from entering. But I was seething with rage, and would have liked most to scream my hatred into the faces of these barbarians. Hate, hatred—since when had that element seized hold of me?—This change had only come over me but a few hours before. This country, this people, which up to then I had loved and admired, had now suddenly become my enemy. So I was no longer a German—or at least was no longer supposed to be one. Naturally, that cannot be arranged and settled in the short span of a few hours. But there was one thing that suddenly I sensed: I was ashamed of the

> trust I had placed in so many, persons who now were unmasked as my enemies. Suddenly even the street seemed to me strange and alien. Yes, the entire city had become a strange and alien place.[17]

The significance of this Boycott Day, its causes, and true objectives are still being debated in the historical literature. Karl Schleunes, for example, argues that the Nazi leadership needed the boycott as a kind of "safety valve" for the accumulated pressure of the party rank and file, which had been discharging itself in violent "individual actions," because at this stage, for both political and economic reasons, there did not as yet appear to be any prospect for intensified official economic measures against the Jews. In this way, Schleunes contends, the resoluteness of the party leadership to adhere to the basic demands of the party program had been communicated to the middle-class Old Guard in the party. The message was that even if it was impossible for the present to achieve a complete realization of those demands, their time would come.[18] Uwe Dietrich Adam contends, in connection with the Civil Service Law proclaimed on April 7, that the boycott was symptomatic of a "tactic of first creating a 'situation' in order then to utilize that for the triggering and justification of anti-Jewish measures."[19] If these assumptions are correct, one would have to postulate an element of goal-directed planning and consistency in National Socialist policy toward the Jews, a notion that both authors mentioned generally reject.

It appears quite possible that reports published in the foreign press were a source of concern for the new rulers, especially those leaders involved with foreign and economic policymaking, and that they believed they might be able to sway the foreign media by means of a massive action directed against the Jews in Germany. It is difficult to say whether the National Socialist top echelon was convinced about its own propaganda regarding the omnipotence of "Jewish international high finance." In any event, there are certain indications that at this juncture they did in fact still regard Jewish organizations abroad as being extremely influential. This might help explain the pressure placed on representatives of the German Jews to take action among their fellow religionists abroad to put an end to the "atrocity propaganda." After a meeting with Göring on March 26, 1933, a joint delegation of representatives of the German Zionist Federation (ZVfD) and the Centralverein (C.V.; Central Association of German Citizens of the Jewish Faith) was in fact dispatched to London to sound out the Jewish organizations there.[20] In addition, Jewish organizations in Germany felt themselves obligated to publish statements in the press denouncing the wave of "foreign atrocity propaganda."[21]

Despite all of these efforts, the events of April 1 were given more detailed coverage in the foreign press than the "individual actions" that had preceded them. Only after this date were the first attempts made in both Jewish and non-Jewish circles (for example, in the British trade union movement) to implement an organized boycott of German goods. The fact that these efforts met with little success and had only a small negative impact on the German economy was due to the indeed negligible influence exercised by so-called international Jewry.[22] In addition, the economic upturn, already in evidence in 1933, was the product of a German economic policy consciously geared toward spurring the domestic market and later on toward rearmament needs. The role of exports in this policy was solely as a source of foreign currency for the purchase of vital raw materials and food supplies and had little importance in connection with eliminating unemployment.[23]

The April 1 boycott was successful in its fundamental and, in the view of this author, *consciously planned* function. It set the stage for tightening the screw of economic discrimination and the ousting of the Jews from the economy. Efforts were made to push on with this process—cautiously, in a veiled manner, yet nonetheless consistently. The earlier "individual actions" could still be viewed as the "excesses" of irresponsible Nazi rowdies or subordinate party organizations. The diverse warnings issued by the Reich Economy Ministry, by Economic Commissioner Otto Wagener, and by Rudolf Hess were in fact commented on in this sense. There could no longer be any doubts within the population about the political objectives after this boycott, which had been organized by the top echelons of party leadership and at least condoned by all government offices. Efforts to oust Jews from active economic life were given their official stamp of legitimating approval by the boycott, even if the temporary postponement of their final realization was explained by an openly admitted "exigency of the moment." Helmut Krausnik has given a precise picture of the interacting factors:

> In this phase when the National Socialist regime was still attempting to consolidate its power, the *pseudolegality* of the entire procedure was both an essential feature of totalitarian rule and an aspect in keeping with the unavoidable consideration given to the foreign policy situation and the attitude of the majority of the population. Because even in broad circles of the German burgher classes, there was probably an emotional aversion to violent actions and the unrestrained character of the anti-Jewish agitation of the NSDAP, especially in its effects on the "individual" Jews. In regard to the so-called "*reduction of Jewish influence in German life,*" as officially proclaimed by the government, corresponding measures—clothed only in a threadbare cloak of formal legality—were not just "accepted as part of the bargain," because of the questionable "national energy" of the new regime. Rather, such measures were also deemed

> necessary, defensible or even acceptable by antisemitically tainted circles—even amongst the "educated" middle classes. . . . If one looks at the subsequent period as a whole, the National Socialist party leadership never chose to *renounce* noisy demonstrations and consciously provoked incidents, let alone vicious propaganda. Yet the focus of official Jewish *policy* up until 1938 lay, on the one hand, in the so-called *legal exclusion* of the Jews; on the other . . . in a step-wise but systematic, relatively *unobtrusive*—yet for this very reason all the more effective—*police-administrative practice* of suppression and terrorizing. The total atmosphere was, moreover, essentially determined and shaped by an unceasing, officially tolerated *moral defamation and discrimination* of Jews by the Party.[24] (emphasis in original)

In this respect, the limitation of the boycott to only one day, which Goebbels had already announced the evening of March 31 and which was finally proclaimed formally by the government on April 4, is of little import.[25] Its function, namely, to legitimize anti-Jewish measures in the economic field, had been fulfilled after the first day. The creeping boycott that commenced at that point demonstrates that this signal was understood by interested individuals and offices. In any event, the somewhat surprising retreat from the public stage indicates that the new rulers were still uncertain about reactions abroad and the potential political and economic consequences. In a discussion in the Reich Chancellery at noon on March 31, consideration was given to a proposal to call off the boycott set for the next day if the governments of the three Western major powers would issue a declaration denouncing the "atrocity propaganda" by midnight.[26]

The "division of labor" between the party leadership, which organized the boycott, and the government, which sanctioned it and in the end proclaimed its termination, may at first glance appear to be a confirmation of those views in the secondary literature that place emphasis on the notion of "dualism." This concept posits the dualism of the "totalitarian state of measures" and the "authoritarian state of norms" as a central defining feature of the National Socialist system of rule and its "Jewish policy." According to Uwe Dietrich Adam, this dualistic structure of rule resulted in "a contradictory mosaic of antagonistic interests and directions in the field of economic and educational policy. Such interests and directions made a preconcieved notion of Jewish policy—and thus its continuity—appear highly doubtful."[27] This is not the place to deal in greater detail with the recent controversy between "intentionalist" and "functionalist" explanatory models of the National Socialist system of rule. In my view, this controversy is ill-conceived and overestimates the importance of individual factors.[28]

Storm troopers on guard in front of a Jewish shop in Berlin on April 1, 1933.

Yet it is important to point out that the initial economic measures of Jewish persecution, as well as the April 1 boycott, do not support this dualistic interpretational approach. On the contrary, an examination of the existing sources and other evidence demonstrates that as early as the first phase, all of those features of the synthesis of ideologically grounded orientation and tactical flexibility in implementation typical of National Socialist Jewish policy were already present. The "pressure from below," which discharged itself with differing degrees of stormy intensity in the streets, the initiatives of party bodies, as well as the laws and implementation guidelines of the governmental agencies, only appear to be opposed forces in this system. In actuality, they supplemented each other and were applied and implemented in accordance with the momentary situation. They were applied in a coordinated and tactically flexible manner, yet they were no less purposeful for that reason. There was no need here for highly detailed blueprints planned years in advance. On the contrary, this mixture of purposefulness and flexibility facilitated the realization of political goals in the most efficient manner.

One of the National Socialist aims was the final ousting of the Jews from the economy and their despoliation. The April 1 boycott had the function of a starting signal. It not only indicated the legitimacy of the process but also marked out the first Jewish targets that had been "released" for such a purpose: retail trade, civil servants, and the free professions. The measures applied were part of a total strategy and supplemented each other. Legislation and the government administration focused on "treating" the Jewish civil servants, doctors, lawyers, and others in the liberal professions. In contrast, retail trade was left to the harassments, annoyances, and boycott initiatives of the central and local-level party organizations. Ernst Herzfeld had this division of labor in mind when he described the April 1 boycott as an important Nazi success:

> Even if the blow intended to reduce "Enemy No. 1" to economic ruin within a short time had not been carried out according to plan, the Nazis had nonetheless . . . achieved significant advantages. The opponent had given in first, and had himself called off his counterattack. In order to protect the "hostages" from even worse developments, the unprecendented signal of April 1 had been countenanced. Not only had the Nazis had the last word on the matter. They had also eliminated all "*Rassejuden*" [Jews by race] from the press, the film industry and the theater. The judicial system had been partially cleansed of its Jews. . . . The unbridled lust for power of the Nazis, however, was not satisfied with this. . . . The barrage of propaganda was directed against the Jews with undiminished vehemence and intensity. In ceaseless repetitions, it was hammered into the heads of the readers and listening audience that the Jews were subhuman creatures and the source of all evil. . . . In other respects, however, the Nazis shifted from an open, frontal "all-out attack" to the less clamorous mode of close-quarter combat and a war of nerves."[29]

The Civil Service Law and the Liberal Professions

One week after Boycott Day, the Law for the Reestablishment of the Profesional Civil Service (Gesetz zur Wiederherstellung des Berufsbeamtentums, or Berufsbeamtengesetz; hereafter Civil Service Law) was enacted. This can be regarded as the first comprehensive law involving economic discrimination against the Jews, though Jews are not specifically mentioned in the title of the law.[30] Its proclamation was preceded by protracted discussions in various ministries. These discussions had little to do with Jews or Jewish policy but were closely connected with the worries, by no means unfounded, of the civil bureaucracy in regard to its constitutional privileges. Once these had been tampered with, even if only as far as Jews and "politically untrustworthy individuals" were concerned, then further interference in the civil service could not be ruled out.[31]

The law issued on April 7 stipulated that civil servants of "non-Aryan" origin were to be retired immediately. The first implementation ordinance on the legislation defined as "non-Aryans" all those persons who had even one "non-Aryan" grandparent. It obligated all civil servants to which the law was applicable to prove their "Aryan" descent. This definition and the exceptions spelled out in the Civil Service Law served as an example and basis for the legal exclusion of the workers and clerical employees in government service who did not have professional civil servant (*Beamter*) status, along with lawyers and physicians. Corresponding regulations and decrees were issued in the course of the ensuing weeks—in express reference to the Civil Service Law and using the same criteria and exceptions—for Jewish attorneys and notaries public; Jewish doctors in state-supported health insurance clinics; medical students, postgraduate assistants, and lecturers at universities; and even members of professional associations such as the German Pharmacists' Association.[32]

Only after long argument and debate did it prove possible to arrive at the exact definition of "non-Aryan" descent contained in the Civil Service Law. Various ministries had, up until April 1, voiced reservations, and Jewish organizations had attempted to utilize established connections with higher government offices to achieve some toning down of its regulations. Symptomatic of the still prevailing feeling of insecurity among the new rulers at this time is the fact that such efforts were actually successful in some cases. The Association of Jewish War Veterans (RjF) was able, with the help of the aging Field Marshal von Mackensen, to induce Reich President von Hindenburg to intervene directly with Hitler. Hitler agreed to limit the scope of the law, reducing the group of those directly affected. Soldiers who had fought at the front, fathers or sons of those who had fallen in battle, and all veteran government workers who had been given civil-servant status before August 1, 1914, were exempted from the purview of the law. The files attest to this decision by Hitler, expressly termed a "gesture of concession" toward the Reich president. The sources do not support the notion, as variously maintained,[33] that the decision was actually forced by Hindenburg's alleged threat to resign, nor does this appear probable.

It would certainly have been more difficult to induce Hitler to make such concessions on this matter if he had had even an approximative idea of just how large the group of these "exceptions" would turn out to be. Apparently, he and those around him were totally convinced by their own propaganda (according to which the Jews in World War I had, for the most part, supposedly been "shirkers" and soldiers who had wangled desk jobs to avoid front-line duty) and believed that the regulations of exclusion would be applicable to only a small number of Jewish "combat veterans." However, after issuance of the law and its various derivative prohibitions on professional employment, it turned out that a quite sizable number of Jews were able to continue working in their professions for several years as a result of the regulations governing exceptions.

The Civil Service Law affected only a relatively small segment of Jewish professionals directly. In the Kaiserreich, Jews had, for practical purposes, been almost totally excluded from holding civil service positions, although this had not been on the basis of formal legal regulations. That situation had not changed significantly during the brief span of the Weimar Republic. At the beginning of 1933, the number of Jews with permanent civil service jobs at all levels of the bureaucracy did not exceed five thousand for the entire Reich. After the Civil Service Law was enacted, the June 1933 census figures indicated that there were still twenty-five hundred Jewish officials in the civil service; of these, some two hundred held senior positions. Despite various forms of harassment and unobtrusive measures to oust them from their jobs, a number of them were able to remain at their desks until the enactment of the Nuremberg Laws in September 1935. Among other things, the 1935 laws were designed to "amend the oversight" of 1933. In any event, those who had been categorized as "exceptions" under the 1933 legislation had the advantage of being able to collect their pensions for a few more years. In this case too, it was probably a concern among "Aryan" *Beamten* about the inviolability of guaranteed privileges as civil servants that was the underlying decisive motive, rather than any solicitude regarding the fate of their dismissed Jewish colleagues. The Jewish civil servants who had been summarily dismissed were cheated out of at least a portion of their entitled retirement pensions by unobtrusive procedural measures, such as a shrewdly devious way of calculating their official age of retirement. This was before such pension payments were completely abolished by subsequent "legal" measures in the following years.[34]

Compared with its immediate impact, the indirect effect of this law was of far greater importance. Since the regulations contained in the Civil Service Law were taken as a model for numerous professions, at least until the enactment of the Nuremberg Laws, the group of those affected was far larger than just those few thousand remaining Jewish civil servants. Jewish doctors and lawyers were among the first to feel its immediate effects. Long before the enactment of the 1933 legislation, there had been a campaign in the courthouses against Jewish judges, district attorneys, and lawyers. Hans Kerrl, Reich commissioner for legal affairs in Prussia, in a radio announcement on the eve of the April 1 boycott, had issued an order enjoining Jewish attorneys from entering court buildings.[35] This led to violent scenes in a large number of courthouses. Kerrl issued a further directive on April 3 banning the appointment of Jewish law graduates as court interns. One day later, he issued a general prohibition barring all Jewish attorneys from entering court premises.[36]

After the relevant national laws and regulations were enacted, the Prussian decrees were probably modified in accordance with the new legislation. Nonetheless, the zeal exhibited by Kerrl, a former minor court secretary, reflects the particular level of aggression against Jewish members of the legal profession. According to estimates at the time, approximately thirty-five hundred such jurists, categorized as "Jewish by religion"—the overwhelming majority of whom were attorneys with their own private practice or employed in private law firms—were affected by the legislation. Only some three hundred Jews held posts as judges or district attorneys.[37] Thus, the Civil Service Law had a direct effect initially on only about 40 percent of Jews in the legal profession. Most of these came under the provisos of the regulations on exceptions as former war veterans or as senior attorneys with long government service records. In addition to the group directly affected, there were, however, another almost two thousand "non-Aryan" legal interns and recent law graduates who now had no prospect whatsoever of finishing their formal professional training and being licensed to practice in Germany.[38]

The League of National Socialist German Lawyers, surprised by the large number of Jewish attorneys covered by the clauses on exceptions, stepped up its efforts for further limitations on Jews in the profession. The Third Ordinance on Implementation of the Civil Service Law, issued May 6, 1933, restricted the scope of the combat-veteran category.[39] Judges who insisted on returning to their court positions after the vacation ordered on April 11 were "encouraged" by means of arbitrary transfers and various forms of harassment to retire "voluntarily." The situation was made so difficult for those Jewish attorneys still in practice that in Berlin, for example, they worked out a system for which days of the week they would appear at court, in order to prevent "seething rage among the populace" from boiling over as a result of an excessive number of Jewish lawyers at court on any given day.[40] The now totally nazified professional association prohibited its members from operating joint practices with Jews or even sharing joint premises with "non-Aryan" attorneys. In addition, all public offices were enjoined from engaging the services of Jewish attorneys.

The boycott propaganda against Jewish lawyers that continued to be spewed out by the newspapers was hardly necessary any longer. After all, what rational "Aryan" plaintiff—or even Jewish, for that matter—would, under the existing circumstances, have let himself be represented by a Jewish counsel? Thus, after a short time, even the Jewish attorneys still licensed to practice found themselves engaged in preparing documents and papers for their mainly Jewish clientele outside the walls of the courtroom. Other lawyers were able to find temporary employment with Jewish organizations or the local Jewish *Gemeinden*.

Bruno Blau has described the situation of Jewish jurists in detail in his memoirs: despite the "general view that to be able to stay in the profession as a lawyer or notary was a special bit of good fortune that should not be foolishly thrown away (e.g., by emigration)," it soon became clear "that those who had been compelled as a result of the first law to quit the profession, and then either to create a new existence for themselves in Germany or leave the country, had drawn the better lot." Blau's own fate attests to the correctness of this assessment: enjoying the privilege of permission to continue practicing by dint of his military service in World War I, he dissolved his practice in 1936 because of a sharp decline in clients. After the Nazis "caught up with him" in Prague, he was arrested; he managed to survive, along with eight hundred other German Jews, in the "hospital ghetto" in Berlin.[41]

The approximately eight thousand Jewish physicians practicing in Germany at the beginning of 1933 fared little better than their co-religionists in the legal profession. They were concentrated particularly in the large metropolitan centers; in Berlin, for example, they constituted, according to unofficial estimates, between one third to one half of all practicing doctors.[42] A number of them had been instrumental in establishing the system of public medical care and occupied senior positions there. In contrast, there were only a few Jewish doctors on the staffs of government hospitals in the provinces. The majority of Jewish doctors were in private practice and operated clinics that generally enjoyed an excellent reputation among the population. Until the advent of the Third Reich, the economic situation of Jewish physicians was correspondingly favorable. They were often those listed with the highest incomes in the tax rolls of the local Jewish *Gemeinden*.

The professional envy of non-Jewish doctors in the Weimar Republic was probably only one of the reasons the League of National Socialist German Physicians developed into the breeding ground for a particularly virulent strain of antisemitism. It would appear that the combination of "racist-genetic" medicine and research together with antisemitism was principally ideological in nature. This thesis is also supported by the fact that a number of high-ranking doctors in the SS, some quite notorious, participated directly in the mass murder of Jews in World War II.[43] Even before the Nazis came to power, the League of National Socialist German Physicians had embarked on an especially vicious propaganda campaign to boycott Jewish doctors. This campaign now reached its high point in a veritable barrage of slander and violence. Many Jewish doctors were shipped off to concentration camps, where they were maltreated and did not return alive.[44]

The first national legislative measure against Jewish doctors was at the initiative of Deutschnational Labor Minister Franz Seldte. On April 22, 1933, he issued an order barring all "non-Aryan" doctors from work at state-supported health-insurance clinics and hospitals, with the exception of those "exempted categories" included in the Civil Service Law.[45] At the local level, several towns and states had anticipated this measure by instituting exclusion decrees on their own initiative. In Bavaria, all Jewish school doctors were dismissed from service effective immediately. In Berlin and many other cities, the welfare offices were issued a directive instructing them not to refer patients to Jewish doctors for treatment. The Physicians' Association in Duisburg, at the instruction of the county chief of the NSDAP, stamped referral slips for appointments with specialists with the words: "Not valid for Jewish doctors." After the Jewish doctors still in practice had made a formal complaint, referring to their seniority and status as war veterans, the party county chief informed the Physicians' Association confidentially that it was apparently compelled to reinstate these doctors. He added, however, that they should take their good time in so doing: in any case, the rubber stamps should be stored safely away for future use. Even though the sources are somewhat unclear on this matter, it appears improbable that the Jewish doctors in Duisburg were ever again able to practice in unrestricted fashion.[46] Similar situations prevailed in numerous other cities.

Along with such open and "legal" measures, the quiet boycott against Jewish doctors and the campaign of intimidation among patients were perhaps even more effective. More than half of all Jewish doctors were forced to abandon the profession by the middle of 1933 as a result of this coordinated process of repression and harassment. In the beginning, they did not yield without putting up a fight. At a time when even the official Jewish leadership still believed it could rely on traditional legal norms of the constitutional state to guarantee the economic basis for continued survival of Jews in Germany, Jewish doctors also made frequent confident appeals on their own behalf to government agencies and the courts. However, they were soon forced to recognize the hopelessness of any prospect for intervention by the authorities and to accept the restriction of their practices to Jewish patients only. Or they could explore another option: namely, emigration. In that respect, Jewish doctors were doubtless far better off than their Jewish compatriots in the legal profession, since their professional skills and reputation allowed them a swifter and smoother transition to building a new existence in their country of emigration.[47]

Along with Jewish lawyers and doctors, there were also some five thousand Jewish university graduates and persons active in other "free professions" in Germany in 1933. In view of the discrimination practiced at German universities well into the Weimar period, the figure of eight hundred university faculty members was indeed a significant number. Jewish writers and journalists constituted a group almost equal in size and included some of the most important names in German literature and journalism at the time. Musicians were especially prominent among the approximately three thousand Jewish professional artists. Like the small number of Jewish "leaders in economic life," this was a numerically modest yet highly conspicuous elite, with substantial influence on the educated urban middle classes and the young intelligentsia.

The German Jews in the Weimar Republic were proud of the achievements of these elite groups; they basked in their fame and repeatedly cited them as living proof of the "German-Jewish symbiosis." The extent to which the intellectual and artistic products of these scientists, writers, and artists were in fact representative of German culture before and during the Weimar Republic is a question best left to cultural historians, as it goes beyond the scope of the present study. In the eyes of the Nazis who had taken power, they were, in any event, the embodiment of a racially alien "Jewish spirit" that was supposedly "polluting" the German folk soul. The party program had called for the immediate removal of Jews from cultural life, and Josef Goebbels, the new Minister of Popular Enlightenment and Propaganda, began its implementation soon after the party took power.

University teachers had been directly affected by the Civil Service Law. Two hundred of these, who enjoyed an international reputation in their fields far beyond the borders of Germany, received appointments at universities abroad during the course of 1933. However, after April 1933, nearly 350 Jewish faculty members were left without jobs.[48] The ousting of the other Jews active in various areas of cultural life was implemented by introducing special legislation. Although the Reich Chamber of Culture Law enacted on September 22, 1933, did not contain any express "paragraph on Aryans," it made any professional activity in literature, the press, the theater, music, and the plastic arts dependent on membership in a corresponding "chamber"—and such membership was denied on principle to Jews.[49] In addition, a special law regulating editorship of publications was enacted on October 4, 1933, barring Jewish or "partly Jewish" newspaper editors.[50]

The Civil Service Law and other legislation enacted in the early months of 1933 affected an estimated 12,000 to 13,000 Jews—that is, approximately 5 percent of the 240,487 gainfully employed Jews listed in the census of June 16, 1933. This fact is sometimes cited by historians as evidence that the economic harassment of Jews in the early period after the takeover of power was relatively mild in its effects. Seen from the vantage of current hindsight, the Nazis even unwittingly performed a service to the Jewish professionals legally excluded from their posts. Those who overnight had suddenly found themselves without any source of income were frequently compelled as a result of circumstances to emigrate immediately—such emigration was indeed a much simpler procedure at this juncture—and many may have saved their lives in this way. In contrast, the majority of gainfully employed Jews, initially unaffected by the official measures, were exposed to a protracted, creeping policy of terror aimed at forcing them out. That policy of terror, at least in the early stage, was partially compensated for by the general economic upswing. They were thus inclined to cling to their economic existence in Germany in the hope of "better times" to come. However, the relatively large group of Jewish white-collar workers was immediately affected by the first legal measures, whose regulations, even without express stipulation, were rigorously applied to them.

Jewish Workers and White-Collar Personnel

The 1925 occupational census listed more than eighty-four thousand Jewish white-collar employees and civil servants and some twenty-four thousand blue-collar workers, including domestics. By June 1933, the corresponding figures had already declined by several thousand. The Jewish workers were employed in the sector of industry and artisan crafts. No special mention was made of them in either National Socialist propaganda or the discriminatory legislation, probably because, in accordance with the antisemitic stereotypical thinking of the time, there simply could be no such thing as a "Jewish worker." Among white-collar workers as a whole, Jews accounted only for something over 1 percent of the total. Among commercial employees, there were some 50,000 in 1933, equivalent to 2.2 percent of the total. During the Depression, unemployment among those in trade and commerce—both Jewish and non-Jewish—was especially high. This group of Jewish employees, up to 60 percent of whom were engaged in trade and commerce jobs even before the Nazi takeover, had been a preferred target for antisemitic boycotts and attempts at economic displacement. The German-National Association of Shop Assistants (Deutsch-Nationaler Handlungsgehilfenverband) was particularly active in this regard. It had been one of the most powerful and influential interest associations of the "new" middle classes in the Weimar Republic and had been infiltrated early on by the Nazis and mobilized to serve their political objectives.[51]

On Boycott Day, April 1, the National Socialist Organization of Factory Cells (NSBO) issued an order to launch a campaign in all factories for the immediate dismissal of Jewish employees. These efforts were continued even after April 1, despite the government declaration on ending the boycott and the unacceptability of unauthorized "individual actions." However, the activity base of the NSBO was mainly in the larger plants and factories, which employed only a negligible proportion of Jewish white-collar workers. Most of them at this juncture were apparently employed in small and medium-size Jewish businesses, and such firms initially were less directly exposed to attacks by the militant Nazi organizations. However, in the larger commercial firms, even those under Jewish ownership, increased pressure to dismiss Jewish employees continued unabated. In most cases, it proved successful. To legitimize this dismissal, reference was made to the Civil Service Law, though its sections on exempt combat veterans or civil servants with seniority were duly ignored. Since most of these white-collar workers were from the younger age groups, such a regulation on exceptions would have been advantageous to only a limited number of them in any case.[52]

Jewish organizations—as well, in part, as Jewish employers—attempted to counteract this pressure in the initial weeks after the Nazi takeover by appealing to the labor courts and government authorities. However, their efforts met with little success. Large Jewish concerns—such as the shoe manufacturer Leiser, the electric bulb manufacturers Osram, the rubber factory Fromm, and the engine works Orenstein & Koppel—had to give in to NSBO pressures and fire a large segment of their Jewish employees. Suits filed in the labor courts resulted, in a number of instances, in basic rulings, according to which the Civil Service Law did not apply to white-collar workers in private commerce and industry. However, such decisions had little practical importance. The Reich Labor Court, which handed down a similar decision, at the same time added that "there was justification for immediate dismissal based on Jewish descent only when the continued presence of a Jewish employee in an individual given case might lead to disturbances in the plant, because such disturbances were intolerable for the employer."[53] The Nazi factory cells had thus been given a green light to stage "disturbances in the plant" in each "individual given case"; such disturbances then led on to the dismissal of the Jewish employees. At best, those dismissed were able, by taking the judicial route of appeal to the courts, only to obtain a certain amount of compensation and ensure that the legal guidelines for notification of dismissal were adhered to.

In mid-1933, 21.5 percent of all white-collar potential employees in Germany were still without work, although the revival of the economy in 1932 and the job-creation policies of the new regime had led to a sharp decline in unemployment. In contrast, the number of unemployed still stood at 28.4 percent among Jewish white-collar workers. When the results of the demographic and occupational census of June 16, 1933, were published by the Reich Statistical Office in 1936, the authors noted with a certain amount of surprise:

> Taking into account only the group of wage-earners who can be affected by unemployment (blue-collar and white-collar workers, domestic employees), what one finds is that the percentage of unemployed among Jews

> at the time of the census—i.e., some four-and-one-half months after the advent to power of the National Socialist movement—is, at 31.5 percent, only slightly above the national average (28.9 percent).[54]

What the official statistics failed to comment on was the fact that unemployment among Jewish white-collar workers was, in contrast to the general trend of development, on the constant rise and that the number of unemployed in the commercial sector was steadily increasing as a result of an influx of those persons previously self-employed whose businesses and shops had been forcibly liquidated or "Aryanized."

The Independent Middle Classes

Of the just under 110,000 Jewish "proprietors and leaseholders" listed in the June 1933 census, more than half were concentrated in the trade sector, principally in the retailing of clothing and household goods. Along with the white-collar workers and the small but highly visible and active group of university-trained professionals, this broad stratum of small and medium-size shop owners and merchants left its decisive imprint on the religious and social life of the Jewish *Gemeinden*. It determined to a substantial degree the political and cultural image of German Jewry—both the way it viewed itself and the way it was seen in the eyes of the world.

Jewish retail trade, about which there is reliable information thanks to the data of Herbert Kahn cited above and the Statistical Department of the Reichsvertretung, had been the principal target of the April 1 boycott. The SA and the SS "defense guards" that had posted themselves in front of all Jewish businesses in every city and even in the smallest village, the schoolchildren who congregated in curiosity around them, and the customers and passers-by, whose reactions were varied, marked street scenes throughout Germany on that particular day. After the boycott had been called off and decrees by the government and party denouncing "individual actions" had been published in an attempt "to calm the economy," the repressive measures against Jewish retail trade were continued by other means—less conspicuous but no less effective.

Despite all official admonishments and warnings from Berlin, however, the open and violent attacks against Jewish businesses went on unabated, especially in the smaller towns. Uniformed men posted before shops prevented customers from entering, and the photographs of those who shopped at Jewish stores continued to appear in the local press or in the *Stürmer* display case, accompanied by captions such as "traitor to the people" and "lackey of the Jews." The Gauleiter in the Palatinate, Josef Bürckel, formulated very clearly the difference between public declarations and practical continuing boycott terror in his reply to "repeated inquiries . . . regarding the question of department stores and the treatment of Jewish businesses":

> Various decrees are cited that could lead to misunderstandings in this matter. The following remarks should be of use to all concerned:
>
> 1. Before the takeover of power, the department store for us was the junk-shop which had brought ruin upon the small businessman. This judgment will stand for all time to come. The same holds when it comes to the treatment of the Jewish question.
>
> 2. We old Nazis do not care at all about the decrees issued by some boastful Nazi upstart or other. For us, there is nothing but the fulfillment of the program in accordance with the wishes of the Führer.[55]

The local party leaders, many of whom had become town mayors and or had advanced to other high positions in administration, had various means and ways at their disposal to discriminate against Jewish businesses and tighten the screw of economic pressure. Despite a guideline of the Reich Cabinet of July 14, 1933, expressly stipulating that public contracts were to be awarded only by the agencies officially authorized—without any interference by other organizations, especially the Kampfbund für den gewerblichen Mittelstand,[56]—Jewish firms had few prospects of being considered for such government contracts. This guideline remained in force until August 1938 but left local agencies sufficient latitude so that they could give preference to the "Aryan" firms in every local posting of a public tender. The available sources make it clear that in only a few cases were Jewish firms able to win public contracts after 1933. Such successful firms were, for all practical purposes, without any serious competitors in a specific area because of their scale and their many years of experience.[57]

Another means of boycotting Jewish retail tradesmen "administratively" was the prohibition by welfare offices and other local agencies against using welfare vouchers to purchase goods in Jewish stores. Such vouchers were issues to recipients of welfare or young married couples. When this practice led in 1933 to complaints to the government by Jewish organizations, it was prohibited by various official agencies, yet was generally continued at local level by other means. In Duisburg, for example, the corresponding rubber stamps were collected from the welfare offices (and dutifully stored away for future use!); at the same time, the welfare recipients were told they had to make their purchases at specific shops—"Aryan," of course. Posters appeared in the welfare offices warning welfare recipients against spending money "from public sources" for purchases in Jewish shops.[58]

A prohibition on shopping in department stores or Jewish shops was also introduced for municipal employees. In a number of cities, there initially were disputes with the old municipal bureaucracy about this measure, which referred to a decision by Hitler in October 1933.[59] However, all evidence suggests that regional and local party offices, as well as government agencies, disregarded such instructions from Berlin after a short time, extending the prohibition generally in effect for all Nazi Party members to all municipal employees in a number of towns. When complaints from Jewish organizations and intervention by the central government in Berlin increased in Westphalia, the district governor (*Regierungspräsident*) in Arnsberg informed the Reich Ministry that the regulations regarding the protection of Jewish economic enterprises from unlawful "individual actions" could not be implemented "without serious disruption of public peace and order." He therefore requested not to be bothered any longer by such matters; they should be dealt with by direct contact with the NSDAP, the SA, and the SS, which were themselves exercising an "open boycott."[60]

In actual fact, the open and violent boycott actions continued unabated throughout the entire year 1933, especially in the small towns but also in the large metropolitan centers. In June, uniformed SA and SS men in Dortmund blocked entry to all Jewish shops for two full weeks, manhandling customers wishing to get by them.[61] The large number of similar incidents, attested to by the available sources, proves very clearly that the actual situation of Jewish retail trade cannot be evaluated solely on the basis of the legal measures in effect or their temporary absence. Likewise, the published reports of the Reichsvertretung, which enjoyed a wide distribution and always showed great caution in their formulation, present only a fragmentary picture of the dire and distressing situation in which the owners of small and medium-size businesses found themselves. Even after the announced end of the boycott, the small retail tradesmen continued to be the principal target of measures of economic harassment. Such measures were practiced by party organizations, generally with the tacit toleration of local government and municipal authorities and with the active involvement of interests deriving a direct financial benefit from the boycott.

On the other hand, as long as the problem of mass unemployment remained unresolved, the large department stores and commercial firms were protected from encroachments for a short time simply by dint of their economic importance and the size of their work force. If they understood how to adapt to the new circumstances, Jewish industrial concerns were also able to profit from the general upturn in the economy. Boards of directors were reshuffled, and in many cases the name of the firm was "Germanized" even before sizable blocks of stock had changed owners—

a common practice in subsequent years in the wake of the intensified "Aryanization" process. In these early years of National Socialist rule, Jewish economic activity at various levels persisted, and the fate of the small bourgeois upper class, even at this time, was by no means identical with that of the Jewish population as a whole.[62]

The Jewish Reaction: Struggle for Legal Rights?

How then did Jews in Germany react to this sudden onslaught and new reality? In answering this question, it is necessary to distinguish between (a) individual reactions and (b) those of the new Jewish organizations that now came into being and began to adjust to the new situation. After the first shock had been weathered, Jewish individuals attempted to come to terms somehow with the new state of affairs—each in his own way, in keeping with his personal situation and based on individual attitudes and convictions, individual strength of resistance, or ability to accommodate. In 1933, nearly forty thousand Jews left Germany, most more or less in great haste. They were generally younger or unmarried persons; whether still employed or jobless, they enjoyed greater economic and social mobility. Those who emigrated in 1933 also included wealthier Jews who had been able to sell their property quickly. This first wave of emigration, which remained the largest emigration in any single year until the November 1938 pogrom, presumably also included an appreciable number of politically active Jews fleeing Germany as a result of their justified fear of the concentration camps.[63]

However, for the great majority of German Jews, the situation was different. Whoever had a family and children of school age, a shop or some other business, a house or other property found himself unable—unless he was immediately threatened—to arrive so easily at a decision to take leave of his homeland. After the first shock waves of the Nazi takeover and April boycott had passed, people began to get used to the situation. Many clung to the illusion that things would perhaps not turn out all that badly. After all, there had been a rapid turnover of governments in the final years of Weimar, and it was thought that Hitler too would not last in power for very long. Others assuaged their fears with a belief in the continued existence of the constitutional state, in which legal norms would finally win out despite all of the revolutionary upheaval of the early weeks of the new regime. In this connection, they were able to point to the numerous declarations by the government denouncing "individual actions," declarations whose real purpose was to help calm down and stabilize the economy.

This attitude is reflected in the many complaints lodged by Jewish individuals and firms preserved in the files of national and municipal government offices. The style and tone of such formal complaints differ substantially. Some of those lodging a grievance point confidently to the civil rights anchored in the constitution. Others cite statements by the government against arbitrary unlawful "individual actions" in the economy. Yet there are also overly zealous assertions of one's contribution to the fatherland and protestations of the strength of one's "national patriotic outlook." In some instances, there are denials that one belongs to Jewry. Half a century after full legal emancipation, these letters reflect the diverse complexity of the Jewish minority in Germany: the attitudes expressed run the gamut from intense assimilationism to the point of self-denial all the way to a proud insistence on one's own identity and the rights that had been won.

A typical example is represented by correspondence between the Dortmund department store concern Gebr. Kaufmann and the local mayor in October 1933.[64] After prior verbal discussion, the mayor's office was supplied by the firm with extracts from and copies of government regulations, declarations by the Trustee for Labor (*Treuhänder der Arbeit*), and decrees and circulars issued by the Economy Ministry in order to demonstrate that "the Trustee of Labor, in matters pertaining to economic measures, is authorized to provide government offices with orders to be passed on to the various agencies." Apparently, the mayor had rejected this, quite in keeping with the sense of Gauleiter Bürckel's position as quoted above. The letter of the Jewish department stores requested the municipality to inform the firm whether it was prepared to rescind the prohibition on purchases by municipal employees, the freeze on placing ads, the exclusion of the firm from bidding for public contracts, and its exclusion as a firm where welfare vouchers could be redeemed.

The reply by the mayor of Dortmund to this very objective and respectful letter is symptomatic of the situation at the time: "Returning your enclosed supporting documents," the mayor informed the firm that all central government ministerial decrees regarding the cancellation of the boycott against Jewish department stores, prohibitions on their placing public advertisements, and so on had also led in Dortmund to a cancellation of local prohibitions. However, the mayor chose to add his own comments regarding each individual point of the complaint "personally, as a National Socialist." As a National Socialist, he found it "difficult to understand how a civil servant could do his shopping in a Jewish department store." He could not imagine "that any newspaper in Dortmund would accept ads from Jewish businesses." Although the firm was free to bid for tendered contracts of the municipality, "you cannot demand from me as a National Socialist that I approve your bid."

One could cite a great many similar letters and grievances from the year 1933, some of which went all the way to the Reich Chancellery. A Jewish meat wholesaler in Wanne-Eickel in Westphalia, for example, appealed directly to Hermann Göring after his local protestations and a complaint to the district governor in Arnsberg had produced no results. Referring to Göring's orders that prohibited "interference in the economy," the petitioner enclosed a letter written by his battalion commander during World War I and stressed his wartime achievements. He then went on: "self-employed here in this town since 1900, I have never been accused of any wrongdoing and have always fulfilled my duties toward the municipality and the state."

In this case as well, the reaction of the authorities was typical. The local Gauleiter replied by threatening physical violence regarding a number of similar grievances that involved sanctions against the Jewish cattle and meat trade in particular. On September 27, 1933, the district governor in Arnsberg wrote to the Reich Interior Minister requesting that he "look once again into the matter of the Jewish question, in detail, and if possible in cooperation with the national head office of the NSDAP and the top command echelon of the SA. . . . Because, first of all, the heads of the local agencies . . . do not see any possibility for doing full justice to the decrees and secondly, it is highly likely that there will be a serious disturbance of public law and order if the decrees are implemented, judging from opinions that have been transmitted to me by party officials." Such statements cannot be viewed as proof of the existence of a contradictory "dualistic" Jewish policy, as the following section of that same letter shows. The district governor indicated his understanding of the need for a "calming down of the economy" and the "struggle against unemployment" yet requested that another aspect be borne carefully in mind: "the extent to which, specifically during the struggle to gain power, the demand was raised for an elimination of the disproprotionate influence of Jews in various areas of the economy, and the fact that opposition to Jewry is the emotional foundation of the movement."[65]

In the light of such experiences, it is understandable that the stream of personal grievances submitted by Jews to the local and central authorities was gradually reduced to a trickle as 1933 wore on. Jews had come to recognize the hopelessness of any appeals to norms of constitutionality in the "new Germany" and attempted increasingly to cope with mounting difficulties on their own and with the assistance of the Jewish community.

Building a Network of Jewish Self-Help

Before 1933, the Jewish *Gemeinden* in Germany had not yet federated into a general representative body to promote their interests. This fact was characteristic of German Jewry, which was dispersed in hundreds of *Gemeinden* throughout the entire expanse of Germany and which was likewise far from unified in any philosophical or religious sense. It is true that there was a State Federation of Jewish *Gemeinden* in Prussia, but that body was more an organizational appendage of the Jewish *Gemeinde* in Berlin, where more than half of all Jews in Prussia lived in 1925.[66] It was also in the Berlin *Gemeinde* that the first foundations were laid for the establishment of an extensive system of self-help for German Jews.

The nucleus around which this organization crystallized was a respected group of young social workers, active for many years in Jewish welfare, whose organizational and ideological center was within the Zentralwohlfahrtsstelle der deutschen Juden (Central Welfare Agency for German Jews). By the 1920s, they had developed an impressive network of modern social welfare services in the poorer Berlin neighborhoods and had successfully applied progressive methods of social work. Their accumulated experiences, after an admirably swift readjustment to the new circumstances, were now utilized for the benefit of a broad and ever expanding circle of German Jews. Among these Jews were many who, just a few short months before, would never have imagined in their wildest dreams that they would someday have to rely on the services of any institution of social welfare.[67]

A call for contributions by the welfare office of the Jewish *Gemeinde* in Berlin in April 1933 can serve to convey something of the attitude that accompanied these first fledgling steps down the path to creating a network of Jewish self-help. The call quoted from an essay by Ismar Elbogen, head of the Hochschule für die Wissenschaft des Judentums in Berlin, which had appeared on April 4 in the *C.V. Zeitung,* the weekly paper of the Centralverein:

> Tens of thousands have been stripped of their source of livelihood and forced out of their profession. Many who were self-employed are now uprooted. It is meaningless to ask today about reasons and causes. There is no sense in accusing ourselves or others. There is but one dictate of the hour: to work and to help!
>
> They can condemn us to *hunger,* but they cannot condemn us to *starvation*! They can squeeze the space that remains to us for living ever tighter, yet in its constricted confines we must join together, and each must try to support his fellow. . . . Think of the history of our forefathers—repeatedly, they experienced such catastrophes, yet did not surrender their will to live! Unperturbed, they searched out and found ways and means for continued survival and the building of a new existence, albeit more modest, in place of that which had been lost. And so we too must, after the paralyzing stupor of these past weeks, once again regain

> our senses and undertake *all* possible efforts to create bread and work for our sisters and brothers.[68]

After difficult negotiations on the bridging of regional, political, and even personal differences, an organization representing all German Jews officially came into being in the autumn of 1933 in the form of the Reichsvertretung der Deutschen Juden.[69] However, the urgency of the need for economic self-help was recognized at an early point, so that a national Zentralauschuss der deutschen Juden für Hilfe und Aufbau (Central Committee of German Jews for Relief and Rehabilitation) was formed as early as April 13. It was later integrated into the Reichsvertretung.[70] The various individual Jewish *Gemeinden* soon put the existing and newly established organizations to work in helping to provide crucially needed assistance. The largest of these organizations was the Zentralstelle für jüdische Wirtschaftshilfe (Central Bureau for Jewish Economic Relief; hereafter Wirtschaftshilfe) opened the beginning of April in Berlin.[71] In its first few days, the offices of the Wirtschaftshilfe were stormed by hundreds of persons seeking assistance, since rumors had spread that the bureau "had large sums of money for support at its disposal."[72] Its actual possibilities were far more modest in scope, yet the extent of relief assistance available at that time appears surprising from a present-day perspective.

The university graduates and civil servants hard hit by the Civil Service Law were in particular and pressing need of assistance. For this reason, their problems also shaped the character and the approach of the Wirtschaftshilfe in this early first stage of its activity. Attempts were made, in a demonstratively legalistic manner, to have "illegal" dismissals reversed by the submission of grievances to competent government offices and, if need be, by the filing of a suit with the labor court. If reinstatement was not possible, an attempt was made at least to assure that the legally stipulated compensation and dismissal notification periods were adhered to. Special legal advice columns were started in all Jewish newspapers. These columns published the full text of new laws and regulations, commented in detail on basic court rulings, and encouraged those affected to insist on their legal rights. Among other things, this may have been a product of the greatly enlarged legal-aid sections in all Jewish organizations: a kind of internal Jewish employment scheme to give work to the large numbers of jobless Jewish attorneys and judges. In addition, this practice reflected a view that was also predominant at the time in Jewish leadership circles: namely, that it was possible to defend economic positions by juridical means and methods. Only in this way can one explain the suggestion advanced then—though soon abandoned—to form a Jewish organization for protecting the interests of Jewish blue-collar and white-collar workers who had been barred from membership in the DAF (Deutsche Arbeitsfront).[73]

During this first stage of development, the other sections of the economic relief network structured along the lines of occupational groups also operated according to the principles described earlier. The Commercial Advisory Office attempted to have the municipal regulations on purchasing restrictions for civil servants and the ban on granting public contracts to Jewish firms rescinded by means of protest and intervention by the courts. In general, such attempts met with just as little success as complaints filed by individuals and firms. Consequently, one soon shifted, out of necessity, to an approach that stressed the practical provision of financial relief aid. These measures, still regarded at the time as temporary, were dubbed "economic first aid." Alexander Szanto, who was active in the Berlin Wirtschaftshilfe, has left a very vivid description of this "constructive first aid":

> For many years, a Jewish restaurant owner had been operating a small pastry and coffee shop, whose clientele consisted mainly of Christians. . . . Since the Boycott Day, [customers] had hardly dared to venture to his shop. . . . At the same time, difficulties started to crop up with the Christian waiter in his employ, and the authorities harassed him with all sorts of chicanery. He became indebted, was unable to find a buyer for his shop and had to close it. . . . The Wirtschaftshilfe assisted him in opening an ice-cream parlor in a completely different neighborhood of town. . . . The ice-cream machine was purchased for him by the Wirtschaftshilfe from a Jewish manufacturer. . . .
>
> The Jewish merchant Y. was a competent and hardworking traveling salesman dealing in textile goods. Since he was on excellent terms with his network of customers—both Jewish and Christian—he initially was able to successfully continue his trips in the rural countryside. But he ran into difficulties in finding a hotel room in the small provincial towns, where hotels and inns tended more and more toward a policy of refusing a room to Jewish guests. The Wirtschaftshilfe provided a car for him, and later on a delivery van. In this way, it proved possible for him to organize . . . his trips in such a way that in the evening . . . he could manage to get to a larger town, where accommodations were still available. When this became impossible as well, he used to spend the night in his van by the side of the road, preparing a meal from canned goods he had brought along. . . .
>
> The press photographer Z. was fired as a non-Aryan from his well-paid job with a newspaper publisher. The Wirtschaftshilfe provided him with a loan for the purchase of his own high-quality photographic equipment, and helped him set up his own studio. . . . When he decided to

> emigrate and the loan had not as yet been completely repaid, he returned part of the equipment to the Bureau, which then was able to utilize that equipment in its own retraining courses.[74]

In view of the economic structure of German Jewry, it was likely that the Commercial Advisory Office would soon become the most often consulted section of the Wirtschaftshilfe. The discussion regarding the legal situation and the juridical struggle for every position it was still possible to salvage went on for a time, but practical assistance became an ever more important focus.

> It was the "little guys"—the craft artisans, tradesmen and shop owners—upon whom the Commercial Advisory Office bestowed its assistance . . . on the assumption that even in the framework of the National Socialist state it would be possible for Jews to survive economically. . . . In answer to all those who criticize the fact that we wished from 1933 to 1941 to give economic assistance to persons who were in any event condemned to annihilation after 1941, one thing must be said: such a criticism rests on an interpretation after the fact. To be wise in hindsight is an easy matter! For us then it was simply a matter of aiding Jews threatened by hunger and worry and in distress.[75]

The principle of self-help also was adopted within individual occupational groups. In the spring of 1933, Jewish lawyers and doctors spontaneously organized internal collections among themselves for colleagues who had been affected by the Civil Service Law and were without any income. Special gala functions, such as the Jewish "Doctors' Ball" in Berlin, were dedicated to raising contributions for the various relief funds. A Jewish Artists' Relief Organization founded by middle-class women supported needy artists by organizing lectures and artistic performances in restaurants and private homes. In addition, the Artists' Relief supported its own soup kitchen and a club, from private contributions, before the Jüdischer Kulturbund (Jewish Cultural League) that was established in Berlin and other cities was able to offer jobs to artists. Ernst Loewenberg, a teacher and member of the board of directors of the Jewish *Gemeinde* in Hamburg, reports about this type of assistance:

> In April 1933, Jewish lawyers, doctors and teachers set up special committees in order . . . to help colleagues affected. . . . As a coordinator for the teachers, I . . . probably interviewed in my office all those teachers who had been forced in Hamburg to leave the school system . . . [in order to] place colleagues from Hamburg in newly established Jewish schools via contacts with the school section of the Reichsvertretung. . . .

In search of work: the unemployed crowd the office of the Berlin Jewish *Wirtschaftshilfe* in 1937.

> Among the many visitors . . . the memory of one in particular remains vivid. In the autumn of 1933, a haggard old woman teacher came to me and explained straightaway that she had never had anything to do with Jews, but that she was desperate. She had been a village teacher for many years in Schleswig-Holstein . . . and was from a strict Protestant family. . . . However, she had discovered when trying to prove her Aryan descent that her father—who himself was the son of a Protestant minister—was Jewish by race. So she had been dismissed from her job. Distant friends had taken in the totally destitute woman. Her brothers lived abroad. She found it impossible to grasp the idea that Jews, with whom she had never had anything to do, should now help her, a German Protestant. . . . I gave her the streetcar fare to go to the advisory office. Later on, her passage to America was paid by a general foundation and from Jewish sources.[76]

This Professional Self-Help Section was also involved in trying to locate jobs abroad to make it possible for persons trained in the free professions and now unemployed to emigrate. In those days, that was a difficult task even when it came to doctors because very few of them were willing to relocate to underdeveloped countries and areas where they could gain entry and acceptance. Palestine was an exception. Many Jewish doctors chose to emigrate there and made outstanding contributions to the establishment of a modern health system. Other Western countries placed the greatest obstacles in the path of doctors wishing to immigrate and obtain a work permit.[77] Thus, in its first few weeks the Wirtschaftshilfe in Berlin had to deal with almost four thousand doctors in need of support, half of whom no longer had any income whatsoever. Only gradually were some of those doctors who remained in Germany able to find work in Jewish *Gemeinden,* schools, and sport associations or to earn something by substituting for doctors on vacation or by temporary employment in the offices of Jewish doctors still able to practice. In a similar fashion, many attorneys also found employment in the administrative bureaucracy of Jewish *Gemeinden* and other organizations.[78]

In all of these measures, the borderline between "constructive help" and actual welfare assistance remained fluid. Until that time, the welfare activities of the Jewish *Gemeinden* had been a well-developed system geared to providing financial support to poor or low-income marginal groups in the Jewish population, though such groups had increased in number dramatically during the Depression. Most individuals in these groups were already recipients of public welfare assistance, and relief funds provided by Jewish welfare were meant as supplementary assistance. The Jewish *Gemeinden* maintained special institutions for such assistance, and it was on these that they expended the largest proportion of their welfare budget: day-care and convalescent homes for children, clinics and old-age homes for the indigent elderly, and so on. There was need for an immediate response to the sudden distress in which many Jewish families, who previously had never had any contact with welfare offices, now found themselves. That privation was ameliorated by financial relief to assist with daily needs, although initially there was not a large amount of funding available for such types of aid. This was compounded by the fact that the Jews dependent on public welfare, who were subject to various harassments and restrictions, also had to be supported by Jewish welfare as well. As a consequence of these heavy burdens, many *Gemeinde*-linked institutions, such as nursing and convalescent homes, now found themselves in economic straits and were forced to close down.[79] In the past, the public welfare agencies had even assigned non-Jewish needy persons to these homes, and they had been able in this way to help cover part of their operating costs.

At the start of 1933, there were twenty-five small Jewish credit associations in existence. These were viewed more as means to provide "constructive welfare assistance" than as credit institutes. The independent capital of all of these associations amounted to a total of only approximately RM 750,000 and was used for providing small, interest-free (or almost interest-free) loans of from RM 100 to RM 200 to small-enterprise artisans and tradesmen. Such credit associations had initially been set up in the 1920s in Eastern Europe by the "Joint" and spread from there to Germany. They had fulfilled an important function, particularly in Poland, where there was a large impoverished Jewish middle class suffering from an antisemitic boycott that had been openly endorsed and supported by the government. In Germany, such loan associations had had a much smaller circle of beneficiaries until 1933, consisting principally of Eastern European artisans and small tradesmen who could indeed be materially assisted by such modest loans.[80]

Jewish self-help efforts were also able to link up with already existing initiatives in the field of occupational/vocational training and counseling. During the Depression years, job placement bureaus had been set up by the *Gemeinden* to assist school graduates and jobless youngsters in choosing a vocation and to provide help in locating jobs and apprenticeships. In addition, the Zionist youth leagues maintained agricultural training farms that prepared young people for emigration to Palestine. At the beginning of 1933, these institutions, which until then had served only a small number of Jewish youth, were literally swamped by a sudden deluge of applications from thousands of young and even older Jewish men and women. The Jewish job placement bureaus and training centers formed the nucleus of a comprehensive system of occupational counseling and job retraining. Many placed their hopes in learning a new profession in order to be able to build new lives for themselves later either in Germany or abroad. The available places were far too few, even if it had proved feasible to multiply their numbers quickly. By the end of 1933, the system of organized vocational training encompassed more than six thousand people, including a number of older persons. Thirteen hundred were studying and living in communal training centers, mainly on the agricultural teaching farms, the so-called *hachshara* (Hebrew for "training") program of the Zionist leagues. The others received training in individual teaching centers. Almost half of the training courses were devoted to agriculture and gardening; the remainder were in areas such as artisan crafts and even in the field of domestic help.[81]

The impressive figures indicate just how swiftly the respective organizations responded to the new circumstances. Nonetheless, only a small number of people could be accommodated. In earlier years, the greater proportion of Jewish youngsters leaving school and entering the job market, as well as older persons who needed to learn a new trade, had made their vocational choices individually, and then had found for themselves a suitable place for training. In 1933, however, despite the upswing in the job market, it became more and more difficult for Jews to find apprenticeship places, even before the introduction of official sanctions. Under these circumstances, the various services expanded by the Jewish *Gemeinden*—such as the occupational counseling and job placement bureaus, as well as the training/retraining courses in agriculture and the craft trades—all took on a growing importance. After a certain amount of time, it proved possible to mollify the German authorities,[82] particularly the Gestapo, who had initially viewed these efforts with skepticism and had interfered at various points. This was done by repeatedly emphasizing one salient argument: vocational training served to prepare people for later emigration.

Beginnings of a "Jewish Economic Sector"

The efforts of the Jewish job placement bureaus were focused after January 1933 mainly on Jewish firms. Increasingly, Jewish blue-collar and white-collar workers could hope to find jobs only with Jewish employers. As long as the number of independent Jewish firms and businesses was still relatively large, it was possible to facilitate procurement of many jobs and apprenticeship positions in this way. This then represented the beginning of the development of an independent—though by no means autarkic—Jewish economic sector previously nonexistent in Germany. The more the vocational and job prospects of Jews were restricted as a result of legislation, "spontaneous" boycott, or administrative measures and chicanery, the closer the Jewish community joined together, closing ranks in economic respects as well. And the more hopeless the legal battle to maintain existing positions in the economy proved to be, the clearer was the recognition by ever increasing numbers of Jews that in their struggle for economic survival they could rely only on themselves and perhaps on the support of their co-religionists abroad. Jewish economic life thus began to undergo a restructuring: more and more, Jews were now working for and employing Jews, assuring themselves a livelihood by means of economic intercourse among themselves.

As in other areas, Jewish young people here too showed themselves to be more inventive and farsighted than many adults or than a number of the Jewish organizations. As early as May 1933, an appeal was circulated by the National Committee of Jewish Youth Leagues, signed by Ludwig Tietz and Georg Lubinski. It called on the local branches of all Jewish youth organizations to take an active part in efforts to procure jobs for the Jewish unemployed. Each member was obligated to locate at least one vacant job or apprenticeship by making inquiries among friends and relatives. An effort was to be made to find places for individual agricultural training ("individual *hachshara*") among local farmers—if necessary only in exchange for food and lodging and even with the supplementary payment of a small sum of money to the farmer. In the course of a few weeks, several hundred positions, mainly agricultural apprenticeships, were located and arranged in this manner.[83]

Beginning during the Weimar Republic, appreciable numbers of Jewish blue-collar workers and even more white-collar personnel had found employment in Jewish-owned firms. This was one by-product of the antisemitic boycott that had already intensified at the time of the Depression; it was also a consequence of intentional efforts undertaken by the Jewish job placement offices. A large proportion of these workers were dismissed during the course of the April boycott under pressure from NSBO officials and other Nazi functionaries. Attempts by large Jewish concerns to reemploy them after Boycott Day were unsuccessful. The Jewish placement bureaus thus concentrated their efforts principally on small and medium-size Jewish plants, in which as a rule there were no NSBO factory cells and the supervision by the DAF was less effective. In a number of cases, the employment of new Jewish workers was combined with the awarding of contracts by Jewish institutions to the employment firms. In this way, both the new Jewish employee and his or her Jewish employer came to benefit economically from the arrangement.[84]

The Jewish newspapers were also mobilized in the search for jobs. The success of recurring appeals in the press appears to have been only negligible in the early period, when circulation figures for the Jewish press had just started to climb at a slow pace. But it was at this juncture that the importance of Jewish newspapers for the subsequent development of the Jewish economic sector began to emerge and make itself felt. Clearly articulated in the columns of these papers were the urgency of the need to procure gainful employment for Jewish workers and an appeal to the feeling of Jewish solidarity: as, for example, in an article published in September 1933 with the characteristic title "We accuse!" The article criticized Jewish master craftsmen, cooks, barbers, tailors, and other artisans because they were prepared to take on Jewish apprentices only in exchange for the payment of an apprentice fee. This was denounced as an attempt to try to profit from the distressful hard times. Where should these people, who sometimes did not even have enough for a warm meal, get the necessary money to pay such fees?[85]

Along with press releases, the Wirtschaftshilfe issued a mimeographed bulletin entitled "Vermittlungsdienst" (Exchange Service). Its first issue in the spring of 1933 reflected the desperate situation faced by the jobless and impoverished. Doctors and lawyers appealed to their colleagues in particular, requesting to be kept in mind when they were buying tea, coffee, or soap. Their wives advertised assistance with various types of written work and knitting. Dismissed judges and state attorneys offered their gowns for sale or their legal libraries "at bargain prices." The mimeographed pages also carried requests for and offers of capital investment, ranging from RM 3,000 to RM 40,000, although there were more requests than offers. Frequently, factories or shops were offered for sale at what appeared to be completely ridiculous prices: for example, a "shipping firm in Mannheim" for the incredible sum of RM 1,000; or a doctor's practice, completely equipped and with a family home, in an office whose rent was prepaid until April 1935—RM 5,000 to RM 6,000![86] The sources do not indicate whether buyers were found for the properties. Yet how desperate must the situation have been for those who had placed the ads.

And so it was that the Jewish economic sector came into being—unplanned and by no means conceived as the long-term solution to the crisis situation of German Jewry—in the early months of the Nazi regime at the initiative of individuals and groups who suddenly found themselves jobless and without any income. Many may have taken the assurances of the new rulers at face value—namely, that Jews had nothing to fear in the field of the vocational trades—and thus ventured in such trades to build a new basis for their continued economic existence in Germany. Others sold off their legal or medical practices in order to emigrate to a new homeland. It seemed reasonable to everyone in need of help to turn first to their own community.

Yet the ensuing joining of hands economically also marked the beginning of a new process of intellectual and organizational self-assertion by the Jewish community, which had been left to fend for itself. Individual Jews reached a decision, sometimes earlier than those in positions of leadership in the community: to liberate themselves from the sway of the arbitrary measures introduced by the new rulers, to contend to the best of their abilities with the new circumstances, and to cope for the present with their new lot—whether in order to remain in Germany, economically active and productive despite everything, or to rescue and transfer as much as possible of their capital at the time of their prospective emigration.

First Attempts to Salvage Personal Assets

The difficulties inherent in transferring assets abroad originally had no connection with the Nazi policy of persecution of the Jews. In 1931, the Brüning government had imposed legal restrictions on currency export to prevent the calamitous flight of capital during the Depression. Even the Reich Flight Tax (*Reichsfluchtsteuer*), later utilized by the Nazi regime to rob and despoil departing Jews, had already been introduced at that time.[87] In 1933, capital transfer abroad was almost completely suspended. The new rulers issued regulations on exceptions pertaining to the transfer of Jewish assets in order to accelerate Jewish emigration. In the first two or three years of the new regime, it was still relatively simple, despite the tense currency situation, to transfer funds abroad. For this reason, it proved possible during this period to salvage a certain amount of Jewish capital and spirit it out of the country, in contrast with later years.

Affluent and farsighted Jews tried to utilize the existing possibilities for immediate or imminent emigration. Heads of large industries and bankers with the advantage of foreign business and financial connections were naturally in a far better position to do this than the great majority of the middle classes, whose capital was largely tied up in business and real estate. In the first few months of the new regime, before the complete nazification of all government offices, an appreciable number of wealthy Jews appear to have found ways to liquidate their assets and emigrate without absorbing any large capital loss. For this reason, there were a good many affluent Jews in the first wave of emigration.[88] Members of the Jewish upper class who chose to remain in Germany for the time being began to spirit their capital abroad by means of trading deals and the investment of foreign firms in their companies. In addition, the transferal of their firms, even if only to partial foreign ownership, afforded them the advantage of a certain protection from boycott measures and other encroachments, at least for a brief period of time.

By 1933, something tantamount to a new "branch" of financial consultants and transfer experts had come into being. The Gestapo files report on their activities. Thus, a letter written by a Berlin financial adviser was confiscated in the offices of a Dortmund businessman and then passed on to the Gestapo. The writer of this letter offered his services "to preserve Jewish capital, especially legal investment abroad"; this "naturally would have to be compatible with German interests." In addition, he claimed to have also "arranged conversions of Jewish businesses and industries, so-called '*Gleichschaltungen,*' without the Jewish partner having lost influence in the firm." This economic adviser informed the Berlin Gestapo, in written reply to an inquiry, that he had "gotten the idea of *Gleichschaltungen* because I wished to give Aryan friends an opportunity to find a position. It is a matter of general knowledge that non-Aryan businesses can be bought very cheaply today, since a large number of the owners are contemplating emigration. I am involved in arranging *Gleichschaltungen* in order to enable non-Aryan entrepreneurs to emigrate, while at the same time helping my previously unemployed friends to find a position." The Gestapo appears to have found this double motive understandable and convincing. It is characteristic of the situation at the time that this economic adviser was under constant Gestapo surveillance until 1941 but was allowed to continue his activities, as indicated by regular entries in Gestapo files. In 1935 and 1937, he was repeatedly interrogated and was briefly taken into custody. He had been anonymously accused of "camouflaging Jewish firms as Aryan, buying up patents with Jewish money for illicit sale abroad, as well as engaging in the illicit sale and transfer of assets outside the country." Yet in none of these cases could any punishable charge be proved against him.[89]

This instance has been described here in detail because it presents a realistic picture of the concrete cooperation between German and Jewish official agencies, including the Gestapo, in promoting Jewish emigration. Such cooperation was already in effect by the beginning of 1933. Nourished by totally opposed motives, it led to an agreement that made possible the transfer of a portion of Jewish assets to Palestine and other countries. Only after it was stabilized and had been strengthened by its successes on the economic front and in foreign policy did the Nazi regime switch to a policy of expropriating Jewish capital and forcing Jews whose assets had been plundered and who were now destitute to leave the country. Earlier, when such an approach did not seem feasible, the regime was prepared to deal flexibly with the existing laws in the interest of accelerated Jewish emigration. Not only did this attitude lead to the conclusion of various agreements with representative Jewish bodies—such as the Haavara Transfer Agreement discussed below—it was also a key factor operative in individual initiatives. In the summer of 1933, the director of the Anglo-Palestine Bank in Tel Aviv, who had come to Berlin to participate in negotiations on the transfer of capital, wrote in his July 1933 confidential report:

> Practical action goes its own ways. It does not wait for the official bureaus, and can achieve a great deal. There are many avenues for individual action . . . such as private agreements with persons or corporations who have payments to make in Germany, etc. It goes without saying that there is also the illegal way. Naturally, a businessman who has maintained contacts abroad over the years, the man who knows his way around the government agencies—and any clever and resourceful person—have things easier in this regard than some simple fellow, say a university graduate, who has twenty or maybe fifty thousand marks in liquid assets and is waiting for some administrative office that will arrange to get the money out of the country for him.[90]

The Haavara Transfer Agreement[91] came about through an initiative that was originally private. Sam Cohen, director of Hanotea Ltd., a firm dealing with citrus plantations in Palestine, concluded a kind of clearing agreement with the Reich economy minister in May 1933. According to that agreement, every Jew wishing to emigrate was permitted to deposit a sum of up to RM 40,000 in a blocked account. In return, they received from Hanotea the full equivalent value in Palestine currency, based on the official exchange rate (similar to the pound sterling), in the form of real estate such as a house or a citrus plantation in Palestine. Hanotea in turn obligated itself to use the funds in the blocked account for importing German goods to Palestine, mainly pipes, pumping equipment, fertilizers, and the like. In July 1933, the agreement with Hanotea was expanded to the sum of RM 3 million on the condition that the official Zionist organizations be involved in the scheme.[92]

These negotiations sparked vehement discussion and dispute within the Jewish public in Palestine and in other countries. An arrangement that directly or indirectly helped promote German exports contradicted all efforts to organize a worldwide boycott of German export goods as a protest against the persecution of Jews in Germany, including efforts by non-Jewish organizations such as the British trade union movement. The Haavara Agreement was the subject of public controversy and heated discussion in the Jewish press and at the Prague Zionist Congress in August 1933. The executive of the Zionist World Organization initially hesitated to accept the transfer agreement and take over its implementation. However, when the financial situation of the German Jews continued to deteriorate and the urgent necessity for them to emigrate became absolutely clear, the 19th Zionist Congress in Lucerne decided that the entire activity of the Haavara scheme should be placed under the official control of the Jewish Agency for implementation. The desire was to rescue at least a portion of Jewish assets and to give German Jews the possibility of emigrating to Palestine. According to the regulations of the British Mandatory government for Palestine, there were annual immigration quotas for Jews without means; so-called capitalists who had the sum of least £1,000 Palestine (approximately RM 15,000 at the time) in their possession, were issued a "capitalist immigration certificate." That certificate enabled them to immigrate without any restrictions.[93]

The circular letter issued by the Economy Ministry on August 28, 1933, informing all foreign currency bureaus about the signing of the Haavara Agreement, reveals something about the possible underlying motives of the German government. It is stated there, among other things, that the agreement "had been concluded with the official Jewish organizations involved . . . in order to continue to promote the emigration of German Jews to Palestine by granting the requisite sums—without putting an excessive burden on the foreign currency reserves of the Reichsbank, while at the same time increasing German exports to Palestine."[94] The "granting" of the "requisite sums," which constituted a clear exception under foreign currency regulations in effect at the time, referred to the amount of at least £1,000 stipulated by the Mandatory authorities. In the first few years, this was provided by the Reichsbank in foreign currency at the official rate to emigrating Jews.

It is true that the Haavara Agreement did not promise the German side any additional influx of foreign currency, since all goods exported to Palestine were paid for in reichsmarks drawn from the blocked Haavara account. However, the Economy Ministry was doubtless banking on the anticipated stimulus for employment of the increased volume of exports. The government, overestimating the financial might of "world Jewry," also appears to have had definite fears about the impact of a worldwide boycott of German products. It expected the foreign boycott efforts would be more successful than they actually turned out to be. The German consul general in Jerusalem, Heinrich Wolff, who actively supported efforts for the agreement, may have shared this apprehension, or may have been cleverly playing on such fears, when he pointed to the danger of further drops in exports as a result of the Jewish boycott in an April 1933 report to the Foreign Office in Berlin.[95]

After the agreement had been concluded with official Jewish representatives, including the German Zionist Federation (ZVfD), the Palästina-Treuhandstelle (Palestine Trusteeship Office, abbreviated "Paltreu") was set up in Berlin. Two Jewish private banks—Warburg in Hamburg and Wassermann in Berlin—also had financial involvements with the Paltreu Office. The Haavara, registered with the Anglo-Palestine Bank, functioned as partner in Palestine. By the end of 1933, these institutions had already transferred some RM 1.255 million; this sum had risen to nearly 140 million by the outbreak of the war in September 1939. The monies transferred considerably eased the burdens of emigration to Palestine for approximately fifty-two thousand German Jews and their subsequent absorption there. In many cases, such emigration was possible at all only as a result of the Haavara scheme.

This agreement must likewise be evaluated in the context of the reaction of German Jews to the catastrophe that had befallen them. Despite the political turbulence and constantly exacerbating antisemitism in the Weimar Republic that had preceded the National Socialist regime, the Jewish population and its leadership were almost completely unprepared for that catastrophe. Today we can only admire the ability they evinced to adjust swiftly to the changed situation, rely on their own wits and resources, and proceed to create a comprehensive and relatively well-organized system of Jewish self-help. Not all of the problems could be solved in this way, even though many of the new programs and initiatives of the year 1933 were improved and expanded in the ensuing period. Later on, German Jewry would find itself facing ever new forms of repression and persecution in the economic sphere and beyond—repression against which it ultimately proved unable to muster any defense.

2

1934–1937
The Illusion of a "Grace Period"

Only a superficial observer could regard the four years from 1934 to 1937 as a period in which Jews in Germany were able to pursue their economic affairs undisturbed and without molestation. It is true that, after the regime had established itself, open violence against Jews was confined to sporadic incidents. Legislation likewise dealt only rarely with Jewish economic activity. Even the announced and anticipated new economic restrictions in the wake of the Nuremberg Laws of September 1935 failed to materialize. Among many contemporaries at the time, there thus arose the illusion of the advent of an economic "grace period"—a view that even today is widespread in the historical literature. In actual fact, however, the process of ousting Jews from the economy in Germany and expropriating their assets pressed ahead with inexorable consistency.

Initially, the brunt of this process was felt more in the smaller towns and rural areas of the provinces than in the large metropolitan centers, and it generally was carried out in quiet and relatively unobtrusive ways. The Nazis had understood that Jewish owners of small and medium-size shops and firms could be motivated to sell their businesses for a mere fraction of their real worth—without the introduction of legislation that created a stir or public proclamations but rather resorting to threats, intimidation, and small-scale violence wherever deemed necessary. In the early period, nonetheless, many Jewish firms improved their economic situation. They too were able to profit from the general economic upturn, insofar as it was possible for them to continue to operate their businesses. Yet the process of displacement was the dominant feature in these years, and by 1937 the Jews were already a crushed and significantly weakened group, both demographically and economically.

Emigration and Its Consequences

The Jewish population shrank during this four-year period by about 130,000. This constituted some 27 percent of the 470,000 to 480,000 Jews who were still living in Germany at the end of 1933. Approximately ninety-two thousand had emigrated, and the remainder can be accounted for by the difference between the birth and mortality rates.[1] More than 60 percent of those emigrating were between the ages of twenty and forty-five, and this group had a higher percentage of males than females. This process enhanced the demographic trends of overaging and an excess of women that had been observed earlier in the Jewish population in Germany. The ratio of women to men in 1933 was 1,093 to 1,000; by 1939, the comparable figure for women had soared to 1,366! In 1933, 29 percent of all Jews were over forty-five, and 10.5 percent were above the age of sixty-five; by the end of 1936, the corresponding figures had climbed to 35 percent, and 20 percent, respectively.[2]

This demographic development did not take place uniformly. In numerous rural communities, the Jewish population was heavily diminished, whereas losses in the large cities were partially compensated for by urban migration. Many Jews chose to move to the principal cities, where they felt more secure in the bosom of a larger Jewish community, could send their children to Jewish schools, and could make better preparations for their ultimate emigration.

There are detailed and informative figures available for Berlin, the main goal of Jewish internal urban migration, for the months of August 1935 to March 1936. They derive from a pilot survey conducted by Department II/112 of the SD, the Security Service of the SS. This was the predecessor organization of the notorious Department IV B4 in the later Reichssicherheitshauptamt (Reich Security Main Office; hereafter RSHA).[3] The participants in a training course in the department had been asked, among other things, to collect detailed data on the movement of the Jewish population—age, sex, family status, and occupation of Jews who had moved to or from Berlin—classified according to municipal districts. This data indicates that in the eight months covered by the survey, forty-six hundred Jews had relocated to Berlin, and seventy-four hundred had left, most of them emigrating abroad. The study also found that 67.7 percent of those who had left and 65.3 percent of those who had moved to Berlin were under the age of forty, most of them even younger than thirty. Women accounted for 53 percent of persons relocating to Berlin but only 48 percent of those who had left. Some 60 percent of both sexes were unmarried. Of those Jews who had relocated to or left Berlin, 38 percent were children and dependents; 18 percent of in-migrants to Berlin were blue- and white-collar workers, whereas the comparable figure for those leaving was 23 percent. Fourteen percent of those moving to Berlin were teenagers in occupational training; 11 percent of out-migrants were in that category. Six percent of the newcomers to Berlin were teachers and members of the free professions, compared with 9 percent who had emigrated.

This picture of Jewish migration into and from Berlin can be regarded as representative for all of Germany during the period surveyed. Quite naturally, young, unmarried individuals, young families, and employees or those still studying a trade or profession were more mobile, for example, than self-employed older tradesmen. Such tradesmen relocated to the large cities or emigrated abroad only later on, generally after liquidation of their businesses. Members of the free professions still in Germany were represented in somewhat overproportionate figures in the migration movement. The especially strong influx of female domestic help (approximately 7 percent of all those migrating to Berlin) was a product of the prohibition contained in the Nuremberg Laws on employing "Aryan" domestic servants in Jewish households.

"Spontaneous Popular Anger" and Legal Restrictions

Until September 1935, very little new legislation was introduced aimed at restricting Jewish economic activity. Such new laws basically confirmed the existing status quo. In March 1934, by decree of the Finance Minister, the exclusion of Jewish firms from the program for redemption of welfare vouchers became official policy.[4] Similarly, the banning of Jewish doctors or doctors related by marriage to Jews (*versippt*) from the various government-supported health insurance schemes, even if they had been World War I veterans, became official with the issuance of an order by the Reich minister of labor on May 17, 1934.[5] A corresponding exclusion order barring dentists was issued in February 1935.[6]

A new wave of violent boycotts erupted in the summer of 1935. Although these boycotts took place throughout the German Reich, they are known in the research literature by the name "Kurfürstendamm riots." At the time, these disturbances caused a minor sensation in the foreign press. Numerous historians have viewed these events as staged incitement of "spontaneous popular anger," a preparation for the Nuremberg Laws that Hitler was to proclaim at the Party Congress in September of that year.[7] It is true that, at about the same time, the Reichsbank president and economy minister, Hjalmar Schacht, had been contemplating the introduction of new laws restricting Jewish economic activity. Such laws had been fearfully anticipated by the Jewish community, yet they were not introduced at that juncture. For this reason, I would argue that it is inaccurate to view the events of the summer of 1935 or the Nuremberg

Laws as constituting some sort of caesura, or change of direction in the process of ousting the Jews from the economy.

The Nuremberg legislation, in particular the Reich Citizenship Law (Reichsbürgergesetz) of September 15, 1935,[8] provided a basis for further economic measures. Such measures, however, were not introduced until a much later date. Those who felt the pinch initially were the remaining Jewish civil servants and members of certain selected professions, such as pharmacy, in which only a few Jews still remained active.[9] The violence of the summer of 1935 was brought to a quick end because of the imminent approach of the Olympic games. Nor had those violent actions been necessary for spurring the process of the displacement of Jews from economic life. Though these actions in some localities may well have motivated Jewish business owners to a more rapid liquidation or "Aryanization" of their businesses, they represented little more than a way station within the broader general development.

Along with apprehensions lest unfavorable impressions be created among foreign visitors to the Olympics, there were also purely economic reasons for this reserved policy. Unemployment in 1935 had still not been completely eradicated, and the situation in respect to foreign currency reserves could only have been worsened by sanctions against large Jewish concerns with a high export volume and important connections abroad. It was not until 1936, when the German economy had reached full employment, that the Nazis began to plan and, beginning in 1937, to implement the complete and total removal of Jews from the German economy, the envisioned *Entjudung der deutschen Wirtschaft*. That marked the actual turning point and is treated in detail in the following chapters.

Naturally, the events of the summer and autumn of 1935 were by no means inconsequential for the German Jewish community. The new outbreaks of violence awakened concern in the Jewish public in Germany and abroad. The simultaneity of these events in many localities across Germany proves that they were not "spontaneous," and the role that Goebbels's propaganda apparatus played in their instigation has been sufficiently documented.[10] Moreover, those with economic interests at stake did not pass up an opportunity to harm their Jewish competitors. For example, a day report of the state police from Dortmund in August 1935 mentions "distasteful forms" of boycott activity:

> Not always did the boycott limit itself to avoidance of Jewish businesses. It also manifested itself in numerous attacks directed against Jewish shops, whose show windows were defaced with slogans or smashed in. In many instances, customers were also photographed or publicly denounced in some other manner. These attacks were generally disapproved, since one

> suspected that the NS-HAGO was behind them, and assumed therefore that their real reason was competitive envy.[11]

Whether such attacks were so "generally disapproved" remains an open question. In any event, the local paper, *Westfälische Landeszeitung—Rote Erde,* reported on August 13, 1935, with obvious relish, about a "prank by frolicsome schoolkids out for a holiday romp." "Working systematically and with precision," they had pasted stickers on the backs of unsuspecting passers-by with the caption: "I am a traitor of the people, I just shopped at a Jewish store." "Shortly thereafter, they appeared in front of another Jewish business, and the whole spectacle was repeated."[12]

Munich, the "capital of the movement," had once again set a bad example. The new boycott action had begun there in April 1935 with the nighttime defacing of show windows. In May, display windows had been smashed, and there were violent boycott riots during the period May 18 to May 28 on the streets and in front of and within Jewish shops. Covered by Gauleiter and Bavarian Interior Minister Adolf Wagner, the police took a "reserved" stance toward these excesses, and petitions by Jewish firms to the government authorities were fruitless. When reports began appearing in the foreign press as well, the Reich economy minister finally found himself obliged to direct an inquiry on the matter to Bavarian Minister-President Siebert. In his evasive reply, Siebert relied on an enclosed report by Wagner, a copy of which was also forwarded to Minister Frick and to Hitler personally. Gauleiter Wagner explained the antisemitic riots as being the result of, among other things, the fact that the government "had not concerned itself as much with the furtherance of the antisemitic idea as would be in keeping with National Socialist ideology."[13]

In his reply to Siebert, dated June 24, 1935, Schacht disagreed with Wagner's "mistaken views." In so doing, he quoted a report submitted by the German consul general in New York, who had called the reports from Munich a "considerable source of danger for German exports to the United States." This danger obligated him, "in the interest of the government program for labor and raw materials . . . to point out these harmful consequences of such news reports."[14] When the antisemitic boycott riots did not subside even after this, but rather spread throughout all of Germany, Schacht convened a discussion among ministry heads on August 20, 1935. In the literature, this meeting is often cited as a proof of the "protective hand" that Schacht held over the German Jews and their economic activity. It is therefore useful to examine in greater detail the behavior of Economy Minister and Reichsbank President Hjalmar Schacht during the period of the events described.

Schacht's "Protective Hand"?

Schacht's role in Jewish policy, as well as in many other areas, does not appear as yet to have been fully researched. Before the International Military Tribunal in Nuremberg, which acquitted him, as well as in his memoirs, Schacht repeatedly maintained that he had endeavored as best he could to shield individual Jews and Jewish economic activity in general from attacks and measures aimed at ousting the Jews from economic life. However, the number of sources that might be able to document the truth of this assertion remain extremely small. Nonetheless, such scanty documentation has generally been accepted by research. Uwe Dietrich Adam notes, for example: "Jews active in economic life had been guaranteed a basically unrestricted practice of their professions down to the beginning of 1938 as a result of Schacht's long opposition to the Aryanization plans of the [Nazi] party." According to Adam, Schacht's dismissal from the post of Reich economy minister at the end of 1937 was the decisive turning point and "proves at the same time how much the implementation of racial policy can be dependent on the existence of a single individual."[15] The same view can be found articulated even more distinctly in a recent, unmistakably apologetic presentation based on autobiographical statements of former officials in the Reich economy ministry: "One day after Schacht's dismissal . . . the millstone of antisemitism was set rolling in the direction of the economy, the last 'reserve' of Jewish activity."[16]

Schacht was a complex personality and certainly had the moral courage of his convictions. There is no doubt that he showed personal courage in several situations connected with persecution of Jews. For example, he had the branch of the Reichsbank in Arnswalde (Brandenburg) closed in July 1935 because the wife of the director had been publicly pilloried in the *Stürmer* display case after shopping in a Jewish store.[17] In other cases as well, Schacht attempted to protect Jews he was familiar with who had turned to him for help. Yet these episodes are not sufficient proof that, as he stated, he "prevailed in each and every case in appeals to Hitler, against the opposition of the Gauleiter and functionaries, though I did find it necessary to threaten my resignation."[18] Rather, Schacht's principled opposition to the economic discrimination against Jews must be called into question on the basis of his testimony at Nuremberg. He did not contest in Nuremberg that he had agreed with the legal measures against the Jews; rather, he admitted that he had endorsed a guaranteed special inferior legal status for Jews and that he had been opposed only to their forcible and unlawful ousting from economic life.[19] Moreover, Schacht also made no secret of his conservative-antisemitic views in his memoirs written after the war:

> In Germany, the Jew [*sic!*] was rooted only to a negligible degree in the working class and artisan crafts. No one begrudged him the fact that he could freely engage in commerce and industry. But when the legal and medical professions showed an unusually high percentage of Jews . . . [theater, the press, concerts] . . . were under Jewish direction, then this constituted the incursion of an alien spirit into the spirit of the host people.[20]

This was written in 1951 or 1952. It is not difficult to imagine the Schachtean "spirit" in those years when he was still a willing servant of the Nazi cause.

Later research, if indeed deemed desirable, will perhaps emphasize different aspects of the picture. However, Helmuth Genschel appears to me to be basically accurate in his differentiated and balanced assessment of Schacht's role.[21] Yet the fact underscored by Genschel—namely, that Schacht "succeeded" in preserving three Jewish banking houses until 1938—says nothing about his fundamental perspective on the Jewish question. The Reich loan consortium was a group of banks formed to handle the Reich loan (*Reichsanleihe*), which was of crucial importance for the financing of rearmament. The Jewish capital that had accumulated in Jewish private banks in the course of the sales of businesses by Jews and the "Aryanizations" was quite welcome for investment purposes, and the financial columns in the Jewish press recommended the Reich loan as a safe investment with a relatively handsome return on capital. One should also be cautious in evaluating the statements of the Jewish bankers cited in Genschel regarding Schacht's basic attitude toward Jewish issues and concerns. In any event, Schacht did not repudiate the small circle of Jewish bankers and large entrepreneurs he was personally familiar with; in part, he continued to maintain contact with them. This gesture would, under the prevailing circumstances at the time, not be underestimated.

Yet in all available and attested statements by Schacht on the general treatment of Jews in the economy, he referred solely to the current concrete economic situation and emphasized only the harmful impact extreme antisemitic measures were likely to have on foreign policy, the exports situation, or the foreign currency reserves. This is reflected in the well-known Schacht memos of May 3, 1935, and July 7, 1938. Perhaps this can be viewed as expediency, and the only possible tactic for argumentation at the time. Nonetheless, all of Schacht's attested statements of opinion are characterized by the fact that he always directed his criticism only at the violent and "unlawful" excesses, never at the official and "legal" measures at displacement of Jews in the economic sphere. In the light of the views he was still espousing in the early 1950s about the place of "*the* Jew" in Germany, this is certainly no accident.

Schacht's contradictory attitude was also manifested during the events of the summer of 1935, which are repeatedly cited as proof not only for the thesis of Schacht's "protective hand" but also for the perspective of "dualism" in Jewish policy more generally.[22] Of chief interest here are his Königsberg speech of August 10, 1935, and the top-echelon discussion in Berlin two days later. In Königsberg, Schacht had spoken out against "chaotic individual actions," which constituted a serious destabilizing factor for the economy, as long as "Jewish businesses were permitted to go about their commercial activities . . . in accordance with the current state of legislation." Yet in that same speech he also declared that "the Jews would [have to] make their peace with the fact that their influence in our country was now permanently at an end," and he mentioned the possibility of new laws on Jews relating to economic policy.[23]

Schacht's role appears equally ambiguous in the discussion meeting he convened on August 20. In the invitation of May 13, 1935, he stressed that "it was of special importance [for him], in recognition of the primacy of politics, to be informed about the position of the ministries responsible for dealing in future with the Jewish question in the economy." He requested that "a representative be sent . . . who is authorized to present me with an authoritative statement of position." An amended invitation on August 15 termed the proposed meeting a "top-echelon discussion," and in line with this, the ministers or their deputy ministers met in Berlin on August 20. Adolf Wagner took part as "Deputy of the Führer"; Wagner, in addition to his posts as Gauleiter of Upper Bavaria and Bavarian interior minister, served on Hess's staff as "Plenipotentiary for the Rehabilitation of the Reich." The detailed minutes of the meeting[24] quote several sharply worded statements by Schacht regarding the harmfulness of "lawless riotous actions against the Jews," which made it "completely impossible for him to solve the tasks placed upon him by the Führer and Reich Chancellor to procure the necessary funds for creating jobs and the necessary raw materials for rearmament." He pointed in particular to actions against Jewish foreign representatives and the prohibition in Leipzig against Jews' use of public bathing facilities. He also questioned the legality of prohibitions on shopping in Jewish stores for non-party-members such as himself.

Yet the minutes of the meeting show that Wagner clearly dominated the proceedings. He argued that a "gradual calming of the population" was dependent on "further progress in the Jewish question" by the government. He also declared that "approximately 80 percent of the people [were desirous] of a solution to the Jewish question in the sense of the party program; the national government would have to take this into account—otherwise, it would suffer a loss of authority." Nor does the "agreement" with which the discussion ended, according to the minutes of the meeting, constitute any sort of proof that Schacht had "prevailed." It was decided that no new Jewish businesses could be opened and that no public contracts should, if at all feasible, be awarded to Jewish bidders. It was specifically Adolf Wagner who was given the task of submitting to the Reichsbank president, as soon as possible, new suggestions that would "facilitate legal advances in combatting Jewry." The Nuremberg Laws were promulgated a short time after this. There is no documentary proof of any further such discussions.

It is possible to concur in Helmuth Genschel's final judgment that Schacht had "attained his objective" in that "the matter had been left to the bureaucracy" on only one condition: that Schacht's original intentions did not go beyond this and that he had not anticipated any significant change in economic displacement. On the basis of the situation in Munich, Peter Hanke sums matters up in a far more decisive way:

> In the light of presently available sources, it is no longer possible to contend that the Reich Economy Ministry maintained a moderate and objective attitude in respect to the Jewish question down until the middle of 1938. Special considerations of foreign and economic policy compelled adoption of the official attitude, which began to coincide less and less with historical reality. In contrast, the initially hesitant tendency favored action only by subordinate offices and especially by the free economy, which did considerable harm to Jewish economic life. That "objective" attitude was retained in Berlin even after far more radical currents had, under its cloak, come to play a key role. Based on the Munich sources, this behavior, to date insufficiently acknowledged by the research literature, would appear to have a certain rhyme and reason.[25]

The ambivalent attitude of Schacht toward the regime's economic policy vis-à-vis the Jews must be viewed in the context of his increasingly contradictory attitude toward government policies as a whole. As long as he believed himself able to maintain his position as economy minister and president of the Reichsbank, his rejection of the brutal methods being used against the Jews apparently did not bring him to the point at which he was ready to put his career at risk. When, at the end of 1937, he was obliged to give up his post as minister, that had nothing to do with his attitude toward the Jews. At the end of 1939, when his position as Reichsbank president was likewise no longer tenable, he spoke out at the customary Christmas celebration of the Reichsbank against the excesses of the November pogrom: "The setting fire to Jewish synagogues, the destruction and plundering of Jewish stores and businesses and the mistreatment of Jewish citizens was such a shameless and outrageous action that every decent-minded German must blush in crimson shame." At about the same time, Schacht initiated negotiations with George Rublee on a financial solution to Jewish emigration. Those negotiations are discussed in Chapter 4. It is quite possible that, as Heinz Pentzlin, with a certain amount of exaggeration, has contended: "his actions were . . . influenced in part by the decision to challenge Hitler, to break with him openly—in order to escape from the contradiction of belonging to a government whose policies he was fighting against as best he could."[26]

No comprehensive assessment of Schacht and his role in the Third Reich can be attempted in the framework of the present study. The economic measures against the Jews were terrible enough during his tenure in office, and Schacht's "protective hand" is little more than a legend concocted later for purposes of apologia. Nonetheless, Schacht's personal statements decrying the most unbridled and vicious antisemitic excesses should not go unmentioned. In any event, they stand in marked contrast to the silence of other "Deutschnational" fellow-travelers who were not NSDAP party members, such as his colleague from the nobility in the Finance Ministry, Count Schwerin von Krosigk. Insofar as such persons are the criterion, Schacht was indeed a "laudable exception."

Creeping Displacement by Means of Administrative Measures

Even the most rabid Nazi had no reason to complain about gaps in anti-Jewish legislation in the economic sphere, and complaints to this effect were in fact very rare. On the contrary, everything would appear to indicate that it was precisely the lack of clarity in regard to legislative measures that created the best atmosphere for gradually excluding Jews from active economic life.

At party level, the *Gauwirtschaftsberater* (district economic advisers; hereafter DEAs) in particular were officially responsible in all matters relating to the ousting of Jews from the economy. This position of adviser had been created within the framework of the Economic Policy Section in the Munich national headquarters of the NSDAP even before the 1933 takeover in order to advise Gauleiter about economic questions in accordance with guidelines issued by Munich. After 1933, the DEAs were under the control of the Commission for Economic Policy directed by Bernhard Köhler until his death in 1939 and subordinate to the dynastic power of the respective Gauleiter. Only future research will be able to clarify what roles they fulfilled in other areas, but there is no doubt about the decisive function that the DEAs and their bureaucratic staffs had in implementing economic policy toward the Jews.[27] Extensive files were assembled in their offices covering every single Jewish business in their area of authority, and the development of these businesses was carefully monitored. Sources included reports filed by "inside planted informers" and information from competitors, as well as data supplied by tax offices and the local chambers of commerce and industry. The intimate level of cooperation between party and administrative bodies, documented convincingly by these files, made the offices of these economic advisers ideal executive organs in the continuing process of displacing Jews from economic life as well as in the "Aryanization" of Jewish businesses.

The anti-Jewish boycott was not a one-time or sporadic phenomenon but rather a process that spread and deepened at a slow, steady pace. It was promoted systematically by its adherents. The trade associations and the DAF attempted to prevent the forging of business ties with Jewish suppliers by perusal of the account books of non-Jewish firms. Specialist associations, such as that of the egg and poultry importers, many of whom were Eastern European Jews, excluded Jews by means of an arbitrary "Aryan Paragraph" in their statutes.[28] Although there was no "legal" basis for such regulations, a prohibition on purchasing at Jewish stores was put into effect for civil service workers, and labor courts accepted its violation as grounds for dismissal.[29] Middle-class credit institutions denied loans to Jewish businessmen, and outstanding loans and mortgages were canceled for the most minor reason. This method was also recommended in the press as an effective way of plunging Jewish business owners into liquidity problems and then forcing them to sell their businesses "at bargain prices" to "Aryans." In contrast, however, the newspapers explained that one could borrow money from Jewish banks without any ideological qualms and feel free to supply these banks with information about German loan applicants if this could facilitate the final granting of the loan.[30]

Since there was no basis in law whatsoever for all of this chicanery, individual Jews and Jewish organizations still tried to defend themselves by filing grievances with government offices or resorting to the courts, with ever diminishing success. Thus, for example, a Jew with Dutch citizenship filed a claim against the district government in Arnsberg, requesting compensation for the damages he had suffered because of the boycott "defensive guards" posted in front of his shop in 1934. The complaint was rejected with the argument that the police had no authority to interfere with the party. If he so wished, he could file a suit against the NSDAP! Appeal proceedings to the next higher judicial authority, supported by the Dutch consulate, were suspended by order of the Justice Ministry.[31]

In contrast, government authorities were swift to react to individual attempts at a Jewish counterboycott, such as were undertaken in the early period. In January 1935 in Dortmund, the state police initiated a large-scale investigation on the basis of a complaint by a local mover and shipping agent. Jewish families had supposedly organized a boycott against the plaintiff because he had canceled his contracts with a Jewish cobbler. Since his firm had numerous Jewish customers and also arranged the long-distance moving for Jewish emigrants, he appeared to have suffered heavy losses as a result of the counterboycott. Though the investigation by the state police was unable to demonstrate that any punishable offense had been committed, the frightened Jewish families proceeded to break off the counterboycott.[32]

Under these circumstances, one needed a powerful sense of justice as well as a good deal of personal courage to appeal to a government office or to the courts as a Jewish individual, firm, or organization. Sometimes such appeals were successful: As late as September 1938, a Jewish wholesaler for fats won an administrative suit filed against the mayor of Bochum, who had ordered a prohibition barring Jews from entry into the municipal slaughterhouse. A district administrative court in Arnsberg rescinded the original order, but it was later upheld in a new decree by the mayor. The justification given was that "should the persons named possibly gain entry into the premises, public order would be threatened." In this instance, the administrative court saw no need to take any further steps because "the matter had become objectively meaningless" in the wake of the November pogrom and the measures that followed it.[33] Earlier, repeated complaints of the State Association of Rhineland-Westphalia and the local Essen branch of the Centralverein, directed to the district governor in Arnsberg regarding boycott measures in the district, fared little better. Even in cases where the administrative office felt it necessary to take certain actions, such as ordering the removal of boycott placards and boards for public denunciations, such orders were circumvented by the local authorities.[34] Nonetheless, the official Jewish organizations did not completely abandon the submission of such grievances, even if they had few illusions about their ultimate effectiveness.

An outstanding example of this kind of intervention is a longer memorandum by the Reichsvertretung dated March 8, 1935, and addressed to Berlin Staatskommissar Lippert. Lippert had asserted before the U.S. Chamber of Commerce in Berlin that Jews in Germany enjoyed equal economic rights. The memorandum expressed understanding and even support for efforts "to overcome certain psychological inhibitions standing in the way of sales of German products, especially to America," but apparently Staatskommissar Lippert was poorly informed about the true state of affairs. This was followed by a detailed description of the conditions at the time:

> Numerous Jewish businesses were also forced in Berlin, under pressure from key party offices, to be sold or transferred to Aryan hands. . . . An

exclusion of Jews from economic life is now taking place in massive proportions as a result of administrative measures. . . . No foreigner can comprehend a situation where creative artists . . . are prohibited from practicing their profession. . . . The Jewish distributors of agricultural products . . . are being put to such an extreme disadvantage . . . by administrative means that sooner or later they will be forced to close down. . . . The DAF is seeking a monopoly position for its members even when it comes to jobs . . , which is tantamount to an exclusion of Jewish workers. . . . However, in practical terms today Jews are not being accepted on principle as workers or apprentices in all enterprises which are under any sort of state or municipal government influence, as well as in many large concerns—due to the attitude of the factory cells and works committees. . . . The NSDAP has forbidden party members from having any business contacts with Jews, or using the services of Jewish doctors or lawyers. . . . In many instances, this prohibition has been extended to include all government employees. . . . The executive director of the economic group Garment Industry . . . reported recently in a letter to the specialist group Cloth and Clothing Materials Industry that members of the NSDAP buying in Jewish firms or receiving Jewish representatives are to be suspended from the movement. . . . It is known that this same organization supports the unification of Aryan factory owners in the clothing industry in every respect. It is necessary to counter the claim that this procedure is necessary because Jews are heavily represented specifically in this branch of the economy: it should be pointed out [that] a policy of forcing Jews to leave economic branches in which they are heavily represented, while at the same time completely denying them acceptance into branches where they have been considerably underrepresented to date in comparison to their percentage of the population (agriculture, artisan crafts, industrial working class) is tantamount to the destruction of the economic existence of a large segment of the Jewish community. . . .

In Berlin too, there is no lack of calls for boycotting of Jewish firms . . . [such as] posters with the caption: "Whoever shops at a Jewish store is a traitor" or fliers containing the names of all Jewish businesses and doctors . . . in order to "protect *Volksgenossen* from shopping by mistake at Jewish stores." In Frankfurt am Main, almost all stores that are not owned by Jews are marked "German shop." This is also true in Nuremberg, Stettin and in a large number of smaller towns. . . . The situation is even worse in numerous rural areas. In Franconia, Hesse and Hesse-Nassau, broad circles of the Jewish population have been destroyed economically and plunged into hardship and the most bitter distress as a result of the struggle which has been waged against Jews for over two years now, uninterrupted, using all means of boycott and defamation. But conditions are also very difficult in Brandenburg, parts of Pomerania,

> East Prussia, Hannover and Westfalia. . . . In hundreds of localities, large signs set up at the entrance to town proclaim "Entry prohibited for Jews", "Jews not wanted" or "Jews enter this town at their own risk." As a result, the Jewish population in these regions has been cut off from any commercial contacts. It is devastated psychologically, and often enough is even subjected to purely physical threats.

The beginning of the memorandum, encompassing more than seven pages, explains that the propaganda of the *Stürmer,* "which strikes the eye of every foreigner coming to Germany," and the "purely economic situation of the German Jews," which "catches the attention of the traveller crossing through the countryside," is of greater importance for influencing the attitude of other countries toward Germany than "direct calls for the boycott of German goods." The writer concluded the memorandum with the following courageous words:

> Of no less importance than the uncertainty of economic existence and the lack of any future for the young are the unceasing defamation of the Jewish race and religion, and the banishment of Jews from the cultural life of their fatherland. If it is indeed true that foreign observers tend to judge Germany by the way it treats its Jews—and if one believes it is necessary to change the outlook of the countries abroad—then there is no other way to do this except by removing the underlying causes.[35]

Copies of this memorandum were forwarded to the Reichsbank president and to the Foreign Office. Lippert's lecture obviously had served only as a pretext for its composition; Schacht and the Foreign Office were the real addressees. The memorandum is quoted at length here because it is little known in research and presents an impressive and authentic picture of the views held by the Reichsvertretung, then still proud and confident. Moreover, it disproves the notion, still dominant in research, that until the end of 1937 Jews in Germany had been comparatively well off in economic terms, and it does so from the perspective of the Jewish top leadership echelon at the time, persons who were intimately familiar with the prevailing conditions.[36]

Although unemployment was generally declining and the economy recovering, a large proportion of German Jews were in an extremely difficult economic situation at the time this document was written. The continuing boycott had forced Jewish businesses to set even lower profit margins, and by the middle of 1935, the number of Jewish businesses had already suffered a substantial drop as a result of emigration, business liquidations, and the policy of "Aryanization," which had been initiated much earlier.

Practitioners of the free professions, who had been the first target group for "legal" exclusion in 1933, continued to be harassed. By January 1937, only thirty-three hundred doctors out of an original group of some eight thousand were still practicing. There were just under twenty-two hundred attorneys out of an original figure in the vicinity of four thousand. Since, in both professions, the only persons allowed to continue practicing were former World War I veterans or individuals who had been in practice before 1914, the remaining attorneys and doctors were inevitably older individuals. Emigration was especially difficult for them, and practicing their profession in the land they would emigrate to was nearly impossible, particularly for attorneys.[37] In the wake of the Nuremberg Laws, the sphere of activity of Jewish attorneys, who even before that had had practically only Jewish clients, was circumscribed even further. From that time on, they were prohibited from representing even those remaining Jewish clients as court-appointed lawyers for the indigent, as defense counsel, or as trustees in bankruptcy proceedings.[38] The League of National Socialist Lawyers was still not satisfied; it spared no efforts to scrutinize Jewish lawyers individually and to prohibit them from practicing their profession in any way. For example, the Essen branch of the league filed a formal complaint with the Gestapo against a lawyer who had been forced out of practice in 1933—he was still listed as a lawyer in the local phone book in 1935. Only after laborious explanations was it possible to convince the Gestapo that this was indeed an oversight, and it was decided not to arrest the lawyer in question.[39]

The last university teachers and government officials who were still in their posts were dismissed on the basis of the Nuremberg Laws. By a series of technical administration manipulations, they were then often cheated out of their pension rights, either completely or in part.[40] Jewish teachers were soon teaching only at Jewish schools; because of the high level of antisemitic incitement among schoolchildren, such schools had had an increased number of pupils even before the official exclusion of Jewish children from the public schools. More than two thousand Jewish artists found employment in Jewish cultural life, even though such jobs were insufficient to live on. The Reich Chamber of Culture was busy devising ever new methods to cut off all possibilities of gainful employment for Jews "creative in cultural life"—from artists to newspaper vendors. In the autumn of 1935, the press reported with satisfaction that all stages of film production and distribution, previously an area in which Jews were heavily represented, were finally "free of Jews" (*judenrein*) and that the remaining 140 Jewish motion-picture theater owners would soon be dealt with as well.[41]

The worst off were the blue-collar and white-collar workers. At the end of 1937, thirty to forty thousand of them were out of work, even though there was already a lack of workers in certain sectors of the economy.

Among their ranks were many who had previously been self-employed and who were now dependent on the labor market after having given up their businesses.[42] Only those employed by small and medium-size Jewish enterprises were able to profit from the general economic upswing. In the large firms, even those owned by Jews, more and more Jews were dismissed under the pretext that it was too much to ask of "Aryans" to work together in the same firm with Jews. This was accepted by the labor courts as grounds for dismissal. In the civil service, a similar reason for dismissal was the argument used against the few remaining Jewish government workers that they could not be expected to swear the legally required oath of allegiance to the Führer and identify with him and his philosophy.[43]

Foreign workers, or those who had been made stateless by the July 1933 law rescinding naturalizations of the foreign-born, were in particularly dire straits.[44] Even before the Nazi takeover, foreigners had had to renew their work permit on an annual basis, but those who had lived in Germany for more than ten years were generally released from this regulation. Beginning in 1934, such certificates of release were no longer issued. The Eastern European Jews, who were in any case among the most impoverished groups within German Jewry, were thus deprived of any possibility for legal gainful employment and became increasingly dependent on public and Jewish welfare. In addition, the threat of deportation hung over them, although such deportations were rare before 1937 out of consideration for bilateral agreements with countries with a large number of resident German citizens.[45]

"Aryanization" as a Race for Personal Enrichment

The opinion is still widespread in the historical literature that Jewish businesses were not transferred to non-Jewish ownership until relatively late (i.e., during the final years prior to the outbreak of the war) and that this transfer was generally carried out by administrative means. In actual fact, "Aryanization" had already begun in 1933 in the form of "voluntary" sales. In the course of the accelerating process of displacement of Jews from economic life, the number of these "transfers," at prices that were more and more unfavorable for the Jewish sellers, increased from year to year. Old Guard party stalwarts and middle-class party functionaries were the principal gainers. In reality, the supposed "grace period" was in fact "open season" for Nazi owners of small businesses who were out to make a "killing" in the property market.

The approximately one hundred thousand independent Jewish firms in 1932 were distributed roughly as shown in Table 2.1.[46] This estimate may

Table 2.1. Distribution of Jewish Firms in 1932

Area of Business	No. of Firms
Retail trade	55,000
Wholesale and export	8,000
Artisan crafts	9,000
Industry	8,000
Free professions	12,000
Other	10,000

not be exact, but it presents a fairly reliable picture of the actual relative figures. The borders between categories are also a bit fuzzy in these statistics. For example, the approximately twenty thousand cattle trade firms are not listed as an independent occupational category. They have apparently been included among the butchers (as craft artisans), the meat wholesalers, or the agents and middlemen listed there as "Other." In addition, these figures include only Jews classified as "Jewish by religion," so-called *Glaubensjuden*. Persons "Jewish by race," so-called *Rassejuden* (i.e., those of only partial Jewish descent and/or Jews not professing the Jewish religion) were not listed in the 1933 census as Jews.

In the autumn of 1935, the periodical *Deutsche Zukunft* estimated the number of still-existing Jewish firms and businesses at seventy-five to eighty thousand and assumed an approximately equal number of firms owned by "Jews by race and Jews from mixed families (*Mischlinge*)."[47] The second figure is doubtful and impossible to verify, but the first can be regarded as relatively reliable. Thus, according to these two estimates, a total of some 20 to 25 percent of all Jewish businesses had either been liquidated or transferred to "Aryan" hands by the middle of 1935. Apparently, these were businesses located largely in villages or small towns, where Jews were much more at the mercy of the boycott campaign and had less capacity to resist in economic terms than Jews in the metropolitan centers. One consequence of this was the mass migration of population to the cities, which is also confirmed by demographic statistics.

Attempts to feign a change of ownership by altering the firm name—a fairly common ruse in the early years after January 1933—were now a rarity. The Nazis and interested middle-class buyers had soon uncovered these "attempts at camouflage," as they called them, and had endeavored to prevent them by all possible means. A corresponding ordinance was not enacted until April 1938,[48] but great efforts had been made even before then to foil such attempts, regardless of whether or not they were completely in accordance with existing laws.

Data in the files of the DEAs and the Gestapo present a vivid picture of this situation. For example, a Jewish commercial concern in Essen, which had added the words "German . . . company" to its official name in July 1933, was carefully investigated by the Gestapo until they finally unearthed the fact that there had been an earlier bankruptcy of the firm. The owner was then taken into "protective custody," and the firm was dissolved by administrative means.[49] The Jewish press and Jewish organizations also condemned such specious "transfers of businesses" as "not only unlawful, but lacking in dignity."[50] Such "attempts at camouflage" were a temporary and marginal phenomenon, and most probably had little influence on the reported statistical data.

Small businessmen whose stores appeared especially attractive to local party functionaries as "objects for Aryanization" were slowly worn down and demoralized by other means as well, such as the phony charge that health regulations had been violated. After passage of the Nuremberg Laws, many Jews were arrested under suspicion of "race defilement" (*Rassenschande*) and then "persuaded" in jails or concentration camps to sell their businesses. At the beginning of 1936, the Hannover section of the DAF reported with obvious glee the successful "rescue" of numerous German jobs: A Jewish owner of a large firm had intended to dismiss German workers and employ Jews in their stead; he was arrested, and his firm was transferred to "Aryan" ownership.[51]

The methods used appear at times to have been distasteful even to high-ranking Nazis. A letter sent by Generalreferent Herbert L. W. Göring on July 27, 1933, to Reinhard Heydrich, head of the SD of the SS, presents a vivid and "knowledgeable" description. Angered that "the party program of combatting the Jews was being exploited by certain circles, using their position at work or in the party for unfair advantage," he goes on to say:

> One method is apparently to approach Jewish firms with an offer to help them as party members by joining their board of directors, administrative board, executive board or in some other "advisory" capacity, naturally in return for a fee. It is suggested that any difficulties arising could then easily be cleared up as a result of existing close ties and cooperation with the party and government administration. Once the ties to the Jewish firm have been firmly established and people have managed in some way to "get inside," then difficulties of a personal or political nature are soon created for the Jewish owner. One wishes to help as a friend of the firm, but the situation, it is alleged, appears very serious, since it is known that the matter is already being looked into at a high level. During the

> next phase, the Jewish owner or owners are arrested by senior-level officials, but one goes to great lengths to aid them after their arrest. In the meantime, the agent for sale or transfer of the properties makes his appearance. After release—generally the person is not held in custody longer than three days—the Jewish proprietor or proprietors are informed about what great efforts were made to help get them released. Without the personal assistance, without the aid of the office of Gauleiter, where one has excellent connections, the Jew(s) in question would undoubtedly have been placed in a concentration camp. Thus, it is wise for the Jew to show his gratitude to his helper or to the district office in a concrete manner—i.e., to pay. This formula can be played out in a great many different variations based on the same principle.[52]

The DEAs had been instructed in the case of "Aryanizations" to assist "old-time party stalwarts" wherever possible in becoming independent owners of business firms. Party organizations and chambers of commerce openly discussed suggestions for establishing special investment funds, which were to place the necessary money at the disposal of potential buyers with insufficient capital who were interested in purchasing such firms. "Aryan" businessmen were urged to contribute to these funds in order to rescue the "German *Volksvermögen* [property of the German folk]."[53]

Larger firms with many employees were subjected to relatively less harassment until the end of 1934, as long as economic policy was still saddled with the problem of resolving the high level of unemployment. The large department stores were an exception to this: The 1920 NSDAP called for their "immediate communalization and leasing at cheap rates to small tradesmen." Hardly anyone was still talking along those lines, yet the department stores were vehemently attacked in the party press and were off-bounds to party members. Four of the five biggest department store concerns were owned by Jews or had Jews among their largest shareholders. These were now gradually put under mounting pressure. The consolidation loan granted in 1933 to the firm of Hermann Tietz, expressly approved by the Führer himself, had resulted in the takeover by the banks of a portion of its stock. In the course of 1934, the Tietz brothers sold their shares and resigned from the board of directors of the corporation. It now took on the name Hertie AG. The owners of the firm Leonhard Tietz in western Germany had taken similar action at the end of 1933, and the family emigrated. In Berlin, the assets of the Wertheim family were transferred to the name of the "Aryan" wife of Georg Wertheim in 1935 but were later taken over by completely different parties. The department store firm of Schocken was initially an exception because it was partially owned by British nationals. It was not until the summer of 1938 that its main shareholder, Salman Schocken, sold the company to a German bank consortium for a price that was later estimated to be no more than half of its real worth at the time; Schocken and his wife emigrated to Palestine.[54]

It is interesting to note that a number of party organizations, in particular those of the middle classes, viewed the transfer of these department stores to "Aryan" ownership with mixed feelings. Since these department stores were now shielded against the effects of the antisemitic boycott, the continuing propaganda on promoting small retail trade was far less persuasive and effective. For example, the Römischer Kaiser department store in Erfurt was "Aryanized" in 1937 against the clear and express opposition of local retail trade representatives. The arguments they presented were (1) now the "Aryan" owners were in a good position to increase sales volume at the cost of small retail trade, whereas the former Jewish owners had suffered from steadily declining turnover figures as a consequence of the boycott; and (2) it was likely that the Jewish owners, continuing to operate at a loss, would have been prepared at some future date to sell the store at an even lower price. Despite these objections, the party agreed to the purchase on the condition that the new owners would not utilize the fact of "Aryanization" for increased advertising. In addition, the DEA suggested to the new owners that they delay their payment of the purchase price because he had initiated a tax-evasion investigation that might reduce even further the final negotiated terms of sale. Similar demands not to "misuse Aryanizations" of large department stores, at least for purposes of advertising, were also voiced by middle-class interested parties in Duisburg.[55]

For reasons of employment policy already alluded to, large industrial concerns were generally able to survive longer, as were wholesale trade companies, especially if they had foreign connections and promoted exports. Jacob Toury has demonstrated this convincingly in his highly detailed study of Jewish textile firms in Baden and Württemberg. According to Toury, just under 60 percent of the large textile concerns in this area were not *entjudet* ("cleansed of Jews") until the years 1938–39. In contrast with the more general trend, it was precisely the factories in smaller localities that were able to stem the tide and survive longer. The reason was that Jews had established important centers for the textile industry, particularly in rural areas of Württemberg, beginning with the second half of the nineteenth century, and a large segment of the local population was employed in these enterprises. Employment policy and scarcity of foreign exchange appear in this case to have combined as factors enabling the large Jewish textile firms to survive somewhat longer. There was apparently a similar development in the ready-made garment and fashion clothing field in Berlin.[56]

After the German economy had regained full levels of employment toward the end of 1936, and earlier in some individual areas, the larger concerns were put under mounting pressure. Now, however, the applicants for "Aryanization" were not those party functionaries from the middle class who had gained power and influence as a result of the "National Socialist revolution" but rather respected industrialists and heads of firms, men of a quite different caliber. For that reason, "Aryanization" in these cases had more "legalistic" features and was accompanied by orderly negotiations and "civilized" final agreements. Only in special cases, at least until 1938, was application made of the time-tested methods of "protective custody" and incarceration in a concentration camp.

One of the best-known examples of this is the "Aryanization" of the Simson armaments plant in Suhl (Thuringia). Private buyers such as Flick and Kloeckner had been unable to persuade the Jewish owner, who had been pressured by Gauleiter Sauckel, to accept the purchase price they offered, even after the owner was arrested in May 1935. The plant was then expropriated with Hitler's express authorization—and without any compensation whatsoever—and taken over by Sauckel in December 1935. Later the factory was named Wilhelm Gustloff Foundation, and through merger with additional "Aryanized" plants, it became one of the biggest machinery manufacturing concerns.[57]

Helmuth Genschel, who has documented this case in detail, regards it as an individual example that should not be generalized "because of its special importance for defense policy at a point where rearmament was still disguised." Yet he too underscores the methods that "already at this point in time were also being applied by the Reich against continuing opposition," methods that did not differ essentially "from those of the large-scale Aryanizations of 1937/38." "A noteworthy cooperation between the district and national direction of the NSDAP, the Army Weapons Office, the Prussian and Thuringian state governments and the police and justice authorities made it possible to Aryanize a plant with a value of more than RM 10 million without any investment of capital or formal expropriation by pseudolegal means!"[58]

However, the case of the Simson weapons factory was not quite such an isolated example. In December 1935 in Hamburg, the directors of a large department store were arraigned in court on the charge of *Rassenschande*. After all of those accused had been acquitted, the "angered population" demonstrated in front of the store until the owners finally agreed to "Aryanization." A further example is the "Aryanization" of a company that processed scrap metal in Essen, with branches in Berlin and other cities. The Gestapo decided in October 1937, based on accusations by an "informer" planted in the firm, to proceed "with lightning speed" against the company because its owners were supposedly making preparations to transfer it abroad and then to emigrate themselves. After this, everything went according to the proven method: The owners were arrested, and a thorough check of their account books was undertaken to determine whether there had been any wrongdoing in the past that might furnish a basis for a compulsory "Aryanization." It was especially resented that in 1936 the Jewish owners had been awarded a contract tendered by the navy for the scrapping of old warships because there apparently were no serious competitors for the job. In this case, however, the "Aryan" buyers—respected large concerns in the metal industry, still in business today—evinced greater agility and acquired the main portion of company stock before the entire assets of the previous owners had been confiscated. The price paid was probably correspondingly low. It is not known how much of this the emigrating owners were able to retain.[59]

These few examples shed light on the differences, as well as the shared features, in individual Jewish fates during this period. Large and small entrepreneurs who made an early decision to sell were able to get a better price and transfer a larger proportion of their assets to their land of emigration. Whoever hesitated and waited was generally completely plundered in the end and was happy to escape with his life after a stint in "protective custody" and a concentration camp. When it came down to it, the distinguished and well-educated "Aryan" large entrepreneurs behaved no differently from the small middle-class Nazis. If there was a chance to grab Jewish assets, they were, in the final analysis, not finicky in their choice of means and methods. At the most, they tried not to dirty their own hands too much. So too in the case of Flick, who had waited too long with the purchase of the Simson factory in Suhl but who was recompensed with a profit of $9 million in connection with another deal: the "Aryanization" of the Petschek firm. Flick's friendly relationship with the owners did not prevent him from suggesting to Göring the promulgation of a general "Law on Aryanization." When the conclusion was delayed, his deputy, Steinbrinck, suggested that violent measures or nationalization be considered.[60] In the "Aryanization" of another large concern, the metal ore dealers Rawack & Grünfeld, things apparently proceeded in tamer fashion. There too, however, Flick appears to have made a handsome profit.[61]

An informed estimate counted more than 260 larger Jewish firms that had been Aryanized by the autumn of 1936.[62] One year earlier, the *Kölnische Zeitung* had reported a "heavy shift of property from Jewish to Aryan ownership" and had expressed fears about "unfavorable consequences of such sales for the market," that is, a drop in share prices. It reported on the "Aryanization" of two large concerns in the electrical industry that had been bought by Siemens and mentioned the "change in ownership" at the firm of Orenstein & Koppel AG. In addition, it reported that negotiations were underway regarding other businesses. The paper warned about "undue haste" because the banks still had "Jewish creditors with large outstanding debts, whose rapid eradication [*sic*!] would require very substantial write-offs. An *Auffanggesellschaft* [a special company formed for the explicit purpose of taking over "Aryanized" property] for Jewish firms . . . could be highly useful."[63]

There were still a large number of Jewish firms in the banking industry. In general, there had been a decline in private banking concerns since the end of the nineteenth century, but the high proportion of Jewish-owned banks had dropped only negligibly in the postwar period. In keeping with custom and protocol in these business circles, the formal "transfer" here was generally carried out with great discretion, behind closed boardroom doors. This occasionally proved to the advantage of the Jewish owners, who were familiar with unobtrusive ways of transferring assets by means of foreign business partners. Friendly agreements concluded with "Aryan" partners or directors, with whom one had worked together for decades, were not uncommon.[64] According to a statement of the former director of the Gebrüder Arnholds bank, there was an intriguing paradox here: the banks, which were indeed a near personification of the despised bugaboo of "Jewish finance capital," were treated with relative indulgence and consideration by the Nazis. The reasons for this lay naturally in the state of foreign cash reserves and the ties between Jewish banks and interests abroad. Nonetheless, the dwindling deposits both by "Aryan" customers—and, with mounting emigration and deepening pauperization, by Jewish clientele as well—undermined the basis for continued survival of the Jewish banks. Small provincial banks were liquidated in the early years of the Nazi regime. Toward the end of 1935, large old and well-known houses began the process of liquidation or transfer: Gebrüder Arnholds (Berlin and Dresden) in December 1935 and A. Levy (Cologne) in February 1936.[65]

One of the last remaining Jewish private banks in Germany was the firm of M. M. Warburg in Hamburg, which was not "Aryanized" until 1938. Max Warburg, who was its director until the end, was not only a respected banker in financial and business circles but also an active leader in Jewish public life. Since 1928 he had held the post of executive director of the Hilfsverein der deutschen Juden and was one of the initiators and founders in 1933 of the Zentralausschuss as well as the Reichsvertretung. His bank was centrally involved in implementation of the Haavara Transfer Agreement. This, along with hesitancy about "giving up"—and thereby demonstrating for all to see the hopelessness of any future life for Jews in Germany—was probably among the reasons for the later transfer of the bank. In the course of the Nazi period, the bank had acquired more and more Jewish customers and had become the preferred bank of the Jewish economic sector. The types of business transactions had changed; the main focus now was on handling Jewish blocked accounts and financial implementation of "Aryanizations" and liquidations. When these fields also shrank as the process of ousting of Jews from the economy reached an advanced stage, and as the general situation for Jews in Germany became more and more threatening, Warburg was compelled in 1938 to give up the bank and emigrate.[66]

The Daily Struggle for Survival

Between 1933 and 1938, German Jews experienced alternating phases of hope and despair. A few calm months were enough to awaken optimistic expectations for stabilization, which might, in spite of it all, make economic survival feasible in Germany even if such a life would now be more laborious in its demands and stintingly modest in its rewards. The outbreak of boycott actions, on the other hand, helped to lend credence to pessimistic assessments. Optimists and pessimists differed primarily in respect to the intensity of their preparations for emigration. Initially, however, all had to invest the bulk of their energies in the daily struggle to scrape together enough to allow themselves and their families a relatively decent level of existence.

Jewish occupational structure underwent an accelerated process of restructuring, though this had very little to do with the earlier "productivization" aimed at by various groups in the Jewish community. Along with the restructuring organized by Jewish self-help associations, a spontaneous and more regressive occupational restructuring process took place, in which the old vocation of peddler once again became a respected calling after having almost totally vanished from Jewish occupational statistics since the end of the nineteenth century. Former doctors and lawyers, as well as junior- and senior-level officials, now turned itinerant, traveling through the countryside or from house to house with their goods and samples. Because this activity required a permit for trade or peddling, it was listed in the statistics of the government offices as the "establishment of a new business" by Jews, just like the transfer of a store into one's private residence. Party offices and interested middle-class businessmen, especially in the retail garment area, believed they could see in this a sign of an increase in Jewish economic activity and were correspondingly alarmed. In reality, the volume of business transacted by Jews was shrinking steadily. The turnover in sales outlets that had been shifted to private dwellings declined, despite the general pickup in overall demand. Jewish traveling salesmen, who often were the victims of dishonest swindlers, were in many cases unable to cover even their transportation expenses.[67]

The shrinking of business volume also necessitated a reorganization of the form of the business in order to economize. The family business was the most suitable modus because women and young school leavers had few prospects for employment in any event. The shift of commercial and artisan shops into one's private residence made this transition easier. Doctors and lawyers who still had a small practice employed members of their families as extra help during office hours. The Jewish press regarded this phenomenon as an expression of the strengthened "community of fate" (*Schicksalsgemeinschaft*) of the Jewish family and proof of its will to survive. In distress and under duress, the Jewish family had abandoned its resistance to the idea of married women going out to work. The ancient Jewish tradition, according to which the woman in the devout family often provided a living for her Talmud-studying spouse, was cited as a laudable example.[68]

Soon after 1933, there was a change of direction in organized Jewish financial assistance. There were hardly any illusions about the value of legalistic intentions. If one applied at all to the authorities, an attempt was made to locate those case workers who "were prepared, as decent human beings, to help Jews in a difficult situation, if they could in any way."[69] The principal efforts were increasingly aimed at providing direct financial assistance. In the first few years of the Nazi regime, there was still hope to provide a secure, albeit altered, basis for the continued existence of German Jewry for many years to come by means of an "economic rehabilitation program." By the end of 1936 at the latest, people became convinced that emigration should be regarded as "the most comprehensive form of a constructive program of economic aid." However, in view of the structure of the German Jewish community and the restricted possibilities for immigration in other countries, "a substantial Jewish population was likely for some time to come, consisting of individuals who were subjectively and objectively unable—or not yet able—to emigrate."[70]

Offices of the Wirtschaftshilfe could now be found throughout the country. The district centers served Jews resident in smaller localities in particular. The circle of those needing assistance had a different composition compared with 1933 and was now broader in compass. In 1936, more than sixty-two thousand persons received advice and relief aid. The proportion of those from the free professions was considerably smaller as a result of emigration and the absorptive capacity of the developing Jewish educational system and network of Jewish cultural institutions. In contrast, there was a steady rise in the number of jobless self-employed and white-collar workers as a consequence of the process of "quiet displacement."

The Jewish credit associations attempted to provide support for the self-employed. They distributed two types of loans: "category A" loans, lent against collateral and at an interest rate of 3 to 6 percent, and "category B" loans to businessmen who were economically worse off. The latter were interest-free and generally did not require collateral; they were repayable "according to ability" and without any due date. In both cases, only small sums were involved, and the distinction between the two categories blurred over the course of the years. This division into categories was abandoned completely in 1936, since only a few of the applicants were able to provide the necessary collateral according to rules that had been laid down by the "Joint." A new version was now introduced, "category Z" loans, designated almost exclusively for use in covering moving expenses or in connection with the liquidation of existing businesses.

Between 1933 and 1938, the credit associations distributed 12,200 individual loans totalling RM 4.5 million. This amounts to an average of about RM 370 per loan, a sum that can serve better than any description to characterize the modest clientele of these credit associations. Human beings in deep financial straits, facing the total collapse of their economic existence, were sometimes also helped by loans of just RM 100 or RM 200. The associations often provided indispensable financial first aid. The capital of such loan associations was insufficient for long-term activity or for credit needs of businesses. Their clientele consisted almost exclusively of individuals on the economic margins of society; small tradesmen and house-to-house and market peddlers, including a large number of Eastern European Jews. Accordingly, these credit associations should in retrospect be viewed as an institutional component of the broader welfare system.[71]

A number of Jewish cooperative banks served the credit needs of the wealthier middle classes. A few such banks had been in existence for some time but really came into their own only during the Nazi period. One example was the Ivria Bank in Berlin, principally for Zionist-oriented circles; another was the Jewish Credit Association, which catered to the liberal circles around the Centralverein. There were Ivria banks in Leipzig and Chemnitz as well, not surprisingly, as these were cities with a high proportion of Eastern European Jews. Despite the uniform name, each of these banks was an independent cooperative with its own capital funding. Their importance for the system of economy and finance in the Jewish community in Germany was greater than that of the credit associations. The Ivria in Leipzig, for example, reported capital assets in 1935 of RM 1.35 million and a volume of 59 million.[72] Nonetheless, the cooperative banks covered only a small portion of the credit needs of Jewish businesses. The upper middle classes and the Jewish large entrepreneurs calculated their needs in quite different and much larger figures. They continued to obtain loans for a time from the general banks and increasingly from the Jewish private banks, for which there is no available data on total volume.

At an early point in developments, offices and organizations involved with providing economic assistance were aware of the obligation to assure as orderly a liquidation of the Jewish enterprises in Germany as possible. This is reflected in the establishment, initiated as early as 1934, of a special "Society for the Promotion of Economic Interests of Jews Now or Formerly Resident in Germany, Ltd."[73] This long and complicated name had been invented by the official charged with registering the organization, who even in 1934 apparently had trouble imagining there could still be anything like "German Jews" in the country. The complete name was almost totally unfamiliar among the Jewish public, the organization being known by its familiar abbreviation, F.W.I. The declared task of the society was to prevent the hasty sale of Jewish enterprises and to salvage as large a portion of Jewish assets as possible by means of expert advice and orderly handling of all transactions, using domestic and foreign financial institutions.

The society was apparently thought of as a tool to serve larger business enterprises. Its offices were located on the Kurfürstendamm in Berlin, and it tried to project an image that was solid and inspired trust. There were leading Jewish personalities on its board of directors. The banking house of Gebr. Arnholds was likewise involved and had a financial interest in the initiative. Despite all of this, the society was unable to point to any substantial success, a result of the initially hesitant attitude of Jewish entrepreneurs and of the differences of opinion within the board of directors regarding the economic future of Jews in Germany. Even after these differences had become irrelevant under the pressure of events, and there was general recognition of the necessity for business liquidations, the F.W.I. never really came into its own. The large Jewish entrepreneurs went their own way in arranging transfer of capital and assets, and those with medium-size and small businesses found solutions in the framework of the Haavara Agreement or parallel organizations, which is discussed later (see "Emigration and Transfer of Assets," pp. 99–106).

The Expanded "Jewish Economic Sector"

> Only a smaller number of the large Jewish department stores and businesses were able to retain their Jewish directors and a clientele not directly exposed to the pressures of the party. With this one exception, the Jewish community must now live in its own framework, and is increasingly taking on the character of a new type of ghetto. A ghetto which is admittedly not surrounded by walls, yet which is cut off from economic as well as social and intellectual contact with the surrounding world. The typical German Jew today is a middle-aged man, whose children have

emigrated and who ekes out a meager existence as a small businessman in one of the larger cities.[74]

This description, taken from the 1937 annual report of the major British assistance organization for German Jewry, the Council for German Jewry, paints an accurate picture. The developments described had been forced on the German Jews by external circumstances, and the "Jewish economic sector" had evolved over the course of the years against their will. At the end of 1936, voices still could be heard among the Jewish public decrying a Jewish "economic ghetto" and rejecting any abandonment of positions still in Jewish hands.[75] Yet the pressure of circumstances proved to be stronger.

Naturally, it is impossible to speak about any sort of autarky of the Jewish sector for the simple reason that Jews were dependent on goods and services that they were unable to manufacture or supply themselves. However, as producers and employees, they were increasingly dependent on the internal "Jewish market," which was becoming ever smaller. Those who had left active economic life lived first off the proceeds from liquidation and lifelong savings and then off their very bone and substance. Or they were dependent on Jewish welfare, financed by funds from Jews still able to contribute, or, to a lesser extent, by assistance from coreligionists abroad.

The administrative bureaucracies of the Jewish *Gemeinden* and organizations had not only been enlarged to help cope with the growing tasks, they represented a kind of "scheme for creation of jobs" from the funds of the Jewish public sector. These monies derived largely from tax revenues paid by the German Jews themselves. Jewish doctors found work in an impressive publicly supported health system, equipped with hospitals and clinics, children's homes, homes for the aged, and rural convalescent homes. Former lawyers were able to make use of their knowledge and experience in Jewish administration. Teachers were placed in the significantly expanded Jewish educational system and in adult education, often as language teachers in courses preparing for emigration. Writers and journalists worked for the Jewish press and in Jewish publishing houses, which flourished on a scale hitherto unknown.[76]

This development was also reflected in the ad sections of Jewish newspapers, which published the addresses of still practicing Jewish doctors and dentists and of attorneys whose licenses were still valid. Even without any special appeal, most Jews frequented Jewish physicians and specialists. Jewish boardinghouses in spas announced the availability of kosher cuisine. They were preferred by non-Orthodox clientele as well, even before signs proclaiming "Jews not wanted" made their appearance in most hotels. The advertisement sections of the papers became more and more voluminous and reflected all facets of the "Jewish economic sector": ads from job seekers and, far less frequently, want ads for vacancies, announcements concerning stores and artisan shops and businesses of all kinds, apartments and rooms to rent—a diversified picture of everyday occupations and needs, which necessarily brought together again individuals who had long been estranged from the Jewish community. The process of economic liquidation was also manifested in the pages of these papers: businesses and properties, furniture, and concert pianos were offered for sale at bargain prices "due to emigration."[77]

The bureaus of the Wirtschaftshilfe increasingly became offices for the provision and coordination of services in the "Jewish sector." The bulletin *Vermittlungsdienst* stopped publication in 1936 because no corresponding responses were forthcoming from the numerous ads offering something for sale or requesting capital. Jews who had capital as a result of liquidation of businesses or other sources generally were chary of investing it in Jewish enterprises. They increasingly preferred various forms of liquid accounts, which were then available to them whenever needed for emigration or purposes of everyday living. On the other hand, the Wirtschaftshilfe bureaus and the Jewish *Gemeinden* and organizations now had at their disposal a large number of newly established direct contacts as well as persuasive "means of advertising" in order to stimulate mutual Jewish economic intercourse. Loans could be granted in the form of shipments of goods from Jewish commercial firms and manufacturers. The extensive orders placed by Jewish institutions were also given, wherever possible, to Jewish suppliers. Jewish sales representatives and agents were furnished with recommendations to Jewish firms. The agricultural teaching farms and artisan crafts training centers bought their supplies from Jewish firms; in turn, they passed on their own produce and products wherever possible to those same concerns for distribution and sale. This is also true in the case of hospitals, schools, and welfare organizations—in short, the entire Jewish "public" sector. That sector, taken as a whole, represented a quite sizable market in its own right.[78]

Since more and more Jews were being turned away or placed at a disadvantage by the German banks, the Jewish credit institutions gained in importance. The already mentioned cooperative banks tripled their deposit accounts and loan volume. The existing mutual insurance firms were also able to show substantial growth.[79] However, the statistical data on the number of insured and the principal of the policies prove, like the data from the Jewish cooperative banks, that in both instances only a fraction of total amount of Jewish insurance or loan credit was represented here. As a consequence of the liquidation of firms, Jewish entrepreneurs apparently were no longer in need of credit. On the contrary, they now had liquid reserves at their disposal or were able for a time to make use of both general and Jewish banks for their needs. In any case, the insurance companies were by no means equipped to take on a substantial proportion of Jewish insurance requirements.

An arbitration office was established in the Berlin Wirtschaftshilfe, in which Jews were able to resolve business disputes by working out an arbitrated compromise. In view of the prevailing atmosphere in the German courts, this was a welcome alternative.[80] Orthodox Jews, especially in the Eastern European milieu, had always preferred the traditional religious rabbinical court system internal to the Jewish community; in a revised and secular form, a new version of this ancient judicial custom was now adopted by less religiously observant Jews.

Jewish workers, both blue- and white-collar, were even more dependent on the Jewish sector than the self-employed. Even after full employment was reached in the German economy, it was almost impossible for them to be hired by non-Jewish employers because the prerequisite for such employment was formal membership in the DAF. Jewish employers, especially smaller firms, figured out various ways to circumvent these regulations. Even larger enterprises sometimes devised ways to retain at least a portion of their Jewish work force and, in some instances, to treat these workers in exemplary fashion. Also, Jewish solidarity was often manifested in working conditions and personal relations on the job, though not in all cases. For example, the owner of the Schocken department store concern assisted Jews in its employ with the preparation and implementation of plans for emigration. Of some 250 Jewish workers in Schocken, 150 had left Germany, together with their families, by October 1935. The owners of the N. Israel department store in Berlin assisted their employees in a similar fashion.[81] There were undoubtedly analogous responses in many other large Jewish-owned firms, but the relatively low percentage of Jews in a work-force numbering in the thousands proves what little importance such still extant firms actually had for the internal Jewish labor market.

Even before the takeover by the National Socialists, there had been a number of job placement bureaus in the larger Jewish *Gemeinden* in Germany. These bureaus were federated together in the publicly recognized United Central Organization for Jewish Job Placement (Vereinigte Zentrale fur jüdische Arbeitsnachweise). Until its forcible dissolution at the end of 1936, this organization took on an increasingly important role in both job procurement and the channeling of internal Jewish migration. Over the course of the years, it became clearer and clearer that its activity was condemned to failure, an unending labor of Sisyphus: thousands of job seekers faced with a steadily shrinking pool of vacancies. No more than 20 percent of the jobless commercial workers, who made up the bulk of job seekers, were eventually placed. A somewhat higher percentage of success was achieved for female job seekers, especially after the introduction of the Nuremberg Laws. The Jewish jobless were not choosy either: Trained bookkeepers were prepared to work as shop assistants or errand boys, and experienced secretaries hired out as domestics. Young school leavers, more and more of whom wished to learn artisan trades, found fewer and fewer available apprenticeships because Jewish craft trades were also on the decline.[82]

Along with the organized system of job referral and placement in the Jewish *Gemeinden,* the internal Jewish labor market expanded perhaps even more via the network of official, often personal connections. One was given employment by friends and relatives and, increasingly, in the business directly owned by one's parents. Appeals were made to the Jewish sense of solidarity in synagogues and on the occasion of other gatherings; such gatherings also served as places to exchange addresses and suggestions on how to go about finding employment. In Breslau, a program of "sponsorship" was introduced; each sponsor had the task of finding a job for at least one Jewish job seeker.[83]

Paradoxically, the Nuremberg Laws functioned to ease the situation in respect to work for women. In the autumn of 1935, there was temporarily even a surplus of vacancies because the law stipulated that it was necessary to dismiss all "Aryan" domestic servants up to the age of forty-five working in Jewish households. An attempt was made initially to fill the ensuing breach in part by hiring male domestic help. Moreover, efforts were initiated to persuade young Jewish girls of the advantages of such employment. The Jewish Women's League, which had for many years fought for equal rights for working women and access to all vocations, was constrained now to adapt to the new circumstances and organize training courses for domestic help. One could not remain blind to the fact that the process of ousting Jews from the German economy had led also to the exclusion of Jewish working women from many occupations, forcing them into work as domestics, where they could earn a living wage and often support the entire family. Doubtless, it was no easy task for the Jewish proponents of women's rights, compelled by circumstances, to persuade young female school leavers of not only the necessity but also the respectability of traditional female occupations.[84]

In the Jewish public, there were reactions in connection with the attempt to employ men as domestic servants, reminiscent of the campaign against "women with double incomes" during the Depression. Letters appeared in newspapers demanding that, first of all, young girls and women employed in the offices of Jewish organizations should be sent to work as domestics, freeing their jobs to be occupied by older and more experienced male civil servants. Then both sides would be aided in finding their "natural" place in the economy.[85] In actual fact, locating employment for older workers was a difficult problem to solve. Former commercial employees and civil servants constituted the "hard core" of the Jewish unemployed. Younger unemployed persons were at least able to complete an agricultural training course or learn a new trade. Moreover, emigration was easier for them. Some of the older job seekers criticized the Jewish organizations, contending they gave preference to younger personnel or those already on pension, mainly in order to economize, since the latter had lower salary expectations. It was argued that decisions should not always be based just on monetary considerations.[86]

Early in 1935, the regulation of the compulsory employment booklet was introduced. It affected foreign and stateless Jews in particular. Even Jewish employers were prohibited from offering such people legal employment unless they had an employment booklet, and they were usually denied the issuance of such a document. The closing down of the Jewish employment bureaus on January 1, 1937, had even more dire consequences for all Jewish jobless. This had been ordered in November 1933,[87] but the Reichsvertretung had been able to intervene and effect its postponement until the end of 1936. The argument stressed by the Reichsvertretung—namely, that these employment bureaus provided occupational counseling and vocational retraining as preparation for imminent emigration—was only temporarily able to persuade the German authorities and stay their hand. From then on, the Jewish unemployed were dependent on the public employment offices. They had little prospect of being included in the lists there and were often subject to discrimination and abuse. The closing of the Jewish employment offices was only one further step in a continuing process intended to exclude Jews from any active role in the economy. The semilegal, internal system of job referral and procurement, largely without any written documents, was continued, with steadily decreasing success. In view of the rapidly multiplying tasks it had to grapple with, the Jewish economic sector—and thus the internal Jewish labor market—were able to offer less and less assistance.[88]

Vocational Preparation and "Restructuring"

The new employment situation made top priorities of the problems of vocational training for young people leaving school and the possibilities for retraining older workers. As noted above, the beginnings of efforts by Jewish organizations to deal with these challenges can be traced back to the Weimar Republic. Thus, in 1933, without any large-scale preparation, it had proved possible to place some six thousand persons in various collective and individual training programs. Most of these individuals opted for agricultural or other manual occupations for either ideological or practical reasons. After 1933, it soon became more and more difficult to find places for young Jewish apprentices and trainees in the vocational trades. There were few Jewish master artisans in the craft trades, to say nothing of agricultural vocations. Moreover, the non-Jewish members of these middle-class occupations were heavily influenced by antisemitic propaganda, and the relevant professional trade associations barred the employment of Jewish apprentices. Although the economy minister had announced in January 1934 that there was no law "excluding . . . non-Aryans from being accepted as artisan apprentices,"[89] the Chamber of Artisan Crafts in Halle, for example, distributed a circular stating that it "considered it obvious that the craft trades would not employ Jews as apprentices."[90]

In contrast, there was an untapped reservoir of traineeship places in the commercial sector before the displacement process had decimated the number of Jewish shops and commercial firms. The vocational counseling offices found it impossible to close their eyes to these facts. The Jewish press also carried warnings against concentrating too one-sidedly on training opportunities in the craft trades and neglecting training and job opportunities in commerce.[91] An additional factor was that the assumption that artisan craft and agricultural qualifications could facilitate obtaining an entry visa, not only for Palestine but for other countries as well, had turned out to be sadly mistaken. There was still unemployment in the developed industrial countries, but countries in the developing world, especially in South America, were particularly interested in attracting experienced commercial and industrial entrepreneurs with large amounts of capital.

Under these circumstances, a discussion took place between 1934 and 1936 within the Jewish community about the principles that should govern the orientation of vocational education and retraining. Practical-minded "realists" warned about abandoning occupations that had stood the test of time over generations and emphasized the importance of language courses. Future-oriented "ideologues" wished to achieve the so-called productivization of the Jewish occupational structure and prevent any return to "intellectual work" after the tendency to "exaggerated intellectualization now finally [appeared] to have been overcome."[92] There were differences of opinion in the various bodies of the Reichsvertretung, but all were more or less agreed that emigration should in any case be preceded by a solid practical training course in Germany, no matter where the emigrant was headed. Accelerated courses, it was argued, could provide only superficial knowledge and training, and this was not enough as a sound basis for a new existence.[93]

This view, whether it was determined by basic considerations or the illusion that there was still sufficient time left for the Jews in Germany, was quite realistic in view of the existing possibilities for emigration. Only members of certain professions or applicants with large amounts of capital were able, after a great deal of wearisome red tape, to obtain immigration visas for countries in Europe or overseas. The certificates for Palestine as well were issued by the British Mandatory government according to a strict annual quota, except for "capitalists." Thousands of Jewish young people, who were leaving school each year with or without a diploma, were waiting for some sort of job and further training even if they planned to emigrate at a point in the future—an intention that was by no means shared by all in the early years of the regime.

For this reason, the vocational counseling offices attempted initially to utilize the still extant possibilities for an individual apprenticeship or trainee post in the artisan crafts or a commercial shop or office. This was still the most frequent form of vocational training. However, such posts were generally not obtained through the vocational counseling offices of the *Gemeinden*; rather, they were obtained in the early period by means of private connections via friends or relatives or through other initiatives of one's own. Organized vocational training in collective courses, often linked with living away from home, was more costly and required a considerable amount of organizing. Consequently, it was possible to make it available to only a small segment of youth leaving school and entering the job market.[94]

However, the number of individual apprentice and trainee posts also was limited, and the problem of placing school leavers became more and more pressing for Jewish social work and the youth movements. Even the Zionist organizations had no ready answer at first because immigration to Palestine as *chalutzim* (pioneers)—that is, on the basis of the so-called worker certificates (Category C)—was not possible before the age of eighteen. Moreover, even here there were annual quotas. As early as 1932, Recha Freier, the wife of a Berlin rabbi, had sent a first group of teenagers, ranging in age from fifteen to seventeen, to a children's village in Palestine, where they received agricultural vocational training. This was the beginning of the Youth Aliyah,[95] an organization that was expanded in 1933 and that succeeded over the course of the years in bringing several thousand young people to Palestine. Most of these youngsters were placed for training in kibbutz settlements. However, this type of immigration was available to only a relatively limited number of young people, mainly members of the Zionist youth leagues. It was only a partial solution to the intractable problem of viable options for school leavers.

The introduction of a ninth school year in Jewish elementary schools provided a modicum of relief. These schools had experienced a sharp rise in the number of pupils. In addition, a "pretraining course" in artisan crafts was initiated in schools in Berlin and other large *Gemeinden*. These

Table 2.2 Institutions Supported by the Reichsvertretung

Institutions	No.
Agricultural *hachshara* collective farms	32
Centers for "individual *hachshara*"	8
Training courses for craft trades	23
Training courses in home economics	28
Dormitories for trainees	44
Youth Aliyah and other schools	4
Total	139

courses introduced youngsters to the basic principles of the woodworking and metalworking trades as preparation for a future apprenticeship. Courses in sewing and home economics were set up for female pupils. Such courses also included subjects in general education and Jewish studies because many young people, especially those living in smaller towns and rural areas, had been forced to break off their schooling prematurely. Many of them came to the large cities without their parents and had to be housed and taken care of in dormitories. The Youth Aliyah operated a school for continuing education in Berlin; it taught mainly Hebrew and Jewish studies, subjects designed to prepare young people waiting for their immigration certificates for their new life in Palestine.[96] For members of the Zionist youth leagues aged fourteen to seventeen, "Intermediate *Hachshara*" teaching farms for agricultural training were set up in 1935. This program was incorporated into already existing *hachshara* centers for adult *chalutzim* or housed on new training farms that had been purchased or rented for this special purpose.[97]

All of these institutions for vocational training and restructuring required a substantial financial and organizational outlay, yet they were able to assist only a small segment of Jewish young people. Between 1934 and 1937, the number of participants fluctuated between twenty-five hundred and five thousand. One third of these were in collective training courses, mainly in *hachshara* centers; the rest were attending programs in urban teaching centers. The list of institutions supported by the Reichsvertretung at the end of 1936 (Table 2.2) provides some notion of the impressive scope of the Jewish vocational educational system.[98]

The Reichsvertretung spent about RM 1.5 million in 1938 for maintenance of these 139 training centers, a sum amounting to 28 percent of its total annual budget. Yet that covered only a fraction of the total cost for this system of vocational education. A far larger proportion of operating costs for the *hachshara* centers and other training schools was provided by funding from the Jewish *Gemeinden* and from parents still able to contribute to the costs of their children's education. Personal maintenance costs alone amounted to RM 42.50 a month per person. This means that for an average of 4,720 trainees in 1937, RM 2.5 million was required, not including staff salaries and operating costs. In actual fact, the budgetary staff in the Reichsvertretung was upset by these high expenditures, demanded steps to economize, and refused to give its approval to an increased number of trainee places for 1938. Nonetheless, that number rose to 5,520: the ever more threatening situation outweighed the objections voiced by the concerned budget planners.[99]

Along with such *hachshara* centers in Germany, a growing number of "pioneers" obtained training in neighboring countries. These young people generally lived on private farms, were housed in groups, or met daily after work for Hebrew lessons and social get-togethers. In some countries, special *hachshara* farms were leased or made available by Jewish owners. The government in Holland provided 140 hectares of land that had been reclaimed in the area of the Zuyder Zee for construction of a "work village," in which 150 youngsters from Germany took over construction work and operation.[100] In other countries, it was only possible to place individual young people who were robust enough to withstand the strains and rigors of a hard, long day of labor on a farm. In the Eastern European countries, and in France as well, the police and other authorities created so many problems and bureaucratic hassles for German youngsters that the number placed there was never very large.

The activities of *hachshara* abroad were manifold and diverse. The Jewish organizations in Germany were extremely inventive in their search for new possibilities, and young people were prepared to accept tasks and training involving enormous and unusual physical exertion in order to get out of Germany and make their *aliyah* to Palestine a reality. Most of these youngsters were still under the age of eighteen and had left their families back in their former homeland, where they were now no longer wanted. Both in the organized Jewish community and among Jewish youth, the attitude manifested here was a far cry from any passive and resigned endurance of the injustice that had befallen them, but objective opportunities were limited. Nonetheless, an estimated nine thousand young Jews were able to leave Germany with the aid of the foreign *hachshara* program, and most made it to Palestine. When the war broke out, more than one thousand of these youngsters were still living in countries later conquered by Nazi Germany, and they shared the fate of the local Jewish population.[101]

In addition to agricultural training, the Zionist Hechalutz movement also operated a *hachshara* program for seamanship in Hamburg. Twenty-five young people had hired on for work on ships still in the possession of Jewish owners. For a time, they even dreamed about having their own *hachshara* ship, which they wanted to utilize in common to train future deep-sea fishermen and seamen for Palestine. Naturally, these plans came to naught, and the *hachshara* for seamen remained nothing but a brief episode.[102]

In contrast with trends in vocational training for youngsters, there was a distinct decline in the program for occupational training for adults after the first throng of applicants in early 1933. The hope that these measures would enable one to learn an alternative profession in a brief period of time, which could then provide a solid basis for a new existence in Germany or in a country of emigration, proved to be illusory. Even countries granting preference to immigration applications by craft artisans made it known they wanted well-trained craftsmen. Jewish organizations in Germany likewise repeatedly stressed the necessity for a thorough and solid training. A number of earlier applicants had, in the meantime, left the country or found a place in a training program by private means. In any case, not until 1937 was another new vocational retraining course set up—for workers over the age of thirty-five to learn welding.[103] However, it is likely that older and experienced individuals were able to locate private opportunities for vocational retraining. All kinds of private short courses were advertised in the Jewish press: cosmetics and stenography, sewing and other handicrafts, and especially a variety of foreign language courses. Former teachers or artists, who provided instruction in making jewelry and similar artistic handicrafts, particularly for women, found a source of livelihood in this way within the "Jewish economic sector."[104]

There are no reliable figures on the magnitude of individual occupational training and retraining. It is probable that its scope exceeded that of the training program organized by the Reichsvertretung and the various *Gemeinden,* at least in the early period after 1933. Approximately thirty thousand persons had been trained on the various *hachshara* farms and in the urban-based study programs by the end of 1938. Two thirds of them were under the age of twenty.[105] Within this community of peers and coreligionists, these young people also found a sense of security and a certain shield protecting them from the abuse and threats they were otherwise exposed to. The Reichsvertretung and the *Gemeinden,* like the youth leagues and educators, regarded work with youth as the task deserving highest priority on the Jewish agenda. In organized emigration as well, there was heightened emphasis on helping the young to emigrate. Whatever the future might have in store for older individuals, Jewish youth in Germany had no future prospects—that was a view shared by almost all.

For this reason, the largest expenditures were made and the best persons recruited within the program of occupational training and education.

What does the success of these programs look like in statistical terms? According to the census of June 1933, there were 62,200 Jewish young people between the ages of fourteen and twenty-five in Germany at that time. Of the 54,800 children ranging in age from six to fourteen, approximately 20,000 had finished schooling by the end of 1938.[106] Thus, the age groups eligible for all types of *hachshara* and vocational training over the six years from 1933 to 1938 totaled approximately eighty thousand youngsters. Of these, it proved possible to place just under 40 percent in training programs, at least for a short period of time. If one subtracts the figure of approximately nine thousand young people in *hachshara* abroad (who had, in most instances, emigrated from Germany in the two years preceding the outbreak of the war), we find that an average of only thirty-five to thirty-eight hundred youngsters could be placed annually on the various *hachshara* training farms and in the other training courses in Germany itself. The record year was 1938, with a figure of fifty-five hundred trainees. At that time, there were still nearly forty thousand Jewish young people between the ages of fourteen and twenty-five living in Germany, so the system of occupational training was able to reach only some 15 percent of this group on an annual basis.[107]

Consequently, the functionaries and social workers of the Reichsvertretung responsible for occupational training were dissatisfied with the level of success of their work. Georg Josephtal, director of the relevant department within the Reichsvertretung and later labor minister in Israel, noted with alarm that at the end of 1937, based on similar calculations, only some 10 percent of Jewish youth between the ages of fifteen and twenty-five were being trained in such programs. This was far too low a percentage to provide a solution to the problems of unemployment among Jewish youth. To be sure, "the Jewish community in Germany [could] not deal totally with occupation retraining" but had to make all possible efforts for "occupational training for school leavers." "It must be the aim of the Jewish community in Germany to help direct all school leavers, insofar as possible, toward useful vocations. . . . A new social stratum, the children of the socially and culturally advanced middle class, must be included in efforts aimed at productivization." Along with the objective prerequisites, "subjective [preconditions] in public opinion" would have to be created in particular.[108]

Most of the young people reached by the system of vocational education were members of the Zionist youth movement. The small group of non-Zionist trainees, in Gross-Breesen and the rural communal farm Neuendorf, also came mainly from the assimilationist youth movement and had formulated the goal of establishing a communitarian agricultural "settlement," influenced by romantic agrarian ideologies. A Jewish settlement had been established in Gross-Gaglow near Kottbus in 1930. Twenty to twenty-five Jewish families settled there as small farmers until the settlement had to be disbanded in 1935.[109] Not until 1936 was an expressly non-Zionist agricultural training farm with the objective of a common settlement overseas set up in Gross-Breesen, near Breslau. Both the "conscious affirmation of Jewish tradition" and an "avowed attachment to German cultural life" were fostered there. These were intended to shape and determine the behavior of the young trainees "beyond the period of training in Gross-Breesen in the new country of settlement as well."[110]

In all of these cases, only a fraction of organized Jewish youth was included in this vocational training program; the great mass of young people were left to fend on their own. Undoubtedly, financial difficulties also played a role in this connection: applicants on occasion had to be turned away because of a lack of subsidies for operating expenses, even though the youth leagues normally accepted their own members in their *hachshara* centers even without payment of any fees to defray costs. Thus, it was often specifically those young persons from small, rural communities, who had had no earlier ties with the youth leagues, who found they had no opportunity to escape their hostile surroundings.[111] Viewed from the vantage of today, it appears that the organized system of vocational training was of principal benefit to those young people emigrating to Palestine. According to the sources, nearly 80 percent of Jewish youth trained in the state of Hesse between 1933 and 1936 reached Palestine. For the most part, they were absorbed there in agricultural settlements, mainly in kibbutzim.[112] A similar situation probably prevailed in other regions of Germany. In contrast, all of the projects for collective emigration and settlement in other countries failed. For those who completed the training program in Gross-Breesen, we have the results of a survey conducted after the end of the war. These results indicate that only a small proportion of them were able to put the agricultural occupation they had learned to practical use in order to build a new life for themselves outside Germany.[113]

Jewish Welfare and Relief Work

With accelerating displacement from active economic life, the number of Jews directly in need of financial aid rose from year to year. The steadily mounting expenditures on welfare are vivid testimony to the gradual pauperization of German Jewry, though they also testify to its willingness to sacrifice and its sense of solidarity.

According to law, needy Jews were supported until November 1938, and to a limited degree thereafter, by public welfare. Jewish welfare services were actually supposed to provide only additional subsidiary assistance, principally within an institutional framework. In actuality, however, the welfare sections of the Jewish *Gemeinden* had been obliged, beginning in late 1935, to report to the German authorities about the direct support payments they were providing. The public welfare offices then initiated a policy of deducting these amounts from the public welfare payments based on standard schedules.[114] Especially "zealous" offices devised on their own initiative additional ways to harass the Jewish community. Once again, it was the "capital of the movement" that led the way: Mayor Fiehler endorsed the view of the municipal welfare office that welfare for Jews was to be "interpreted according to the basic principles of the National Socialist world-view," even when specific regulations were lacking. According to a communication of the German Gemeindetag (National Association of Municipalities) at the end of 1936, even if needy Jewish applicants "should be supported in accordance with the as yet unrestricted laws," this did not mean that "a non-Aryan necessarily had to be given equal rights with an Aryan member of the community in all areas of welfare." Accordingly, Jewish welfare recipients were excluded from many benefits. An official who had approved a stay in a convalescent home for a Jewish applicant was transferred as a form of punishment. A formal complaint with the police was not filed against him solely because of "individual reasons."[115]

Since Fiehler was also chairman of the Gemeindetag, his devices were soon imitated elsewhere. Standard payment amounts were arbitrarily lowered for Jews, and various occupational groups (e.g., teachers) remained without any support whatsoever. Jews had already been excluded from the special assistance benefits for recently married couples or families with many children.[116]

As a result of this discriminatory treatment and the mounting number of needy Jews, applicants turned more and more to the Jewish *Gemeinden* and the Reichsvertretung for assistance. At the same time, the revenues of the *Gemeinden* were declining due to the fact that often it was precisely the more affluent members of the Jewish community who emigrated. More and more rural *Gemeinden* had to be designated as "*Gemeinden* in distress" because they were no longer able to balance the budget by their own means and had to obtain subsidies from the Reichsvertretung. As early as 1935, almost a third of all German Jews required continuous or temporary financial assistance in some way, such as supplementary relief aid during the winter months, for example. At this time, more than a third of the public funds of the Jewish *Gemeinden* were already being directly or indirectly expended on welfare support. In 1935, such expenditures accounted for 35 percent of the total budget of the Berlin *Gemeinde*; in Aachen, that figure reached a level of 40 percent.[117]

The overwhelming proportion of these funds was supplied by German Jews themselves, with only negligible help forthcoming from Jewish communities abroad. A false picture of the scope of benefits being provided by the Jewish *Gemeinde* system is obtained if one relies only on the documented budget data of the Reichsvertretung. The bulk of expenditures for purposes of religion, education, and welfare was covered directly by the assets and tax revenues of the *Gemeinden*. A certain segment of this income was even transferred to the Reichsvertretung for adjustment purposes and for covering general administrative expenses. Except for a few rare instances, the financial reports of the individual *Gemeinden* from that period, in contrast with those of the Reichsvertretung, have not survived. However, the tax revenues of all Jewish *Gemeinden* for the period 1933–1938 can be estimated at an annual RM 25 million to RM 40 million on the basis of the working reports of the Reichsvertretung and other sources. Naturally, however, there was a tendency toward declining income.

Beginning with the winter of 1935–1936, German Jews also bore the expenses for the program of Jüdische Winterhilfe (Jewish Winter Relief Aid; hereafter JWH), along with the standard *Gemeinde* taxes. In addition, the so-called blue card was introduced to raise funds for welfare assistance; stamps were supposed to be pasted in on a monthly basis.[118] Everyone was expected to participate in this solidarity campaign for donations, and for that reason there were stamps ranging in value from 25 pfennigs to 5 marks. The blue card brought in on average no more than a half million marks annually. Nonetheless, this solidarity action must also be regarded as an impressive accomplishment in material terms, considering the economic situation the German Jews found themselves in.

We do not have exact figures on the total amount of outlay on welfare for the Jewish *Gemeinden*. The data of the Reichsvertretung refer solely to special subsidies, mainly for *Gemeinden* in distress. A cautious estimate, which assumes that the *Gemeinde* expenditures on welfare between 1934 and 1937 averaged some 25 percent of their tax revenues, indicates that RM 25 million was expended for this purpose over the four-year period. In the same period, the Reichsvertretung spent a total of RM 1.3 million for welfare committees and received RM 7.5 million in financial assistance from Jewish organizations abroad.[119]

In these years as well, direct support payments to needy individuals constituted only a limited segment of total welfare expenditures. The bulk of funds continued to be channeled into the maintenance of homes for orphans, hospitals, and homes for the aged and for children. Along with this, the *Gemeinden* maintained soup kitchens and supplied the needy with

Table 2.3. Closed Welfare Institutions

	1932		1937	
Institution	No.	Places	No.	Places
Hospitals	21	2055	21	2003
Convalescent homes	28	1518	15	888
Children's and orphans' homes	36	1655	49	2370
Homes for the aged and the chronically ill	58	2489	76	3771

cheap or free groceries, which were generally provided to them in a discreet manner. The soup kitchens, termed "Baerwald kitchens" after the chairman of the "Joint" at the time, distributed 66,350 warm meals in Berlin in 1934 and sent 11,200 food packets. By 1937, the corresponding numbers had risen to 78,700 meals and 26,400 packets. In relation to the entire Jewish population of Berlin, these figures do not appear very high. But if one considers that the Jewish population was on the decline and that this type of support was meant only for the poorest individuals, the statistics testify to the deepening pauperization of this lowest underclass.[120]

Table 2.3 presents a picture of the development of the closed welfare institutions.[121] In the five years from 1932 to 1937, the Jewish population declined by about 150,000. The most striking change here is the more than 50 percent increase in the number of those in homes for the aged and chronically ill. Most of the new admissions were parents of emigrants who had had to remain on in Germany. The young people taken care of in children's and orphans' homes came in part from non-Jewish institutions. Others were sent by their parents to the large cities in order to free them from the local antisemitic atmosphere and make it possible for them to obtain an education in a Jewish school.

The maintenance of these institutions required a hefty segment of the available funds. In 1932, the costs had still been shared in part by the state-supported health care schemes and the general welfare system. As the years progressed, this proportion dwindled: Jewish workers lost certain of their insurance and pension rights after dismissal, and the discrimination against Jews by the public welfare system placed ever greater burdens on the Jewish welfare programs.

Until the winter of 1935, Jews participated in the general German Winterhilfe relief program as both recipients and contributors. After promulgation of the Nuremberg Laws, they were excluded. Appeals to the solidarity of the German *Volk* played a big role in the propaganda for the Winterhilfe, and the banishment of Jews from the midst of the German *Volksgemeinschaft* was demonstrated here for all to see. National Socialist propaganda had excluded the Jews from the German *Volkskörper* as being "of alien descent" or "alien blood." Now there were juridical consequences: The Reich Citizenship Law classified them as *Staatsangehörige* (German subjects)—that is, second-class citizens.[122] Until their ultimate banishment and extermination, this law and the regulations and ordinances based on it furnished the "legal" basis for the complete liquidation of the economic existence of German Jews and the plundering of their assets. The writer of an essay on the opening of the JWH relief program who expressed his pain and sorrow about the fact that the Jews "had been excluded from a further important sphere of the German folk community" may have had certain accurate premonitions.[123]

The JWH was under the supervision of the Reich Plenipotentiary for the Winter Relief Fund of the German People. The guidelines for the contributions and benefits, which corresponded largely to those of the German program, had to be submitted to him for approval. When the Zentralwohlfahrtsstelle found itself faced in October 1935 with the necessity of creating its own administrative bureaucracy for the JWH, winter was already knocking at the door. An appeal issued by all major Jewish organizations the end of 1935 stressed the "new great moral, financial and organizational task" facing the Jewish community in Germany:

> In the span of a few days and weeks, a system of mutual assistance and solidarity must be established, which will bring our relief aid to the last indigent Jew in the smallest of localities, and which will ask every Jew to make a sacrifice for Jewish Winter Relief. . . . No hungry person in our community should be without proper food this winter, no needy person without clothing, and no one without a roof over their head! No one must be disappointed in the trust he has placed in our willingness to assist. Our community, which has been left to fend for itself in alleviating the privations and burden of the approaching winter, will not abandon a single soul![124]

Like the general Winterhilfe, the JWH also set fixed rates for contributions during the six winter months: 10 percent of the income tax paid by salaried employees, or 1 percent monthly of the annual income tax and property tax in the case of self-employed individuals. During its first year of operation, the JWH was able to mobilize 83 percent of all Jewish salaried workers and self-employed to pay these contributions.[125] Instead of the customary street collections, which were organized as large-scale propa-

"All Waiting for Your Help!" An appeal by the Jewish Winter Relief Action, October 1938.

ganda actions with appearances by party bigwigs, the JWH collected money and food donations, so-called pound donations, from door to door. The entire work was carried out by women's and youth organizations, in large part voluntarily. The first winter, 1935–1936, the JWH assisted eighty-five thousand persons, over 20 percent of the Jewish population at the time. In the winter of 1938–1939, the seventy thousand recipients of relief aid already comprised more than a quarter of all Jews still remaining in Germany. In *Gemeinden* with an especially high proportion of Eastern European Jews, the percentage of those receiving relief aid was clearly higher. This was also the case in the numerous rural communities in distress. The JWH had to support many persons who had never before received any sort of welfare. The voluntary assistants made a very special effort to locate such "bashful indigents" who did not on their own wish to apply to them for assistance. These were principally older persons who, only a short time before, had had large apartments and had been living in modest prosperity. Now they were forced to eke out their days in small, unheated rooms, plagued by hunger and preferring to remain in bed all day rather than to apply to the charity of their co-religionists for aid.[126]

For many of the needy, the Winterhilfe was an irreplaceable source of support. For the Jewish community, it became an important expression of its solidarity, cohesiveness and the collective will to resist the ever more hostile environment. The JWH, however, represented only a part of a ramified welfare aid program. Included indirectly in this assistance were also payments such as the subsidies of the Reichsvertretung to the travel and maintenance expenses of schoolchildren who were no longer able to attend school in their own locality. Here too, personal readiness to provide assistance existed side by side with the organized welfare activities. Families took in children or provided, as "godparents," for their maintenance in a children's home. Jews who were still relatively well off offered their country estates as vacation homes for Jewish children from the cities. There are indeed a sizable number of examples of such voluntary assistance.[127]

However, the most urgent question facing the Jewish welfare system was "What will become of our elderly?" The younger Jews, for the most part, had emigrated or were soon about to do so, and many were forced to leave parents and older relatives behind until they had created a hoped-for economic foothold for themselves abroad. Then the older family members would presumably join them. In the meantime, such older persons moved temporarily to the larger cities, lived in small furnished rooms—for which more and more want ads were placed in the Jewish newspapers—or found a place in a home for the aged. At the opening of the JWH campaign in 1937, Leo Baeck described the situation of these unhappy, lonely people and called for every house and every vacant property lot belonging to the Jewish *Gemeinde* to be utilized to build new housing to provide shelter for them.[128] However, although the existing homes for the elderly had steadily increased the number of places, they were by no means able to accommodate all of those requiring assistance. The welfare offices in the *Gemeinden* attempted to take care of them at home by providing appropriate nursing personnel. The opening of small homes for senior citizens and nursing homes in private dwellings became more and more frequently a new source of income in the "Jewish sector." Single elderly persons received warm meals in the soup kitchens. Such kitchens were set up in all *Gemeinden* and by 1936 had already attained an annual volume of 2.5 millions meals served. Women's organizations established a Jewish Neighborly Assistance program, which aided these persons in the upkeep of their rooms and apartments and in shopping and preparing meals, as well as giving them moral support. In accordance with ancient Jewish custom, an attempt was made to keep such assistance quiet, dignified, and discreet: Good deeds ought to be rewarded in heaven, not trumpeted from the rooftops. The ad placed by a Cologne banker inviting individuals who were ailing and destitute to contact him personally remained an exception.[129]

There had been Jewish welfare even before the Nazi period. What was new here was only the augmented scope and growing importance of the organized welfare system. To the extent that indigence became a mass phenomenon, the barriers fell and the sense of shame dissipated. A person who today was still able to give might by tomorrow need assistance himself. This consciousness of imminent poverty, which seized hold of more and more previously prosperous individuals, is clearly evident from contemporary publications. And that consciousness says far more about the economic situation of German Jews at the time than any statistical tabulations.

Emigration and Transfer of Assets

The absolute figures and percentages of the needy increased from year to year, but not all German Jews were destitute as yet. Many still had property and assets; these could serve as a source for financing emigration but were also key factors in inducing them to stay on. That is particularly true of the broad middle classes. People who had twenty or thirty thousand marks hesitated to separate from a substantial portion of their assets, sometimes the product of generations of toil. And the longer they hesitated, the more they lost.

Along with other emergency legislation, the Brüning government had introduced the Reich Flight Tax in 1931. Its purpose at that time had been to prevent the flight of capital abroad. In its first year, 1932 to 1933, this tax yielded a total of only RM 1 million.[130] Under the Nazis, the tax introduced by Brüning was transformed into one of the "legal" instruments for plundering Jewish property. In the final analysis, this tax accounted for only a relatively small portion of the total pilfered Jewish assets. Yet for the period up to 1938, it functioned as an important factor in the decisions of affluent Jews about whether to emigrate. The tax, which originally was applicable only to assets totaling more than RM 200,000, was levied after May 1934 on all assets of RM 50,000 or more. It was computed on the basis of the last estimated tax value of the property, independently of the sale price actually received. Every sale below real value—and that meant almost every sale due to "Aryanization"—thus significantly increased the real rate of assessment. A compounding factor was that, on the basis of the existing currency regulations, the emigrant could not transfer his money abroad even after payment of the tax but instead had to leave it deposited in a special "blocked account in marks for prospective emigrants." The sale of marks from this blocked account for foreign currency entailed a considerable loss due to the set exchange rate. Until the beginning of 1935, the Reichsbank had paid half of the official market rate of the mark. It then reduced this to 30 percent and continued to lower the figure steadily until it finally reached 4 percent in September 1939! With the outbreak of war, all transfers of capital were prohibited.

According to Hilberg's calculations, which are confirmed by other sources, as long as emigration was still an open option, German Jews paid out a total of RM 939 million in Reich Flight Tax revenues. The rate of assessment was 25 percent, so the total value of assets taxed amounted to approximately RM 3.5 billion. However, this in no way means that the remaining sum was really in the vicinity of 2.6 billion. No matter what that sum was, emigrating German Jews were in actual fact able to take along only a small fraction of this. Again according to Hilberg, RM 642 million of the above sum of RM 939 million, approximately 70 percent, was levied in the period from 1938 to 1940, when the exchange rate for blocked-account marks had already plummeted to between 15 and 4 percent of the official rate. The Flight Tax, special blocked accounts in marks for prospective emigrants, and the arbitrary manipulation of exchange rates were several of the means by which even those German Jews who were able to escape with their lives were systematically plundered by the German government.

Until 1938, a middle-class Jew with a certain amount of assets either had to have some money stashed away abroad or be possessed of a considerable degree of farsightedness in order to make the difficult decision to emigrate. Most had neither, so they stayed on—while the younger and less affluent, who had greater resultant mobility, chose to leave. Emigration to Palestine constituted an exception. The Haavara Agreement signed in 1933 with the Economy Ministry made it easier to transfer capital to Palestine. There was a higher exchange rate than the usual one for the Reichsmark, which in this case also had to be deposited in a special blocked account. Over the course of the years, this exchange rate had likewise worsened markedly: Originally, the emigrating Jews, designated as "capitalists," deposited RM 12,500 (at the official rate) for the obligatory £1,000 in Palestine pounds, the "proof of means" required by the Mandatory government for a Category A certificate. By means of various regulations, the amount had increased by the middle of 1935 to RM 15,000. In 1937, it reached RM 20,000, and by the end of 1938 it had been upped to RM 40,000, a figure that remained in effect until the outbreak of the war—a very substantial sum of money at that time. The devaluation of the Haavara blocked-account reichsmark was thus just under 70 percent at its lowest point. However, the blocked-account mark valid for emigration to countries other than Palestine had plummeted at this point to a value of only 4 percent of the official exchange rate, equivalent to a devaluation of nearly 96 percent!

There are some indications of the reasons that motivated the German authorities to give continued preference to emigration to Palestine. At the time the Haavara Transfer Agreement was concluded, fear of a foreign boycott of German goods was probably the decisive factor, in view of the still high levels of unemployment plaguing the German economy. However, after full employment had been achieved by means of rearmament and a revival of the domestic economy, the boycott argument was basically no longer valid. Moreover, "international Jewry" had proved itself to be far weaker than anticipated by the Nazis in 1933. The crucial factor now was the increasing tendency of the world to slam shut its doors on Jewish emigration. The Nazis wanted to have the Jews out of the country; and Palestine, despite the restrictions of the Mandatory government, remained about the only country in which there appeared to be a possibility for an organized, large-scale Jewish emigration. The Jewish Agency—which, after a certain amount of hesitation, had finally taken over supervision of the Haavara Agreement—was the only Jewish organization capable of implementing and spurring emigration on such a scale to Palestine.

A further reason for giving preference to Palestine as a destination for emigration was mentioned by Undersecretary Stuckart in a discussion on September 29, 1936, dealing with Jewish policy:

> [It] should be borne in mind that the German Jews will generally be superior to the native residents of the country of destination . . . that Jews will gain some influence there, and will form an economic stratum which is hostile toward Germany. For this reason, encouragement to date had been given principally to the emigration of Jews to Palestine.[131]

One year later, on October 18, 1937, the Interior Ministry convened another discussion on the Haavara Agreement. The figure for the extent of Jewish emigration since 1933 given there was "approximately 105,000, of which about half have chosen Palestine as their destination." The person reporting attributed the decline in emigration figures for the previous half year to the unrest in Palestine, the opposition "of a great number of countries to Jewish immigration," and the economic upturn in Germany. On the Haavara Agreement itself, the assembled representatives of the Interior Ministry, the Foreign Office, the deputy of the Führer, and the Nazi Party Organization of Germans Living Abroad felt that "due to the sharp decline in Jewish emigration to Palestine, the disadvantages of the agreement so far outweigh its advantages that . . . there is no longer any interest in the agreement and it no longer appears justified to continue to maintain it in force." In response, representatives of the Economy Ministry and the Prussian minister-president objected that "the Haavara procedure still remains the cheapest way—in respect to foreign exchange—to facilitate Jewish emigration."[132] What that meant was explained by the Economy Ministry in an express letter to the Foreign Office dated October 29, 1937, and thus after Schacht's suspension from duties on September 7:

> The point of departure is the basic principle, approved by the Führer, that Jewish emigration must be promoted by all means. The foreign currency situation of the Reich makes it necessary to find special procedures for this. Emigration to Palestine is being financed principally by the sale of German products. . . . Since the sale of German goods in Palestine can only be maintained—and the continuing threat of a Palestinian boycott averted—if the proceeds from German export are put partially at the disposal of emigration, the foreign currency earned in Palestine is supplementary hard currency.[133]

These differences of opinion were finally resolved in favor of a continued preference for Palestine as a destination, although the *Judenressort* (Jewish Department) in the SD of the chief of the SS (the SD Main Office II/112) rejected the "'Haavara system,' which was nurtured by the Economy Ministry and which we have opposed."[134]

However, the conditions for transfer deteriorated drastically in the course of time. In the years 1938–1939—in which, especially after the November pogrom, emigration reached record proportions—it proved possible to transfer only some RM 27 million. This did not amount to even 20 percent of total funds transferred via the device of Haavara from 1933 to 1939. A total of just under RM 140 million in Jewish assets was rescued over the course of six years by the agreement. The owners of the accounts received approximately £8.1 million in return for this in Palestine, corresponding to an average exchange rate of RM 17.23 to £1 Palestine.[135] Various attempts undertaken during these years to finance exports to other countries via Haavara blocked-account reichsmarks and by means of tripartite trade agreements were largely a failure. Capital transfer was thus basically linked with and dependent on the relatively limited import possibilities of Palestine. Many German Jews who had deposited reichsmarks in the Haavara accounts were obliged to wait a long time until new import orders arrived and had been confirmed by the German authorities. These waiting periods became longer and longer over the course of the years, since so-called negative lists prepared by the German side excluded more and more export goods from this transfer. In a complaint filed in January 1936 with the Economy Ministry, the Jewish Reichsvertretung stated that these extra difficulties were preventing the transfer of up to RM 250 million and thus impeding emigration—precisely at a time when the Nuremberg Laws had motivated many new persons interested in emigration to make deposits.[136] But this intervention was unsuccessful. There were months when up to RM 20 million were deposited with the Paltreu in Berlin, a sum equal to the entire annual exports of Germany to Palestine. At the end of August 1938, there were still some RM 84 million deposited in Paltreu accounts for which no export orders had been received.[137]

Max Warburg made a new attempt the end of 1935 to expand the options for transfer. In a discussion with Schacht, he proposed the establishment of a "liquidation bank," which would transfer Jewish assets—in a way similar to the Haavara procedure—to other emigration countries, thus promoting German exports. Yet these efforts met with failure partly because of the opposition of Jewish organizations abroad, which rejected the notion of taking any part in the distribution of German export goods.[138]

Not until May 1937 did the Reich Foreign Currency Control Office approve a procedure similar to the Haavara for emigrants to other countries. In the same house and with some of the same members of the board, the General Trusteeship for Jewish Emigration Ltd. (Allgemeine Treuhandstelle fur die jüdische Auswanderung GmbH, abbreviated Altreu) was founded in Berlin. The transfer conditions were considerably less favorable than those of Paltreu. The loss due to exchange rate was 50 percent, and the permitted sums for transfer were limited to a maximum of RM 5,000 for individuals and RM 8,000 for families with children. Of these sums, only 50 percent were paid out in foreign currency. In December 1937, the Altreu system was expanded, and the difference in exchange rate was placed at the disposal of the Reichsvertretung in order to promote the emigration of destitute Jews. It is unknown just how many Jews were able to take advantage of this and emigrate in this manner, since the archives of the Altreu did not survive.[139]

Along with the transfer of goods, which accounted for the bulk of rescued assets, the Haavara developed other avenues. An Education Clearing Scheme allowed parents who had remained in Germany to deposit limited sums with Paltreu, which were then paid out to their children who had emigrated abroad to cover the costs of their education and maintenance. In 1936 in England alone, there were some 350 pupils and students who had gotten out of Germany in this manner. A special agreement went into effect in the spring of 1937 allowing for the payment of financial assistance from foreign organizations or individuals to the Haavara in Palestine or in London. These sums were then paid out in Germany by the Paltreu in reichsmarks. Some RM 4.5 million was transferred in this way in the final two years before the outbreak of the war, while transfer of goods steadily declined in volume. Even after the beginning of the war, American financial assistance in particular was able to reach Germany in this manner until the Paltreu was finally closed down in December 1941.[140]

Individuals and various types of organizations also tried through their own initiative to rescue Jewish assets. In 1937, the Jüdische Landarbeits-AG (Jewish Agricultural Work Ltd.), which was affiliated with the Association of Jewish War Veterans (RjF), together with the training farm in Gross-Breesen, started the so-called Parana Project with the support of Max Warburg. The basic idea was a joint settlement of German Jews in Rolandia, located in the jungles of Nordparanà in Brazil and established in 1933 by former Reich Minister and Vice-Chancellor Erich Koch-Weser.[141] An English society was attempting to find new settlers for this project, who were to transfer their assets by the purchase of railroad equipment in Germany. By the time the war broke out, a small group of Jews had been able to relocate as coffee planters to the Rolandia settlement, which was populated mainly by non-Jews from Germany. The Jews purchased their land from the English company, paying in reichsmarks.

Similar agricultural settlement projects were also planned in Cyprus and other countries but failed to materialize. Thus, the Haavara scheme and the Altreu arrangement remained the only legal means for an orderly and organized transfer of assets abroad. However, the approximately RM 140 million which was rescued in this way from the rapacious grasp of the Nazis, constituted only a fraction of the total Jewish assets in Germany, estimated for 1933 to have been RM 10 to 12 billion. Even if the German immigrants forfeited a sizable portion of their assets by means of this procedure, the Haavara was a decisive factor in enabling more than fifty thousand Jews to escape Germany in time and emigrate to Palestine. Some twenty thousand of these immigrated into the country by means of "capitalist" Category A certificates and with the assistance of the Haavara.[142]

The contemporary Jewish press contained numerous references to individual initiatives for the transfer of assets and property, such as by exchange of real estate or other assets with Germans returning to Germany or Germans wishing to sell their property abroad at favorable prices. It is impossible today to determine whether and to what extent such initiatives proved successful. Nor is it possible to determine the exact magnitude of the amount of Jewish capital that was transferred "illegally." Such "illegal" transfer was viewed then as a serious crime, punishable by severe penalties and even internment in a concentration camp. Yet in the light of the legal situation prevailing at that time, it can be seen in retrospect only as legitimate self-defense by persons who had been stripped of their rights and abandoned to the arbitrary predatory acts by the state and its *Volksgenossen*. Nonetheless, in view of the high risk involved, and as a result of their residual respect for the law, the greater majority of German Jews found themselves incapable of having anything to do with such illegal ventures.

Yet they did exploit the still existing legal avenues open to them with remarkable inventiveness. Jewish emigrants, for example, took along expensive furniture, machines, tools, jewelry, and art objects on trips abroad in order to convert them into cash, as long as such an option was still feasible. In the early years, the authorities do not appear to have paid particular attention to such devices to export capital, since their main interest was in increased Jewish emigration. Not until December 1936 did the Gestapo begin a systematic surveillance of Jews preparing for emigration. The tax offices were instructed to keep a watchful eye and to report all cases in which unusual purchases of inventory or professional equipment indicated the possibility of an imminent emigration. The German legations abroad also were diligent in their efforts to close the still open avenues for transfer. For example, the German consul in San Francisco reported on a dispute within the local Jewish community: A Jewish hospital was accused in 1936 of having imported expensive medical equipment from Germany. In his defense, the hospital director explained that the instruments had been purchased from Jewish immigrants; in this way, they had been able to transfer—and thus to salvage—at least a portion of their assets to the haven of their new chosen land.[143]

A circular from the Economy Ministry dated May 13, 1938, contained the first express order stipulating that before shipment of personal possessions when moving abroad, the responsible foreign currency office had to be provided with exact information on the articles being sent and on the capital holdings of the sender. At the same time, special regulations governing the shipping of possessions to Palestine were rescinded.[144] In September 1936, the American press published reports by their Berlin correspondents, according to which affluent Jews had been given a secret order requiring that they deposit 25 percent of their assets as security to cover the Reich Flight Tax in the event of emigration. This, according to the reports, meant for many that they would have to sell their businesses. The reports went on to say that the Economy Ministry had denied this order, which had been quoted verbatim in the American press; yet the tax offices contacted had replied evasively that they were acting "in accordance with the law . . . and not just only against Jews." The Jewish reports viewed this as further proof that now the Jewish question was being liquidated by administrative means, "and without excessive pyrotechnics."[145]

The Creeping Displacement from Economic Life—a Balance Sheet

The community of 350,000 to 365,000 Jews still living in Germany at the end of 1937 differed distinctly in its demographic composition from German Jewry on the eve of the Nazi advent to power in 1933. Even then, the Jews had been a group characterized by declining numbers and a rapid process of overaging. Now, only six years later, these demographic features were far more pronounced. The Jews had also suffered a massive loss in economic power. As a group, they still had quite substantial assets at their disposal, yet many individuals had already been reduced to living off their last savings. The press carried almost daily reports on bankruptcies and business closures, particularly in the provinces. It was almost impossible to obtain credit. German banks no longer issued loans to Jews and foreclosed on their mortgages. The Jewish banks still in existence did not have sufficient funds to replace the credit that had been withdrawn.[146] Nonetheless, the Jewish community had not yet abandoned all hope: Individuals tried by all available means to retain their factories, stores, or jobs. If unsuccessful, they attempted to learn a new profession. The amounts of income tax paid by Jews had declined in some cities by 20 to 40 percent; nonetheless, in 1937, Jews still paid out nearly RM 80 million in taxes. This sum, however, included the substantial taxes levied on proceeds from liquidations.[147]

The economic measures that were feared in the wake of the Nuremberg Laws had not materialized, but administrative practices directed against Jews intensified from month to month. Jews were still legally permitted to practice virtually all commercial occupations. Yet in administrative practice in many localities, they were even denied permits as itinerant peddlers, though this had no basis in law. They were also beleaguered by a crisis in housing: those who were no longer able to afford large, expensive apartments were hard put to find alternative suitable housing. The want ads in Jewish newspapers are wrenching testimony to the harrowing situation: They are replete with inquiries for small apartments, furnished rooms, shared apartments with a common kitchen, and room and board for elderly, isolated individuals. There were even a few offers of corresponding vacancies, a further source of income for some in the Jewish economic sector.[148]

In the Jewish press and the mimeographed annual reports of the Reichsvertretung, apprehensions about the future were formulated hesitantly, with great reserve. Perhaps the intended wish was to avoid discouraging people. Or maybe another fear played a certain role: that one might be accused of spreading "atrocity propaganda" if one protested too vehemently against the harassments by the German authorities. Nonetheless, perceptive observers, Jewish and non-Jewish alike, could read the unambiguous signs of the times. In October 1935, the *Westdeutscher Beobachter* published a "Warning to the Excessively Enterprising" subtitled "Jews Want to Sell." The paper had learned that for a number of weeks, "non-Aryans had been looking for buyers for retail stores, wholesale firms and, in a few isolated instances, for factories, houses and real estate property." In particular, "a large number of non-Aryan business and factory owners in small and medium-sized towns [were attempting] to sell their firms to Aryans." Since these wishes had not been fulfilled, "due to a lack of qualified buyers with sufficient capital," the hope was expressed "that the responsible authorities [were] already dealing with this problem." For the time being, the "Aryan" buyer was advised "to make sure to acquire the entire inventory when making a purchase. In this way, the Jewish owner would be prevented from selling off his inventory at throw-away prices in a liquidation sale."[149]

What is stated here in veiled language is expressed more openly in the files of the DEAs. Those files noted that Jewish sellers had been forced by all imaginable pressure tactics to sell off the remainder of their inventory stock at piddlingly ridiculous prices. For the lucky buyers, this proved to be a welcome extra profit bonus; for the rest of the retail trade, it functioned as a protective measure against price-gouging competition. Thus, everyone got what they wanted. Everyone, that is, except the Jews.

In December 1935, the southern German correspondent of the Austrian paper *Reichspost*—which sympathized with the Nazis but was at that time not yet subject to the restrictions of Goebbels's *Sprachregelung* (centrally regulated information policy)—sketched with undisguised satisfaction a knowledgeable picture of the situation faced by Jews active in economic life. He first offered a description of the growing number of "Aryanizations," the possibilities for emigration, and the activity of the Haavara, which had been responsible for an increase in exports, "sadly enough, specifically to Palestine." The journalist then went on to note that

> . . . among Jews, [it was] likewise not everyone's wish to settle in Palestine. Thus, the question takes on enhanced importance: what is to be

> done then with the remaining German Jews, whose thread of existence has already been severed? . . . Most recently, the pressure to emigrate has also become acute for many Jews active in economic life. However, the Jewish merchants in small and medium-size provincial towns have, for some time now, been fighting a difficult battle. In these towns, the *weapon of the boycott* can be utilized far better than in a place like Berlin, for example. The consequence is that there is now a massive selloff of Jewish retail shops. . . . There are reports . . . from certain areas . . . that an average of 40 to 50 percent of all Jewish businesses have already been transferred to Aryan ownership. Along with this, there are many small towns in which the last residues of Jewish business activity have already been liquidated. This is also the reason for the fact that various small Gemeinden are offering their synagogues for sale. Only recently, a farmer in Franconia was able to purchase such a building for the price of 700 marks—for the purpose of storing grain. . . . The material side of the problem on the Aryan side would probably be well on the way to solution by the establishment of a special *Auffangorganisation,* whose purpose would be to permit capable Aryan qualified buyers lacking the proper amount of capital to purchase larger Jewish enterprises. . . . However, there is no answer to the question about what to do with Jews who are forced to sell their businesses far below true market value, and for whom any further economic activity is extremely difficult. . . . In recent days, the plan has appeared of an international Jewish transfer bank. . . . Should this plan be realized with the assistance of international Jewish high finance, those many thousands of Jews who today are . . . consuming the last remaining residue of their assets would be given a chance to leave Germany—before they have been reduced to total poverty.[150]

Jewish observers outside Germany viewed these events with alarm—and probably with greater clarity than the German Jews and their leadership inside the Reich because they enjoyed the vantage of distance from the scene and an uncensored foreign press. The European representative of the "Joint," Bernhard Kahn, reported at the end of 1935 about a massive sell-off of Jewish businesses at farcical prices and the deepening pauperization of German Jews. According to Kahn's estimate, more than a quarter of German Jews were already destitute and in need of welfare.[151] At the end of 1936, Jakob Lestschinsky, writing from Paris, also viewed the situation with great consternation:

> Some 20 to 22 percent of the Jewish population today is already more or less dependent on welfare. 20 to 25 percent are living on their last savings. People have liquidated or transferred their businesses, and received a bit of money in return: a few isolated individuals got millions, a few dozen

> were handed hundreds of thousands—and tens of thousands received nothing but a paltry few thousand marks. Now this last scrap of savings is being eaten up. Whoever has children and was somehow able to manage, has sent them abroad. His hope now is to receive some good news. And that redeeming message requesting him to come to the new homeland. The homeland of the children. Whoever is childless sits and counts his coins. And prays to heaven that his years will not outlast, God forbid, his handful of marks. Earning a living—and maybe in some cases a quite decent one—that's something only 10 to 15 percent of the Jewish population, at the most, are able to do. The rest have just enough to scrimp by on. But all . . . sense that it is definite now: their fate has been severed from that of the Germans. And is henceforth bound up with another country—of which they only dare to dream. All their thoughts and feelings, all their hopes and longings are fixed on one consuming idea: emigration! So what then is happening: is this the liquidation of German Jewry!?[152]

Lestschinsky had lived in Germany for many years before 1932 and was regarded as one of the most knowledgeable observers of the economic developments among German Jewry. The study cited here also demonstrates a very detailed knowledge of the situation in Germany at the time and has been confirmed by later research. Yet at the end of 1936, even Lestschinsky did not want to think it possible (and hoped against hope he was wrong) that German Jewry, after nearly two thousand years of Jewish life in that land, was nearing the endpoint of its history. This is most probably why he added a question mark after the exclamation point at the end of the above-cited passage. One year later, he would have left out that question mark. By the end of 1937, even the optimistic observer had to admit that economically, at the very least, German Jewry was facing final destruction. Yet the most discerning and clearsighted were unable to foresee the swiftness with which this process would come to its calamitous conclusion.

3

1938
The "Fateful Year"

> The year 1938 . . . marks a historical turning point in the fate of the Jews. . . . Using legislative and administrative means, the Aryanization process had been significantly accelerated. The goal of a complete exclusion of the Jews from economic life was already beginning to crystallize around the middle of 1938. . . . The Reichsvertretung, after a temporary cessation of activity, resumed functioning once again on November 29. . . . [It] had to adjust to the fact that it had been made the sole financial body for emigration, welfare and the school system. . . . In this manner, a "mutual shared responsibility" of the Jewish community in Germany was decreed for the final stage of its liquidation.[1]

The annual report of the Reichsvertretung, from whose introduction the above passage is quoted, was written at the beginning of 1939. It contained only a carefully disguised allusion to the November pogrom: "Never to be forgotten is that strength, those forces, which came to life especially in the closing months of the year 1938 and which, in the awareness of being part of a community of fate, found their expression in the direct help extended by one person to the next."[2] In actual fact, the new phase in Jewish policy had already been introduced at the end of 1937. As 1938 wore on, its impact intensified as progressively more severe measures were instituted. Between 1933 and 1937, legislation, administrative practice, sporadically organized "popular anger," and a process of creeping displacement had undermined the social and economic position of German Jews. There were non-Jews who reacted to these developments with feelings of perplexity and sympathy; the bulk of the population, however, remained indifferent. A substantial number of loyal Nazis, party and government functionaries at all levels, and just plain, ordinary individuals simply interested in pecuniary gain had taken an active part in the process of pushing Jews out of the economy and society. The Nazis had largely succeeded in isolating German Jews, ostracizing them in the consciousness of the broader population from the *Volksgemeinschaft* and branding them as aliens and "enemies of the people."

In economic terms, all preconditions had been created by the end of 1937 for the final "removal of Jews from the German economy," termed *Entjudung* in Nazi parlance. After having been subjected to a successful process of progressive displacement over several years, the economic function of the vast majority of Jews in Germany at this point was limited to their role as consumers. Now one could push ahead with eliminating the last remaining residues of active Jewish economic activity and gaining control of remaining Jewish assets. A string of successes in foreign policy, accelerated preparations for the coming war, and a broad-based domestic political consensus formed the framework for this project—just as the War in the East was later to create the prerequisites for the physical extermination of millions of European Jews. In this context, the November 1938 pogrom was only a signal: a call to complete, within a short span of time, a process that had been set into insidious motion many months before.

The Demographic and Economic Situation

At the beginning of 1938, there were still between 350,000 and 365,000 Jews living in the *Altreich*—that is, within the borders of 1937.[3] The Jewish population had thus declined by between 160,000 and 175,000 since January 1933. Most of that number had emigrated, and the difference in vital statistics between births and deaths is estimated to have been thirty to thirty-five thousand. The Jewish population was still dispersed in some 1,400 *Gemeinden*; however, 612 of these had been classified as "communities in distress," and a further 120 small *Gemeinden* were facing imminent dissolution. Nearly 65 percent of all Jews were concentrated in seven large communities; 140,000, amounting to some 40 percent of all Jews left in Germany, lived in Berlin.

At this point, Jews still holding jobs were, almost without exception, working for Jewish employers. Consequently, the employment situation was largely dependent on the number of still extant Jewish firms and businesses. Some 60 to 70 percent of enterprises owned by Jews in January 1933 were no longer in Jewish hands. This estimate is confirmed by figures given by the *Judenreferent* (Adviser on Jewish Affairs) in the Economy Ministry, Alf Krüger. Krüger listed the number of Jewish firms as of April 1, 1938, at exactly 39,552.[4] Jewish retail trade had been particularly hard hit by this process of liquidation: In July 1938, of the formerly more than fifty thousand Jewish retail shops, there were, according to official statistics, only about nine thousand left in the *Altreich,* including the sales outlets of Jewish craft enterprises. A total of 3,637 of these were located in Berlin.[5] Even these shops were facing a bitter struggle for survival, especially in the smaller provincial towns and villages. Their dire economic situation is carefully noted in the files of the DEAs. In October 1937, the DEA for southern Westphalia conducted a survey in his region within the framework of a "propaganda study" on the Jewish question being conducted by the Reich Propaganda Office of the NSDAP. Tax offices, chambers of commerce and industry, and county economic advisers prepared detailed reports on the economic situation and the "economic influence" of the Jewish firms still in operation.[6] Individual businesses were listed, with exact figures on income during the 1933–1936 period. Thus, for example, the Tax Office for Dortmund, Southern District, reported that fifty-four Jewish taxpayers had emigrated from its area of jurisdiction since "the takeover."

> Of those remaining, owners of concerns that have benefited from the upswing in the economy have been able to enjoy a boost in sales similar to that of the Aryan businesses. In many cases, however, the increase in turnover has occurred at the expense of profits. Profit margins were held to the barest minimum in order to ensure sales under any circumstances. . . . The proprietors of the firms listed in the appendix probably have no appreciable influence. The single Jewish banking firm in this administrative district is of no importance.

The appendix listed the following firms still in operation: four wholesale foods firms, four retail food stores, thirteen textile stores, four shoe stores, and twenty other enterprises of various sorts, including one doctor's office. Only one enterprise, a wholesale foods firm, was listed as having a turnover in excess of RM 1 million for 1936; however, that concern had reported sales of a similar magnitude back in 1933; profits had steadily declined and were given as zero for 1936. Of the other firms, only nine reached profits exceeding RM 10,000, and two recorded income topping RM 20,000 (all statistics based on 1936 tax returns).

The DEA for Bochum mentioned several firms that were "still doing quite well." On the other hand, "other firms at the moment are only able to operate on a modest scale; the bulk of businesses are doing badly, including the well-known firms X, Y and Z." The Bochum report continues:

> In my district, there are no longer any medium-size and larger industrial firms, banks and Jewish companies in shipping and transport. In contrast, Jews are still involved in wholesale and retail trade. The middle of 1933, there were 111 Jewish-owned firms in Bochum engaged in retail trade and crafts; of these, approximately 50 percent have been liquidated or Aryanized. . . . Awarding of public tendered contracts to Jewish firms has long since been halted. . . . It was called to my attention, however,

> that there is no formal regulation barring non-Aryans from participation in bidding. Yet due to the fact that potential bidders are only approved at the suggestion of the Chamber of Commerce, it has been possible to date to avoid approval for Jewish applicants.

The Tax Office in Dortmund-Hörde reported to its superiors in a similar connection that in its district, "apart from one large concern . . . there [were] only a few small firms in Jewish hands, along with a tiny number of medium-size businesses. A substantial proportion of those Jews liable for payment of business taxes have already had to quit the field. . . . There is no Jewish influence in the economy within the Dortmund-Hörde tax district."

The list furnished by the mayor of Soest in Westphalia in the framework of the above-mentioned survey provides a picture—also typical of numerous other small towns—of the especially precarious situation being faced by many Jewish firms in outlying and rural areas.[7] A total of fourteen firms were listed by the Soest mayor. Four of these were larger factories, including a plant manufacturing electric light bulbs, employing a work force numbering 155. In the case of all four firms, it is mentioned that "Aryanization" had been initiated. In respect to the other enterprises, the mayor had the following comments: "virtually no business," "operations shut down almost completely," "only Jewish clientele. No employees," "shut down for business," "business nearly closed," and so on.

The reporting of all Jewish assets and property was ordered by decree in April 1938.[8] The registration took several months and, as preserved documents indicate, no form of property and assets was excluded. The results are summarized in a confidential circular of the Economy Ministry dated November 28, 1938.[9] It stated that the value of reported Jewish assets and property in the entire area of the Reich, including Austria, was approximately RM 8.531 billion gross, RM 7.123 billion net after deduction of debts and other obligations. Of this, RM 112 million were in agricultural properties, and RM 2.343 billion in urban real estate. Active business capital constituted only RM 1.195 billion, approximately 14 percent of reported total wealth. Since the total amount included some RM 2 billion listed as assets of Jews in Austria—where "Aryanization" was only in its early stages at the time, April 1938—the proportion of capital still invested in business firms in the *Altreich* proper was probably even lower. The sum of RM 4.481 billion, equivalent to about 60 percent of the total amount, was listed in the category "other types of assets," and was emphasized as being "vulnerable assets . . . readily seizable." These consisted of various forms of disposable assets, invested in bank notes, securities, and the like, for the most part apparently the proceeds from the sale of businesses already liquidated.

Jewish property and assets in the *Altreich* have been estimated at RM 10 to 12 billion for the year 1933.[10] This had declined to half of that amount by April 1938, whereas only about a third of all German Jews had emigrated within that same period.

The developments documented by these figures serve to disprove convincingly any thesis contending that the radicalization of economic persecution of the Jews that set in in the autumn of 1937 was the product of some sort of internal dynamics of uncoordinated—or even competing—initiatives flowing from a supposed "dualistic" policy toward the Jews. The sources clearly document the many months of coordinated preparations at party and government level for the measures introduced at this juncture.

The Political-Military Background

The Four-Year Plan that ushered in the phase of accelerated rearmament was proclaimed by Hitler at the 1936 Party Congress. Earlier in August, he had written a secret memorandum announcing the goal of readying the German economy and the Wehrmacht for war within four years. The Jews were mentioned only marginally in this memorandum. Hitler called for taking steps, "with iron determination," to assure that Germany was self-sufficient in raw materials and that "the foreign currency owed to the German economy abroad be paid." For this purpose, two laws should be introduced. "1. A law specifying the death penalty for economic sabotage and 2. a law making all of Jewry liable for any damages caused to the German economy—and thus to the German people—by individuals from among this criminal element."[11] The imminent expropriation of the Jews and the seizure of their assets for the purposes of preparations for war are only hinted at implicitly, yet one of the pretexts utilized later for such measures is already given a clear formulation here. Göring, the new "Plenipotentiary for the Implementation of the Four-Year Plan," was now to play the leading role in Jewish policy as well.

Although Hitler's memorandum had been addressed to only a limited circle, it was soon clear that his suggestions for future treatment of the Jews had been noted far beyond the confines of that narrow circle of confidants. In a confidential note dated December 18, 1936, Undersecretary Stuckart in the Interior Ministry informed the economy minister that discussions were in progress on the "formation of a Jewish Guaranty Association" and that the conclusion had been reached that such an arrangement could be worked out best in the sphere of taxation. The Führer, it was stated, had "given his basic approval to the levying of a special tax on the Jews" and had ordered "preparations for such a bill to be speeded up so that it would be possible to proclaim the law soon after the end of the Gustloff trial."[12]

Despite the wishes of the Führer, it took nearly two more years until what had been planned as a "reprisal" for David Frankfurter's action in Davos was finally made a reality following Herschel Grynszpan's assassination of vom Rath in Paris. A corresponding draft bill had been prepared in the Finance Ministry in June 1937, stipulating that a "special fund for the Reich" was to be set up using "tax revenues from the Jews." However, Undersecretary Reinhardt had to inform the deputy of the Führer on December 23 that proclamation of the bill had been temporarily postponed. Göring was worried that "the declaration of the law at the present time might endanger the situation of the Reich in respect to raw materials and foreign exchange."[13]

This postponement of the *Judensteuer* (Jew Tax) did not mean that preparations for a systematic and planned plundering of Jewish assets and a prohibition on any gainful economic activity by Jews had gotten bogged down. On September 29, 1936, Undersecretary Stuckart convened an interministerial discussion to prepare a top-echelon meeting on "the basic direction of the entire policy toward the Jews." The undersecretaries from the Interior Ministry and Economy Ministry in attendance, as well as party representatives, were in agreement right from the start that "the Jewish question could only be considered solved when there were no longer any Jews left in Germany," and that

> economic affairs would also have to be adjusted in conformity with this goal. . . . All measures in the field of Jewish policy should be oriented toward the aim [of total emigration]. Economic activity by Jews should only be permitted to allow them to earn their own living—though their desire to emigrate should not be dampened as a result of their economic and political situation. In the final analysis, consideration would also have to be given to carrying out forced emigration as well.

In the course of the lengthy discussion, consideration was also given to the fact that "affluent Jews are generally not overly enthusiastic about emigrating. For this reason, Jews should not be left with extensive opportunities for economic activity. On the other hand, efforts should be made to prevent the formation of a Jewish proletariat."

In conclusion, following a suggestion of the interior minister on June 3, 1936, a decision was taken to exclude Jews from a number of additional trades, including that of itinerant peddler, a vocation that had taken on steadily increasing importance in the list of Jewish economic pursuits. "Restrictions for party members and civil servants in business transactions with Jews and Jewish firms [are to] apply only to consumers . . . not to the entire field of import and export. Sales to Jews should be basically permissible." Members of the NSDAP, units of the Wehrmacht and the DAF—"associated organizations" excepted—should be subject to the restrictions mentioned. "On the question of extending the prohibition to include civil servants, Ministerialrat Hoppe reported that President Schacht would most likely be opposed to such a prohibition for his own department." Since "special identificational marking of Jewish stores has, by order of the Führer, not been introduced as yet," consideration should be given to introduction of a uniform symbol identifying non-Jewish businesses and to further examination of the plan to prepare a special directory of Jewish enterprises.[14]

Helmut Genschel has dated the "gradual transition from creeping displacement to open exclusion of Jews from the economy" to the period between the autumn of 1936 and the autumn of 1938. He adds, however, that even before this time, "there were deliberations which clearly indicate the change that was beginning to take place in intentions within the top echelons of the party and government." The exact dating and tempo of the open process of *Entjudung der Wirtschaft* is a matter of debate; in my view, it was already indicated at the end of 1937. In any case, Genschel has also emphasized that the intensified displacement policy should be seen in the context of accelerated preparations for war: "If the National Socialist notions about the 'defeatist' behavior of Jews in the First World War were taken seriously—which must be assumed in the case of Hitler and many of his ideological cohorts—this led necessarily to the conclusion that Jews had to be excluded from a German war economy."[15]

The change of ministers in the Economy Ministry should be seen in this light. The underlying cause behind the change in political course, which also had an impact on economic policy toward the Jews, should not be sought in the chain of events involving Schacht's suspension from duties on September 7, his official dismissal on November 27, 1937, and the temporary takeover of his ministerial functions by Göring. Rather, these modifications at ministerial level were only one of its symptoms. Göring's assigned task—to transform the Economy Ministry into an "executive organ for implementation of the Four-Year Plan" before he passed the Ministry on to Walter Funk on February 15, 1938[16]—was part of the extensive regrouping in policy and personnel carried out in November 1937. This regrouping also encompassed the top echelons of the Wehrmacht and the Foreign Office and marked the decisive setting of the course of the Nazi ship of state toward the goal of the planned war.[17]

The Process of Legal Exclusion Is Stepped Up

All preparations for the final exclusion of Jews from the economy had been completed by the spring of 1938; one could now press ahead with their realization. The deluge of measures that followed has often been examined in detail in the relevant literature, and we will restrict ourselves here to the principal measures.[18] On March 28, 1938, a law was instituted governing the legal situation of the Jewish *Gemeinden,* stripping them and their associated organizations of the status of legally recognized, publicly incorporated bodies. The next day, the Finance Ministry announced that Jewish *Gemeinden* would be required to pay a property tax, retroactive to January 1, 1938. A subsequent series of decrees imposed additional taxes on them, from which they had previously been exempt.[19] The 1938 annual report of the Reichsvertretung observed that as a result of this law, which "substantially increases the extra financial burden on the Gemeinden . . . the process of dissolution . . . has been directly accelerated." The process of liquidation of the small communities, which had, until the end of February, progressed "at a relatively quiet tempo"—some seventy *Gemeinden* had been dissolved from 1933 to 1937—had quickened its pace so rapidly that by the time of the writing of the report, March 1939, "almost 90 percent of the member *Gemeinden* in the Prussian State Federation were in the process of liquidation." However, since the beginning of 1938,

> communal life had increasingly restricted itself to provision of social services for members. Religious services could no longer be held, due to the lack of a *minyan* [the ritually required number of ten adult males]. Religious instruction had been curtailed more and more as a consequence of the emigration of school-age children. Cultural programs, actively pursued the previous year by the organizing of cultural evenings, lectures by district rabbis and the like, necessarily had to be more and more restricted. In some localities, the only Jews remaining by November 1938 were aged or destitute members of the community. All these various and sundry formations, which in a formal sense still might be called Gemeinden, were only the dead hulks of what in some cases had been thriving communities in the past.[20]

New regulations also were issued for taxation of individuals: In February 1938, a law on changes in income tax had stripped Jews of benefits for dependent children. Deductions for newlyweds and maternity and other benefits originally granted were now no longer valid for Jews.[21] On April 21, 1938, the Plenipotentiary for the Four-Year Plan issued an "Ordinance against Abetting the Disguising of Jewish Enterprises." German citizens who were implicated in conscious efforts designed to camouflage the Jewish character of an industrial enterprise, or who secretly carried out legal transactions for Jews, were subject to possible fines and jail sentences.[22] Among the public, the fundamental significance of this *Verordnung,* which initiated the registration of Jewish property and enterprises, was well understood. Thus, for example, a daily paper in Salzburg welcomed the ordinance, in an editorial tellingly entitled "Cleanup!," as the "prelude to the basic solution of the Jewish question in the economy."[23]

Four days later, Göring, together with the interior minister, issued the ordinance on registration of Jewish assets and property.[24] Every Jew, or non-Jewish partner of a Jewish spouse was obligated to declare all assets in the country or abroad exceeding the value of RM 5,000. In blunt language, Section 8 formulated the purpose of this *Verordnung*: the Plenipotentiary for the Four-Year Plan "was authorized to take steps to ensure the utilization of assessable assets in the interests of the German economy." A directive issued at the same time subjected "any sale or leasing of an industrial, agricultural or forestry enterprise and the order of usufructal rights" to firms under Jewish ownership to official confirmation by the "higher administrative authorities."[25]

In a secret report dated June 14, 1938, on "Jews in the economy,"[26] Minister Frick elucidated the meaning of the new ordinances. In a discussion held on April 29, 1938 (three days after the order for obligatory declaration of assets), the "solution to the Jewish question in the economic sphere" was introduced after "consideration had been given to how to transform Jewish property in Germany into assets which would preclude any further economic influence . . . in order to achieve a final exclusion of Jews from the German economy." For the immediate future, Frick thought "a regulation necessary which was . . . aimed at a *compulsory* exclusion of Jews" (emphasis in original). After enumerating his proposal in detail and expressing concern about the extremely unfavorable conditions for emigration for Jews, except to Palestine, Frick devoted the final paragraph of his observations to the question of possibilities for gainful employment for Jews who had remained in Germany.

> Insofar as Jews in Germany are able to live off the proceeds of their commercial and other assets, they require strict state supervision. Insofar as they are in need of financial assistance, the question of their *public* support must be solved. Greater use of the various organizations for social welfare appear to be unavoidable.

In comparison with the Gestapo's later concrete "achievements" in this regard, Frick here appears to be thoroughly lacking in manipulative fantasy.

Schacht, in his capacity as Reichsbank president, responded to Frick's suggestions in a detailed memorandum dated July 7, 1938.[27] In his introductory remarks, Schacht assured Frick "that granting of credits by the Reichsbank . . . had long since been adjusted to the intentions of the Nuremberg Laws." He went on to note that "according to the way things stand, without the intended additional legal compulsion, it [will be] possible . . . to free the German credit system from the granting of any credit which is of benefit, immediately or indirectly, to a Jew." In his subsequent comments, however, he advocated a "cautious approach" so as "not to exaggerate the economic and financial (foreign exchange-related) effects on Germany's foreign relations." After discussing the possible effects of the compulsory "Aryanizations" proposed by Frick on the German capital market and German foreign affairs, Schacht declared that it was "indispensable to fix a specific time period—say five to ten years—and then require that Jews sell their businesses within that span. They must be placed in a situation where they are allowed to seek out their own potential buyers, in order to obtain an objectively reasonable, satisfactory sale price." However, Schacht added, "should Jewish business owners be paid, for example, in Reich government bonds . . . there should be a regulation for compulsory deposit of these securities in order to keep tabs on their movement, shifts in ownership, etc." In conclusion, "after the previous measures in treating the economic facets of the Jewish question—measures which I already find deeply disturbing," Schacht warned against "continuing on down that path which the rest of the world will denounce . . . as an arbitrary action devoid of any foundation in law and as a confiscation of property." Schacht must have been well aware that this was precisely what was planned and probably had precious few illusions about the ultimate effect of his undoubtedly courageous verbal objections.

Frick, in his summary report, had pointed to the "working business capital of the Jews" as that category of assets "affording the greatest economic influence." He had welcomed the fact that, "according to the declaration form required, such active business capital must be specially listed."[28] He was therefore probably quite pleasantly surprised by the above-mentioned results of the declaration of assets and the small proportion of active assets they included.

In actual fact, however, the registration of Jewish assets and property had another ultimate aim, the implementation of which lay further ahead in the future. The groundwork was being laid here for the subsequent total despoliation of the German Jews—here still euphemistically termed "utilization of assets," or, more bluntly, as "seizure" (*Erfassung*). The "Sühneleistung" (Atonement Penalty) levied on the Jews after the November pogrom and later special taxes were assessed on the basis of the declaration of assets of April 1938, although it was conceded in the already quoted November 28 circular of the economy minister that since that survey "substantial assets, impossible even to estimate in monetary terms, had been sold below their true value to non-Jewish businessmen."[29]

The official form for registration of assets was a many-paged questionnaire in which it was necessary to list every type of possession, down to the last detail: securities, properties, insurance policies, outstanding unpaid debts, valuable paintings, luxury articles—nothing could be left out.[30] In addition, by means of various semiofficial hints and ambiguous reports in the press, Jews were encouraged not to declare their assets below their true value. Thus, for example, Undersecretary Brinkmann stated in a press conference, attended by foreign journalists, that Jews had been allowed to determine the value of their assets themselves, so that in the event of a takeover, the owner might be compensated by the government in interest-bearing securities.[31] Ernst Herzfeld also reported that the "suspicion, possibly launched by the Nazis, was widespread that there was an intention to 'purchase' Jewish assets in return for complete or partial compensation. Naturally, nothing more than the declared value would be indemnified. . . . These considerations caused a fair number of individuals to declare the value of their real estate and other assets to be higher than the actual taxable worth."[32]

The Third Ordinance of the Reich Citizenship Law[33] was published on June 14, 1938. It defined exactly what sort of industrial concern and what form of business—such as a private trading company or limited liability company—"should be considered as Jewish in the sense of the Reich Citizenship Law." In respect to companies, it was sufficient if one Jew was in senior management or on the board of directors or if one-quarter of its capital was in Jewish hands. In addition, an "industrial firm dominated in actual fact by Jewish influence"—however that was to be interpreted—was classified as being "Jewish." The registration of other Jewish business enterprises was also announced. It remained the prerogative of a decree by the economy minister to stipulate their obligation to be specially marked. One month later, in a circular by the interior minister dated July 14, 1938, the listing of all still existing Jewish enterprises was ordered.[34] By means of detailed individual regulations, the authorities hoped to make sure that not a single Jewish business would be overlooked. The lists were also supposed to include businesses formerly owned by Jews, whose owners had, "for all external appearances," left the firm, "if there is a likely suspicion that they still control the concern's management." In this case as well, the competent authorities were instructed to look carefully into the "dominant influence" in firms belonging to "persons with Jewish relatives" or "of mixed descent" (*Mischlinge*).

The registration form,[35] which has been preserved, contained correspondingly detailed sections on the ownership of each individual firm and its business situation. The fact that it had to be filled out in quadruplicate clearly proves the close degree of cooperation between the party and the tax offices, chambers of commerce and industry and the municipal authorities, who had demonstrated their willingness in previous years to cooperate in carrying out "Aryanizations" and keeping surveillance on business developments in Jewish firms. It is not known whether a summary was ever published of the results of the registration, but on the basis of various later declarations, it can be assumed that such a summary must have been available to the relevant government offices. It is unfortunate that we have neither such a total listing nor a greater number of the original documents. Such documentation might be able to provide a reliable picture of the economic situation of the German Jews at that time.

The Law on Changes in Trade Regulations of July 6, 1938, excluded Jews from various occupations that they were still permitted, at least formally, to pursue.[36] All of those professions and occupations were prohibited that had already been mentioned in the discussion of September 29, 1936, along with several additional job categories: private security personnel (e.g., Jews could no longer be employed as night watchmen), private investigators involved in gathering data on personal and financial affairs (how many Jewish detectives could there have been?), real estate agents, tourist guides, and operators of commercial matrimonial services (except for marriage brokerage between Jews and *Mischlinge*). These professions were of little importance for Jewish occupational activity—with perhaps the sole exception of real estate agents. Trade in real estate was still an option for a few Jewish firms due to the emigration of Jewish property owners. Moreover, who could say how this scurrilous list came about in the first place?

Of decisive and serious impact, however, was the prohibition on the vocation of peddler (itinerant tradesman) and on the "practice of a trade outside one's official town of residence" by the owner of a firm or traveling sales representatives. Many former independent businessmen and unemployed workers had flocked to these occupations as an alternative that held out the prospect of a modest income. The party and middle-class interest associations, the NS-HAGO in particular, had voiced their concern even earlier about this competition. Thus, their publication *Der Aufbau* declared at the beginning of 1938 that Jews made up 18 to 20 percent of all those in itinerant trade,[37] a claim that was not supported by any further data and is today impossible to verify or disprove. The legal changes in the code of trade regulations were probably meant chiefly to close this "dangerous gap"!

The Fourth Ordinance of the Reich Citizenship Law of July 25, 1938,[38] rescinded the licenses of all Jewish doctors still in practice, effective September 30, 1938. However, the interior minister was given the authority to permit an exception: certain Jewish doctors who had lost their positions could treat Jews, using the professional title of *Krankenbehandler,* "practitioner for the sick." All others were prohibited from the practice of medicine, effective immediately. Since January 1, 1938, Jewish doctors had no longer been allowed to treat patients covered by health insurance schemes for white-collar workers. Since May, they had been barred from accepting welfare patients for treatment.[39] At this juncture, the prohibition mainly affected Jewish patients from the health insurance schemes and on welfare; non-Jewish patients were rarely given referrals to Jewish doctors. In many welfare offices, bills and certificates signed by Jewish doctors were no longer recognized as valid. Of the 3,152 Jewish doctors still in practice at that time in the *Altreich,* only 709 received permission to treat Jewish patients as a *Krankenbehandler*; the figures for Berlin were 426 out of a total of 1,623 practicing physicians.[40]

The Fifth Ordinance of the Reich Citizenship Law of September 27, 1938,[41] excluded all still practicing attorneys. Analogous to the special regulation of the Fourth Ordinance, the judiciary was authorized to grant permission to so-called *Konsulenten,* "counsels for legal advising and representation of Jews." At that time in the *Altreich,* there were still 1,753 Jewish lawyers; even before this ordinance, they had had an almost exclusively Jewish clientele. Now, a total of only 172 (40 of them in Berlin) were licensed as *Konsulenten*. Like the doctors, these *Konsulenten* were prohibited from using their earlier professional designation in any form whatsoever on signs or letterheads. The decree also regulated the fee schedule of such *Konsulenten*: a portion of their income from services had to be paid to a Reich Office for Compensation. This office allegedly provided attorneys who had been forced to leave practice and were World War I veterans with a monthly assistance stipend of RM 200 to RM 250. It is not known whether or to what extent any such payments were ever made.[42] We are not familiar with any other professional group, such as the doctors, whose fee schedules were interfered with in a similar manner. It is possible that this was a private initiative of the justice administration. This measure was a harbinger of the future principle of National Socialist policy toward the Jews: namely, to relegate care for indigent Jews to the responsibility of "Jewish shared liability" for co-religionists. The Sixth Ordinance of October 31, 1938,[43] then extended the prohibition on practicing one's profession (*Berufsverbot*) to the patent attorneys and enjoined *Konsulenten* from representing Jews in cases involving patents.

These ordinances represented the policy of the application and extension of the Nuremberg Racial Laws to the economic sphere, an intention proclaimed as early as 1935 by Economy Minister Schacht and other members of the government. Such an extension had been anticipated with trepidation by the Jewish community. The reasons for a postponement of almost three years can only be surmised. Probably the upcoming Olympic games were initially a factor. Later on, as various already quoted statements by Schacht and Göring suggest, the precarious foreign currency situation played a paramount part. Most likely, the recognition that the continuing process of displacement could be effectively implemented even without additional legislation played a decisive role. "Without pyrotechnics"—in the spirit of this slogan, NSDAP and government offices cooperated closely with organized interested parties between 1935 and 1938 in order to push Jews out of the active economy and slowly but surely to plunder their assets.

In addition to the newly introduced legislation, the corresponding administrative pressure was stepped up in 1938 as well. As Ernst Herzfeld has commented, "the conditions for earning a livelihood for Jews were encroached upon, silently and tenaciously. Factory owners encountered difficulties in obtaining raw materials, or procurement was blocked completely. . . . Our grievances fell mainly on deaf ears in the ministries. . . . The ministerial bureaucracy, insofar as it was at all favorably disposed, did not [wish] to go out of its way for Jews." It is interesting that Herzfeld, who was one of the best-informed Jewish functionaries at that time, especially in the economic field, does not consider Schacht's dismissal as economy minister to have been one of the reasons for the step-up in administrative harassment. On the contrary, Herzfeld notes that the credit restrictions and new limitations placed on transfer of capital by the Reichsbank under Schacht were among the "quiet" displacement measures instituted in 1938 that also caused a great deal of trouble for the large concerns, up until then relatively unscathed. Schacht remained Reichsbank president until early 1939.[44]

The restrictions on raw material procurement mentioned by Herzfeld had already been ordered in November 1937 in a secret decree issued by the economy minister to the offices for supervision and control. The Federation of Chambers of Commerce and Industry then sent a circular letter to its members, "not meant for publication or further transmission," informing them with obvious gratification about the decree. It was stated that the federation had already been responsible for the fact that "individual offices for supervision had, on their own responsibility, made efforts to accommodate to the changing economic situation; however, a "satisfactory total solution" had been achieved only by the decree of the economy minister. "The allotments of raw materials and foreign currency quotas released in this way are being placed at the disposal of other firms; the upshot is a very basic loosening up, in part, of the system of allocation."[45]

Even prior to the legal changes in the code of trade regulations, the DEAs had made sure that itinerant trade permits were no longer issued or renewed for Jews. After the issuance of the law instituting changes in July 1938, these advisers were still not satisfied. The Office for Craft Trades and Commerce of the NSDAP in Bochum pointed out that even according to the new law governing practice of the vocation of peddler and sales representative in one's own town of residence, no itinerant trade permit was required. The reporter "had heard" that in Berlin there were still ten thousand Jewish sales representatives earning something in this way! That situation had to be remedied because "it is precisely the Jewish door-to-door salesman . . . who knows so well how to touch the hearts of our housewives with tearful tales of woe about the unfortunate plight of the Jews . . . in order to profit from such for himself and his race."[46]

The small Jewish retailers, who had been able to retain their membership until early 1938 in the cooperative small credit associations, were excluded by arbitrary, "autonomous" rulings of the association management. In this way, they were often plunged into liquidity difficulties, since they were unable to find a replacement source for the lost credit. Moreover, they were frequently hard put to meet the return payments demanded.[47] As a consequence, many businesses were closed down or "Aryanized," which led to the firing of thousands of Jewish employees. Appeals to the labor courts for at least payment of compensation (for "undue hardship") to workers laid off because of "Aryanization" were successful only in extremely rare cases.

One such case was the ruling by the state labor court in Hannover to award the right to reinstatement or RM 200 in compensation to a truck driver fired from a "business previously operated by a Jewish firm" after filing a complaint against the new owner. In its decision, the court stated that the dismissal had been "*unduly harsh,* because the number of Jewish firms had declined to such an extent that it had become difficult for a Jew, even in his prime, to find employment again in the firm of a member of his race." This ruling provoked the indignant protests of the National Socialist *Rechtswahrer* ("guardians of the law"):[48]

> The dismissal of a Jew is not "unduly harsh" simply because a Jew nowadays finds it difficult to locate work, even in the firm of a fellow member of his race. If one wishes to call this dismissal unduly harsh, then one would likewise have to condemn all the measures of the Party and the government, by which the position of Jewish power has now been undermined and Jewish foreign influence is being systematically reduced, as being unduly harsh. [Here follows an enumeration of the already familiar measures "for the *Entjudung* of our economic life."] And given the totality of all these measures, they wish to claim that the dismissal of one solitary Jew is unduly harsh . . . ?

By September 6, 1938, the legal exclusion of Jews from most economic activities had indeed progressed to the point where the arguments advanced by these militant Nazi jurists were not lacking in a certain logic of their own. In any event, they showed a greater sense of awareness of existing reality than the decision handed down by the court in Hannover.

"Popular Anger" and "Aryanization"

> A far-reaching popular mood hostile to Jews must be created in order to form the basis for continued attack and effective pushback. . . . The most effective means for undermining the Jews' sense of security is the popular anger of the people, which vents itself in violent actions. Although this method is illegal, it has, as evinced by the "Kurfürstendamm riots," had a lasting effect. . . . Psychologically this method is all the more understandable, given the fact that the Jew has learned a great deal from pogroms of the last few centuries. He fears nothing as much as a hostile mood that can at any moment spontaneously turn against him.[49]

The method recommended by the Judenreferat of the SS to motivate Jews to give up their businesses by the use of violence was utilized again in more intensified fashion starting the end of 1937. Once again, Julius Streicher, editor of *Der Stürmer* and the Gauleiter for Franconia, seized the initiative with a Christmas boycott in Nuremberg.[50] After other cities had joined in, the disturbances reached a new high point in Berlin in June 1938, with the defacing of storefront windows and violent attacks against Jews. "The present anti-Jewish campaign," wrote the American ambassador on June 22, 1938, to the secretary of state, "outstrips in thoroughness anything of the kind since 1933. . . . Just as the outbursts of 1935 led to the Nuremberg legislation of September of that year, it is expected that the present campaign will also bring forth further legislative measures."[51] The ambassador had thus clearly understood the dual tactic of "popular anger" and "legal" measures of displacement characteristic of National Socialist *Judenpolitik*.

As foreseen and intended, there was a leap in the number of closings and "Aryanizations" of Jewish-owned businesses. The already mentioned cuts in allotments, officially justified by the argument that there had been a "shift in clientele" away from Jewish firms, accelerated the liquidation of factories particularly hard-hit by the scarcity of raw materials and foreign currency. Starting in March 1938, the reports of the DEAs noted the effectiveness of these measures, which would induce the Jewish owners to jettison their firms as quickly as possible.[52] In the autumn of 1937, the Federation of German-Aryan Garment Manufacturers (ADEFA) launched a propaganda campaign in the retail clothing trade. The executive director of this laudable organization, formerly DEA for Saxony, had calculated at the end of 1937 that "even today, there is a lamentable state of affairs: a sizable number of irresponsible retailers are purchasing annually ca. 400 million reichsmark worth of clothing goods from Jewish garment wholesalers, and then passing these on to an unsuspecting public. One could calculate from this figure that an estimated 14 million German Volksgenossen are today still being clothed by the Jew." In order to remedy this situation, the ADEFA was planning to put the label "German-made goods" on all of the products of its members beginning in January 1938. This was to be done "with the support of the Advertising Council for the German Economy and the Reich Committee for Popular Enlightenment." Only those goods manufactured in all stages of production completely by "Aryan" hands would be granted this label. Along with DEAs, the branch offices of the DAF also joined efforts "to energetically carry forward to completion the process of *Entjudung* in the clothing industry."[53] In January 1938, similar labels were introduced in the leather goods industry.

It is no longer possible to determine the basis used by the executive director of ADEFA for his figures or to what extent they corresponded with reality. There is no doubt that there was an especially large proportion of highly labor-intensive Jewish-owned firms in the ready-made apparel industry. They had been largely spared up to then, yet the displacement campaign initiated by "Aryan" competitors beginning at the end of 1937 appears to have yielded results very quickly.

In any event, by September 1938, the press was able to announce, with obvious glee, the imminent "eradication of Jews dealing in ready-made apparel [*Konfektionsjuden*]." Those identified as beneficiaries were the new owners of the "Aryanized" firms, along with interested parties making up the membership of the ADEFA: "persons who up until then had placed their expertise at the disposal of the *Konfektionsjude,* but who now, as independent entrepreneurs, had to subject their work to the professional criticism of the retail trade branch."[54] In 1938, another paper welcomed "the signs of incipient nationalization present in the process of *Entjudung*. Yet there are some who think things are not progressing fast enough. These *Volksgenossen* see a chance to become economically independent, and do not want to let the opportune moment slip by. Frequently, these are executives or other employees of Jewish firms who think that in this way they can advance rapidly to a higher income level and acquire assets. This is understandable, and it would be foolish to ignore such wishes and objectives." However, consideration should be given to the question of how willing applicants are to risk their own capital.[55]

Nonetheless, this "wave of Aryanization" in the ready-made clothing industry, as spectacular as it seemed, represented only the conclusion of a protracted process of liquidation and expropriation that had been going on for several years. By the beginning of 1938, as we have noted, Jewish retailers and members of the free professions had, for the most part, been shut out of the economy, and at least half of all Jewish workers were jobless. It was only the Jewish craft manufacturing firms, the bulk of which were concentrated in the garment field, that had, in the main, been able to stand their ground. By the middle of 1935, there were some eighty-five hundred craft firms listed for the entire *Altreich*; of these, five thousand were still in existence in December 1938.[56]

There were probably two principal reasons for this relative longevity. First of all, the Jewish proportion in craft manufacture was much lower than in the commercial sector. Consequently, it is likely that the limited Jewish presence engendered less antisemitic competitive envy in this branch. The 1933 occupational census had listed 19,319 Jewish self-employed in the entire sector of "industry and crafts"; these, in turn, comprised 1.27 percent of all self-employed in this economic sector; 8,278 Jews were active in the clothing trades, amounting to 1.74 percent of all self-employed in this area. In contrast, the Jewish proportion of those in commercial goods trade in 1933 was 4.21 percent and reached a figure of 7.35 percent among the self-employed.[57]

The second reason was economical: business was bad. The Jewish craft firms, mostly one-man shops operated by small tailors, shoemakers, or hatmakers, had in the meantime fallen upon such hard times that there were hardly any "Aryans" interested in a possible takeover. In Berlin in 1935, almost 70 percent of all Jewish craft manufacturing firms were concentrated in the garment industry; the comparable average figure for the Reich as a whole was about 50 percent.[58] Many of the artisans were Jews from Eastern Europe, who were used to hardship and clung tenaciously to these modest sources of income. In the aftermath of the November 1938 pogrom, the process of *Entjudung* was brought to a swift conclusion: by March 1939, almost all of the remaining 5,800 craft manufacturing firms had been liquidated, and only 345 of these were "Aryanized."[59]

In addition to their importance as a source of employment and foreign currency, the large Jewish concerns enjoyed an additional "advantage of scale." As long as some semblance of legality was preserved, the "Aryanization" of these large firms required substantial amounts of capital. Interested "Aryan" parties with the corresponding capital at their disposal chose in many cases to wait until the purchase price of the businesses had plummeted further as a result of increased pressures. Occasionally, as we have seen, they waited too long, but in general their expectations were fulfilled. The Jewish large entrepreneurs also often chose to bide their time in a mistaken trust in their capacity to endure or because the general upswing in the economy had also meant greater sales volume for them, at least temporarily. Some businessmen likewise tried to utilize contacts abroad in order to arrange more favorable deals and were occasionally successful.

By the end of 1937, both sides understood that the time was past for waiting and for engaging in tedious, protracted negotiations. The Jewish proprietors realized too late that not only did they have to sell their businesses at prices far below their real value, but they would also have to absorb substantially larger losses due to capital transfer—providing such a transfer was still feasible.

The "Aryanizations" carried out during this period were given especial emphasis in the Jewish press, since they frequently involved large concerns that were generally well known. The new "Aryan" proprietors of such firms published large ads in the papers after taking over the businesses. This is what may have given Genschel the impression that the period from the end of 1937 to the middle of 1939 had been the "boom period in Aryanization."[60] Genschel relies in this connection principally on data contained in the *Jüdische Rundschau,* which had reported on the "Aryanization" of 769 Jewish firms between January and October 1938; 340 of these concerns were factories, 260 of which were in textiles and garment manufacture, and 30 were involved in leather goods and shoe manufacture. In addition, 370 wholesale firms were "Aryanized," as well as 22 private banks, including respectable old banking houses such as M. M. Warburg, Bleichroder, Gebr. Arnholds, Dreyfus, and Hirschland.[61] These large or fairly large concerns, which attracted the attention of the press, constituted only a portion of the enterprises then caught up in the throes of liquidation. In Berlin alone, the Chamber of Commerce and Industry had received some 1,000 applications for "Aryanization" since April 1938, of which just under 650 were approved. According to figures of the Reichsvertretung,[62] forty-five hundred to five thousand Jewish firms of all sizes and types were "Aryanized" in the period from April 1938 to the November pogrom—that is, not more than 5 percent of the "Jewish firms" that had been listed by the 1933 occupational census. These figures alone provide a clear indication of just how far the liquidation process had progressed by this time.

The year of the "final dash for the finish line" in the race for Jewish firms was 1938. Suitable "objects for Aryanization" not designated for liquidation brought numerous *Volksgenossen* onto the scene; they had gone empty-handed until then and now wished to take advantage of this last final chance to line their pockets. This was the period of the "unbridled enrichment of those who felt they had had a raw deal, and now belonged to the ranks of the parvenus."[63] The methods of extortion became more and more brutal, and municipal authorities competed with party offices in efforts to intimidate Jewish business proprietors even further and render them tractable. By this juncture, however, special efforts were hardly necessary. The DEA for South Westphalia reported with satisfaction to his superiors in the Commission on Economic Policy at the headquarters of the party in Munich that only in rare instances was it necessary to summon Jews to appear at the mayor's office. "The Jews soften up as soon as they learn that the Party is looking into them personally."[64] In order to make the happy new owners even happier, the sellers were prevented—without the authorities going to the trouble of inventing any legal pretexts for the purpose—from selling off their stock inventory separately or holding liquidation sales.[65]

An instructive, though undoubtedly rare testimony to the frenzy of the time to make a quick mark is the letter of a Munich merchant who had been employed as an expert consultant in "Aryanization" cases. The writer, who described himself as a "National Socialist, member of the SA and admirer of Adolf Hitler," stated in this letter that "[I] was so disgusted by the brutal . . . and extortionary methods employed against the Jews that, from now on, I refuse to be involved in any way in connection with Aryanizations, although this means losing a handsome fee . . . As an old, honest and upstanding businessman, I [can] no longer stand by and countenance the way many 'Aryan' businessmen, entrepreneurs and the like . . . are shamelessly attempting to grab up Jewish shops and factories, etc. as cheap as possible and for a ridiculous price. These people are like vultures swarming down, their eyes bleary, their tongues hanging out with greed, to feed upon the Jewish carcass."[66]

The statistical data from Munich also indicate that the "Aryanization race" of the year 1938 involved only the small remaining number of Jewish businesses still in operation. In February 1938, there were still 1,680 "Jewish tradesmen" in Munich. By October, that number had shrunk to 666, of which two-thirds had foreign passports. Hanke is correct in regarding these figures as proof that even before November 9, "the elimination of the Jews had reached its final stage."[67] In a similar vein, a newspaper article at the time observed that in retail trade, "the number of businesses changing hands [was] not as great, because . . . there had already been a step-up in the number of transfers in recent years." Nonetheless, during the course of the year 1938, a number of larger firms, "both in industry and in wholesale and retail trade, had been Aryanized," and there was "a whole mountain of applications for permits on the desk of the DEA."[68]

In contrast with business properties, the "Aryanization" of real estate and land, especially of Jewish houses and apartments and land ownings in urban areas, had proceeded at a substantially slower pace. By the middle of 1938, pressure from interested parties and the local authorities also increased in this area. For example, a district special supervisor in Bochum—who, not accidentally, just happened to be a real estate agent by profession—stated in a letter written to the DEA in August 1938 that he was "apprehensive that current Aryanizations might be hampered due to a lack of suitable apartments, since there has been a noticeable resistance among Jews in recent days to selling their property: they are worried they may end up without a roof over their heads if they sell their place." He noted that housing police authorities also had no solution. These were "elderly Jews who had sold their business or land in Germany and would, in all probability, not be able to emigrate." After the Jewish *Gemeinde* had also gotten involved in the matter, but without any success, the DEA finally turned on September 23, 1938, to the district governor in Arnsberg with a request that he give his opinion on "the way this question of housing can be resolved or—which would be much more preferable to the Party—the way compulsive pressure [*Zwang*] to leave Germany might be implemented by the authorities. In my view, the question could be resolved in the simplest manner by making it obligatory in the near future for Jews to offer their land holdings for sale; this would doubtlessly serve as a method to spur significantly the emigration of Jewish elements." The district governor passed on the communication to the Economy Ministry with a request for a "general regulation for the entire Reich." On October 5, 1938, however, the district governor had to inform the enterprising DEA of the "decision of the Economy Minister that emigration of Jews could not be implemented to the desired degree at the present time due to the fact that most countries refuse to accept destitute Jews . . . quite apart from this, however, there will be a general arrangement regarding Jewish property holdings."[69]

At this point, there were already very clear indications it was no accident that the "Aryanization" of urban real estate had been postponed. A further postponement was also decided upon in a meeting in the Aviation Ministry led by Göring on November 12, 1938, at which, in the wake of the November pogrom, future "measures for *Entjudung*" were discussed.[70] In February 1939, the economy minister issued an order in a secret memorandum "that the compulsory total *Entjudung* of land not used for agricultural or forestry, in accordance with the express order of the Plenipotentiary for the Four-Year Plan, [could] not be initiated at the present moment in time."[71]

There were two reasons for the postponement: first, there was a desire to curb private enrichment, at least in this sphere, so that the spoils of land that had been *entjudet* would pass over to state ownership. Second, consideration was already being given to the possibility of a "ghettoization" of German Jews in so-called *Judenhäuser* belonging to Jews. A secret express letter from Göring, dated December 28, 1938, reported "the decision of the Fuhrer . . . that Jews be concentrated together in one house, circumstances of rent permitting. . . . For this reason, Aryanization of house property should be left as a final step in total Aryanization."[72]

A further bit of proof of this "farsightedness" can be found in a document that is also quite instructive in other respects and deserves to be quoted at length. The document is a typewritten manuscript contained in the Yad Vashem archives in Jerusalem,[73] entitled "Memorandum on Treatment of Jews in the Capital in All Areas of Public Life." The manuscript has neither an address nor a signature and is not dated. Most probably, it was accompanied by a letter that has been lost. From the content, however, it is certain that the memorandum was written sometime between May 1 and June 16, 1938. Second, it is clear that its purpose was to collate existing measures and encourage further measures that could only be realized at the highest government echelons. Third, there can be no doubt that the writer had detailed familiarity with existing legislation and measures being prepared and that he also included foreign-policy considerations in his purview. On the basis of all of this, it is highly probable that this memorandum was written by one of the *Judenreferenten* for Julius Lippert, mayor and municipal president of Berlin at the time.

The memorandum describes with great accuracy the economic situation of Jews shortly before the introduction of the displacement measures in the summer of 1938. It should be borne in mind that the situation in Berlin was more favorable than in other cities and certainly more so than in the rural areas. This helps account for the migration movement into Berlin from the countryside: Jews felt more protected and socially secure within this large community, and they believed they were more protected from antisemitic attacks because of the anonymity of the big city. Moreover, there were better prospects for earning money in Berlin or finding a job with a Jewish employer. The writer of the memorandum also recognized this. He attributes the "recent unusually strong influx to Berlin" to the fact that "Jews in the outlying areas of the province . . . see fewer and fewer possibilities for earning a living there." He recommends that this influx should not be completely prohibited because there were "better opportunities for preparing emigration" in Berlin. However, a permit should be restricted to certain neighborhoods in town, "with the added stipulation that no employment could be pursued in Berlin." "While it appeared impracticable at the moment to concentrate Berlin Jews in a ghetto, one could assure in this way that there would be no new influx of Jews to certain neighborhoods, thus indirectly creating a kind of ghetto over the longer term." In contrast, he is less concerned about the danger that in-migrating Jews might "become a burden on public welfare," in view of the "to date satisfactory regulation instituted by Berlin welfare offices denying in-migrating Jews any public welfare assistance."

In respect to the Jewish school system, the memorandum notes that in 1937 there were still 2,122 Jewish pupils at public schools and that the Education Ministry was looking into the matter at the moment. "In this connection, consideration should be given to the possibility of cancelling compulsory education for Jewish children altogether." This suggestion appears to have found special favor with the official to whom the memorandum was addressed, because he commented in a marginal handwritten remark: "Yes, very good!! They don't have to be able to read, because ignorance is no protection against punishment!"

The memorandum was apparently written before the Fourth and Fifth Ordinances of the Citizenship Law because the writer deals in detail with Jewish doctors and attorneys. He notes that there are still 742 Jewish lawyers and 1,623 Jewish doctors, but a number of these were "no longer practicing, or only had a very limited practice." There were an "especially large number of elderly [doctors], they were banned from treating welfare patients . . . and Jewish hospital doctors were only working in Jewish hospitals." The memorandum goes on to deal with other professions. Its author does not regard "more extensive measures as . . . necessary" because there were only a very small number of Jews still active in these professions. However, he was concerned about "some 500 German Jews involved in license-free urban peddling at the Berlin markets," whereas "there are hardly any applications . . . for municipal permits for peddlers . . . and the municipal administrative court was denying all applications, due to the lack of any need." The author is somewhat relieved by the fact that "a corresponding change in the law was already being considered by the Economy Ministry," although "this would mean that all Aryan itinerant tradesmen, numbering in the tens of thousands, would also be required to have a permit."

The Jewish peddlers and traveling salesmen also gave the Berlin author of the memorandum cause for thought, since "the number of applications from Jews for license and peddling permits was unusually high." Attempts by police authorities "to deny Jewish applications, in cooperation with the Gestapo, based on the grounds that one is justified in assuming that Jews will use the exercise of their trade for subversive purposes," had not been upheld by the courts. Consequently, the author concludes that "a change in the Reich business code should be recommended in this quite important area. . . . In this connection, one should also consider a general restriction on freedom to trade for Jews by means of a change in the code." As we have seen, the well-informed anonymous Berlin expert on Jewish affairs did not need to wait all too long for this to come about.

We have no reliable statistics on the exact number of Jewish tradesmen still active on the eve of the November pogrom. The 1938 annual report of the Reichsvertretung lists 5,822 Jewish craft firms registered as of December, and 3,750 Jewish retail firms still operating as of November 1.[74] According to other sources, this estimated figure for retail shops is perhaps a bit too low. But even if there were a few hundred more Jewish firms at this point, the process of exclusion of Jewish tradesmen had been largely completed by the time shop windows shattered and the synagogues went up in flames the night of November 9–10, 1938. The November pogrom would not have been necessary for accelerating the "process of

Aryanization." The economic goals pursued by the riots, in addition to their political impact, were of a quite different nature.

The Pogrom: Prelude to Expropriation and Expulsion

On October 28–29, 1938, some eighteen thousand Jews holding Polish citizenship were deported across the Polish border. This first mass deportation to the East was an anticipation of later "deportations" (*Aussiedlungen*) during the war, in its manner of implementation and in the indifferent reaction among the populace and by foreign governments. Jews were arrested at night in their homes, herded together for a short time in jails and at other collection points, loaded onto railway cars, and taken to the border. Because the Polish government, after a brief hesitation, had closed the crossing point into Poland, more than eight thousand Jews were forced back over the German border. They had to stay out under the open sky in a no-man's land between Neu-Bentschen and Zabaszyn in Posen, exposed to the rain and cold, until Jewish relief organizations managed to arrange emergency housing and food for them.[75]

Among the Jews expelled to Zabaszyn was the family of Sendel Grynszpan (Grünspan) from Hannover. Their son Herschel, who had already emigrated from Germany, fired the shots on November 7 that killed the German legation secretary, vom Rath, in Paris. According to Herschel's own testimony, this was to avenge the injustice suffered by his parents. That assassination served as the direct pretext for the pogrom of November 9–10, 1938, euphemistically and bizarrely termed *Reichskristallnacht.*

The night of November 9–10, most of the still existing synagogues in Germany and Austria went up in flames. The police and fire department had received instructions only to protect adjacent buildings from a possible spreading of the fire; otherwise, they were advised to let "popular anger" take its course. According to Heydrich's instructions, "Jewish stores and homes [should] only be destroyed, not plundered." "Special care should be taken in business streets to make sure that non-Jewish shops were definitely protected from possible damage." In addition, the Gestapo ordered "the arrest in all districts of as many Jews—especially prosperous ones—as could be accommodated in the jails" and to "establish immediate contact with the relevant concentration camps regarding the quickest possible internment of Jews in these camps."[76]

These instructions, except for that pertaining to plundering, were adhered to in exemplary fashion. Almost one hundred Jews were murdered that night, and thirty thousand largely affluent Jews were placed in concentration camps. It is not known how many of them perished there. Seventy-five hundred Jewish businesses were demolished during the pogrom, and there cannot have been many more than this figure still in existence at the time.

There are various, in part contradictory descriptions of the details of the pogrom, its underlying causes, the question of who gave the direct order, and the reactions of the population. It is certain that Goebbels played a central role in organizing the "spontaneous" excesses after having obtained Hitler's consent at the annual meeting of the party Old Guard in Munich. There is clear evidence for both the participation of the SA and SS and the passive complicity of the police. In contrast, Göring claimed that the reports had taken him totally by surprise. Yet what angered him was only the destruction of property and the expected financial burden for the insurance companies as a result. In his own words, he would have much preferred that, instead of this destruction, two hundred Jews had been murdered instead.[77]

There are quite differing reports as to the behavior of the population. For example, the writer Jochen Klepper entered in his diary on November 10: "All the store windows of Jewish businesses were smashed today, and fires set in synagogues, though without any danger [to life]. A short walk through Jewish neighborhoods is enough to show one that once again, the population does not condone what has happened. I was able to see that with my own eyes." One day later, he noted that "what Hanni [his Jewish wife] has to report today about the reactions she heard from . . . the wife of the naval officer, women at the bakery, men down at the newspaper stand, and even the next-door neighbor of the demolished Jewish shop (probably the last) is sufficient proof: now as before, there is no need to despair when it comes to the true intentions of the German people."[78] The British consul general in Cologne reported on November 14, 1938, that "there is nervousness amongst middle-class Germans, who in general disapprove. They dare not, however, voice their disapproval. . . . The industrialists say that they have no influence with the party, who have made such a point of racial purity that the Fuhrer must carry his theories to their logical conclusion. . . . Yet I am inclined to think that the Fuhrer knows his Germans. Amongst the masses of Germans who have nothing at stake, there is observable a certain amount of 'Schadenfreude' ('joy in mischief')."[79]

Undoubtedly, these and all other conflicting reports, based on the personal experiences of their authors, possess a certain kernel of truth. However, the timing of the pogrom was by no means accidental, and the shots fired in Paris served only as a convenient pretext. Beginning in the autumn of 1937, the radicalization of public antisemitism functioned to promote the propagandistic preparations for a series of measures and laws directed against Jews. The effect on various groups in the population may well have differed. The declared goal of Jewish policy was the final prohibition of any kind of economic activity by Jews—in order to pressure them into emigrating more quickly. However, there was a desire to retain Jewish assets and "utilize" them for war preparations. The temporary conclusion of this process was the prospective immediate expropriation of a portion of Jewish assets and the freezing of the remainder. Detailed plans had been drawn up for this. The following quotation from a newspaper proves that these plans were being prepared with public knowledge, and that their implications were also correctly understood by contemporaries:

> For a long time now, National Socialism has been making preparations to take decisive economic measures in the wake of the political conclusion it has arrived at in dealing with Jews. . . . The regulation on inventory-taking introduced this year by the government [indicates] the coming efforts to enhance economic performance and the necessary exclusion of Jewish influence in the economy. In one or another form, therefore, the special utilization of Jewish capital would have come about anyhow, sooner or later. The shots fired in Paris . . . however, have triggered an early start.[80]

The author of this article was mistaken only in the last sentence. The Nazis had not been able to foresee the shots in Paris, but those shots did not come too early. Rather, all indications are that not only did the assassination provide the pretext for the pogrom, but that it occurred at a quite suitable time. Three weeks prior to the pogrom, and fourteen days after conclusion of the Munich Agreement, Göring had declared in a closed meeting that "Jews now must be driven from the economy." Their assets would have to be transferred in orderly manner to the Reich and not be squandered as a "welfare system for incompetent party members."[81] The German Federation of Banks and Savings Associations had informed its members on October 28 that the Foreign Currency Control Office, headed by Heydrich since July 1938, was preparing "security orders" for Jewish assets, "by which the control of the owners over their various assets is to be restricted."[82] On August 19, the Economy Ministry had ordered those offices dealing with registration of Jewish assets to finish the work by September 30, if necessary by engaging additional personnel, "in order to make preparations for a possible seizure of part of Jewish assets for the purposes of the German economy."[83] In the tax offices and at the Gestapo and police offices, bolstered by assistance from the respective chambers of commerce and DEAs, lists of affluent Jews were drawn up. Fifteen hundred Jews arrested in July and already in concentration camps were required to build additional barracks.[84] In view of all of these preparations, the shots in Paris would appear to have been a bit too delayed in coming.

Immediately after the pogrom, the measures that had been prepared

After the pogrom: a Jewish shop in Berlin, November 10, 1938. (Photo: Abraham Pisarek)

were set in motion. Hitler's notion of a "Guaranty Association for Jews" (*Judengarantieverband*) could finally now be made a reality: the "special taxation" approved by him two years earlier was now levied as a "Sühneleistung," in the form of the one-time penalty of RM 1 billion. In addition, Jews were required to "restore the appearance of the streets" without being paid the insurance claims they were entitled to; those insurance monies had been pocketed by the state on the basis of a special decree. This sum is estimated at RM 225 million; it was, in effect, an additional penalty exacted of the Jews. In the meeting held on November 12, 1938, in the Aviation Ministry, there was an exchange with the representative of the insurance firms; they were then allowed to retain a portion of this money, thus also profiting from the transaction.[85]

That same day saw the issuance of the First Ordinance on the Exclusion of Jews from German Economic Life.[86] This ordinance prohibited almost all still extant options for gainful employment and ordered the dismissal of employees without any right on their part to claim pensions or compensation. On November 21, an implementation order by the economy minister[87] stipulated that the Sühneleistung penalty was to be in the form of a tax amounting to 20 percent of the assets reported in April, quite

Jewish men and women scrubbing a street in Vienna, guarded by Hitler Youth, March 1938.

independent of whether the respective Jew was still actually in possession of such declared assets. Any changes that had occurred since were subject to affirmation only by the higher administrative office. In October 1939, the tax was hiked to 25 percent of reported assets, since the total of RM 1 billion had supposedly not been reached.[88]

In actual fact, however, RM 1.127 billion was collected, leaving aside the sum of RM 225 million in confiscated insurance. If one adds to this the Flight Tax payments levied on emigrants from November 1938 until the outbreak of the war, the resultant total is a figure of an estimated RM 2 billion in Jewish assets that flowed "legally" and directly into the coffers of the Reich in this brief period. If this amount is compared with the figures based on the registration of declared assets in April 1938, and allowing for accelerated plundering in the meantime, this RM 2 billion probably constituted half or more of the total assets still in Jewish hands. This does not include "profit from Aryanizations" pocketed by individuals or Jewish "contributions" to party organizations.[89] How these "contributions" were "encouraged" is reported by the Reich treasurer of the NSDAP to Reichsleiter Bormann in a letter of December 2, 1938:[90]

> A few members of the Party from the district headquarters appeared at the homes of the Jews in question. First of all, they proceeded to cut the telephone wires. Then they presented the Jew with "contribution certif-

> icates" which had been prepared by a notary. The Jew was told that he had an opportunity to make a contribution. If he dared to resist, they responded by threatening to shoot. Later . . . the assets taken from the Jews were returned by the state police in Stettin. These included houses, automobiles and radios.

It is not clear from the letter whether or to what extent Jewish assets were retained, but the Reich treasurer must have had a similar suspicion:

> In some districts, there are organizations implementing the liquidation of Jewish assets; in other districts, this is basically dependent on the DEA. . . . The great danger exists that the Gauleiter may in some cases take advantage of the situation to set up "black" slush funds which they control independently, without my approval.

The Ordinance on Utilization of Jewish Assets of December 3, 1938, marked the temporary conclusion of this phase.[91] It stipulated the "forced Aryanization" of all Jewish firms that were still in existence but had been prohibited from operating since the pogrom. At the same time, an order was issued requiring the deposit of cash, securities, jewelry, and other valuables in blocked accounts, and control over these assets was made subject to a formal permit. Trustees appointed by the authorities directed the "Aryanization" of Jewish businesses that were still deemed useful. "Unjustified profits due to *Entjudung*" were not seized by the Reich until February 1939.[92] Since the ordinance was not retroactive, it was tantamount to locking the stable door after most of the horses had already escaped—or in this instance, had been stolen.

The tactics of the German rulers aimed at driving Jews out of the country by means of increased economic and physical pressure had the desired effect. In the years 1938–1939, approximately 120,000 Jews left Germany, almost as many as in the entire preceding five years.[93] Most of them had been a short while before still relatively affluent individuals who had hesitated to part from their possessions; now they fled the country penniless. They had been literally fleeced, stripped of their possessions by "legal" means. What remained to them after the "treatment" they were accorded by the tax offices had to be left in blocked accounts, which were almost completely inaccessible. Such accounts were then confiscated by the Reich at a later date by means of new "legislation." The henchmen of the SA and SS also got their spoils: Despite the fact that they had valid emigration papers, many thousands in KZ-camps were able to get out only after they had left sizable sums of money, cars, and other property to local party groups or even individual Nazis as "voluntary contributions."[94]

Emigration and Jewish Self-Help in a Race against Time

TO JEWS IN GERMANY[95]

The Central Committee for Relief and Rehabilitation of the Reichsvertretung of Jews in Germany can look back, in the calendar year of 1938 now beginning, on a period of activity spanning five years. During this period, it has developed in the five main fields of its activity—migration, occupational training and retraining, schooling, economic relief and welfare—into a central organization which is now indispensable as a source for economic and social relief work for Jews in Germany.

The process of dissolution of Jewry in Germany continues unabated. Approximately a third of the former Jewish population has already left Germany, many are just about to emigrate, and many more will be obliged to follow them. There is a continuing need to guide this process purposefully and in a orderly manner by suitable occupational training and appropriate planning for migration, and to pave the way into the future by planned rehabilitational work.

In like measure, there remains the obligation to meet the exigencies of the hour and to care for those who will remain behind. It is therefore necessary for Jews in Germany to maintain and strengthen their great enterprise of rehabilitation. The finding of solutions to problems that remain must be approached with that same degree of resolute determination and self-confidence with which all those forces have labored which have assisted and worked constructively in recent years in creating and maintaining our activities. Our work is to be carried forward in 1938 in the spirit of the slogan "Five Years of Relief and Rehabilitation." The purpose of this slogan is to remind us of our obligation to keep our energies alert, not to fall prey to any unwarranted mood of despair—and not, due to the weight of personal worries and concerns, to grow forgetful of the need to care for the fate of the community.

Once again, we appeal to Jews in all Gemeinden and groups to remain aware of what this community can demand of them. And what it must continue to demand of them. Our experience with "relief and rehabilitation" over these past five years must preserve and help to expand a sense of Jewish responsibility and sacrifice.

5 YEARS OF RELIEF AND REHABILITATION!
CONTINUE TO HELP!

Berlin, the end of December 1937
Reichsvertretung of Jews in Germany

The events of the year 1938 already confirmed the insight formulated in this appeal: it was impossible to halt the process of dissolution of German Jewry. During the course of the year, the hope to "guide this process purposefully and in a orderly manner by suitable occupational training and appropriate planning for migration" finally proved to be illusory. By the end of 1938, no responsible Jewish organization would have issued any warnings about an "unwarranted mood of despair."

In January 1938, in a unique gesture, the Reichsvertretung Council appealed publicly to the German government:

> Even a continuation of orderly emigration—and only such an emigration will assure that the gates of immigration remain open for any length of time—is solely possible if the basis for economic existence for Jews in Germany is not further restricted.
>
> Now that Jews have been excluded from political, cultural and social life and from all leading positions in the economy, we therefore request the Reich government that measures be taken to stem further reductions in possibilities for gainful employment for Jews in Germany. It is, moreover, our hope that options for contact between those who have emigrated and their relatives who have been obliged to remain in Germany are not prohibited.[96]

By this time, the reference to the promotion of emigration accompanied all efforts undertaken to convince the authorities to tolerate still existing Jewish organizations. It is unlikely, however, that the actual addressee of this appeal was in fact the Nazi government. At this point, even optimistic representatives of German Jewry no longer expected anything positive from that quarter. The appeal was not given much emphasis by the Jewish press in Germany; abroad, however, it was accorded top billing by both Jewish and non-Jewish papers. Thus, a Jewish paper in Vienna saw in this "a sign of the unendurable distress being suffered by Jews in Germany . . . [namely, the fact that] the highest representative body for Jews in Germany [had directed] an appeal, officially and publicly, for the first time in its existence, to the government of the Third Reich to prevent the situation from deteriorating to a final crisis; and, at the very least, to allow the older generation an opportunity to live out its last days in peace in Germany." There were similar commentaries on the appeal in other foreign papers.[97] Presumably, this was precisely its principal purpose: to call foreign attention to the dramatically worsening situation of German Jews.

In Germany itself, interventions by Jewish organizations and individuals with government offices and courts had become more and more infrequent over the course of the years; though attempts were occasionally made here and there and sometimes even resulted in success. Increasingly, the main effort was devoted to preparations for emigration. The immigration regulations, applied by many countries in ever more restrictive fashion, also led to the appearance of fraudulent emigration agents; the Jewish papers carried repeated warnings about swindlers.[98] By the end of 1937, there was no longer any argument within Jewish leadership circles: Jews in Germany had no prospects for any sort of future. In earlier years, this point had been much discussed; and even after emigration had been recognized as inevitable by most Jewish spokesmen, both Zionist and assimilationist, there had been warnings, out of a sense of "responsibility," against hasty and inadequately prepared emigration. Some historians have maintained that emigration counseling was more often an attempt to persuade people not to emigrate.[99] Survivors of this period, who are unable to view events with the "objective distance" of the historian, often voice considerable criticism of themselves and others in this regard. One of these contemporaries wrote in 1969:

> Nothing was done, at least in the province, by those Jews who had recognized the Nazis' true intentions, to make clear to their uneducated coreligionists . . . that there was no future in Hitler's Germany for Jews and "non-Aryans." . . . Instead of trying to make life for Jews under Nazi tyranny as pleasant as possible, everything, and every possible pfennig, should have been invested in attempting to get Jews out of the country. . . . People were far too concerned with trying to give life under Nazi rule some content and meaning and to make it as pleasant as possible. The efforts undertaken by Jewish organizations were also in this direction—instead of forcing people, possibly with Nazi assistance, to emigrate.[100]

The author of these lines, Hans Winterfeldt, initially survived the war inside Germany, as a forced laborer and in hiding; later on, he was in the camps at Auschwitz and Mauthausen, and he emigrated to the United States in 1948. The small number of survivors from Jewish leadership circles have been tormented by similar pangs of conscience and self-reproach down to the present. The following remarks by Friedrich Brodnitz, made at a conference organized by the Leo Baeck Institute in Berlin in 1985, are representative of this attitude. Brodnitz was the head of the press office of the Reichsvertretung after 1933.

> In the years after the war, the small number of us who survived the camps or death elsewhere, often sat down together and asked each other the question: were we right in trying for all those years to defend and maintain our position? Many of you will recall the famous article by my friend Robert Weltsch entitled "Wear it with Pride, the Yellow Star!" I don't know how many of you spoke with him about this in his later years. He

> was always embarrassed when people would ask him about this article, because he said—and this is the question which all of us who worked in the Reichsvertretung and survived have asked ourselves—Did we do the right thing? Shouldn't we have said immediately at the start of it all: "Everything is lost. Each person has got to try to save his or her own skin! Get out now!"? We didn't do that, because we were unable to foresee future developments. . . . I often have labored under this feeling of guilt, a feeling of guilt where I ask myself: Didn't we lose people by trying too hard, trying too long to maintain our position and stem the tide?[101]

By the end of 1937, even the most optimistic representatives of German Jewry were convinced that there were no longer any "positions that could be maintained." If many nonetheless did not succeed in emigrating, this was due principally to the tightening of immigration regulations abroad. From January 6 to 15, 1938, a conference called at President Roosevelt's initiative met in Evian on Lake Geneva to deliberate on a "solution to the refugee problem." The Reichsvertretung also sent a delegation to the conference and distributed a lengthy memorandum. The only result to come out of the deliberations in Evian was the establishment of an Intergovernmental Committee on Refugees. The committee met on August 3, 1938, in London and elected George Rublee the director of its London office. After all efforts to ease immigration restrictions had failed, Rublee resigned on February 9, 1939. Leopold Schwarzschild commented on the Evian conference in the *Neues Tage-Buch,* published in Paris:

> [The civilized world] suffers embarrassingly from its bad conscience. It knows . . . that the acceptance of several hundred thousand emigrants . . . is actually *not* a genuine "problem," but rather a minor matter. . . . But despite all this bad conscience, no one has the will to act differently, even from now on. . . . 31 governments, deeply moved, sent delegations—each of them is convinced the situation is truly a disgrace—and each is animated by the hope that the thirty others are the ones who will eliminate the situation and the disgrace.[102]

The German Jews by this time were no longer in the least bit choosy about their destination for emigration. Just under 130,000 Jews had emigrated in the five-year period from 1933 to 1937. Another 118,000 emigrated in 1938–1939, and an additional 30,000 to 31,000 succeeded in getting out of Germany after the beginning of the war. Even before the November pogrom, emigration had taken on the character of an attempt to flee, to escape; now, occupational or language preparation hardly played any role. Even the transfer of assets, which had become almost an impossibility in 1938, was a factor of diminishing importance. "The destination for emigration depends more or less on personal accidents," Werner Rosenstock wrote in March 1938.

> The constant changes in the individual lands of immigration bring about a situation where many are forced at the last moment to alter their route and to suddenly go to another country, instead of the one prepared for over a long period of time—or even another continent. The crucial importance of such a shift in destinations is something we are often not fully aware of, and we exchange boat tickets in many ways not much different than we used to on a brief excursion out of town, after we had missed our original train and opted for another destination instead.[103]

Until 1936, Palestine had been number one on the list of countries for emigration promoted by the Jewish organizations. The quota for "certificates" set by the Mandatory government was filled completely, but by the introduction of categories such as "capitalist" and "youth *aliyah,*" it was possible to create additional opportunities for emigration to Palestine. In this way, a total of 38,400 German Jews had found a new home in Palestine by the end of 1937.[104] In contrast, until 1938, German Jews did not even manage to exhaust the full quota set by the American authorities for immigration from Germany. Until the end of 1937, only some twenty-nine thousand Jews from Germany and Austria had emigrated to the United States. There had been no lack of applicants, but the numerous difficulties and delaying tactics of the American consular and immigration authorities required great tenacity on the part of applicants and the endurance of a protracted waiting period. Only after the *Anschluss* of Austria and the November pogrom did Roosevelt introduce an easing of regulations; this made possible the immigration of nearly one hundred thousand additional Jews from Germany between 1938 and 1944. Great Britain also absorbed some forty thousand Jewish refugees from Germany in 1938 to 1939.[105]

It was clear to all Jews in Germany in 1938 that their days there were numbered. More and more Jews now went wherever they could: to Shanghai and Trinidad, to Kenya and Rhodesia, and, above all, to South America, where one might be able to rely on support from experienced Jewish relief and resettlement organizations.[106] After 1937, the chance to transfer assets hardly played any role in the decision to emigrate. Naturally, every person who had received an immigration visa to some country tried to salvage a portion, no matter how negligible, of his or her possessions. People wandered through the advice bureaus of the Hilfsverein or the Palestine Office, tramped for days or weeks on end through the tax and foreign currency offices, only to discover in despair that most of the few assets they had managed to preserve had been taken away from them.

Until the November pogrom, it had still been possible to take along movable goods and merchandise up to a value of RM 1,000 and also to pay for the tickets in German currency. After that, this loophole was also closed. The office of Paltreu in Berlin was literally swamped with applicants for Haavara transfer. At the end of August 1938, there was a total sum of some RM 83 million deposited in Paltreu accounts, whereas for that entire year only RM 19 million had been approved for transfer.[107]

Like the Haavara, for emigration to Palestine, the Altreu had been created to deal with emigrants to other countries. The Nazis could now rest assured that the Jews were so amply "motivated" to emigrate that they would also abandon their assets in order to save their skins. Thus, there was no longer any reason to promote Jewish emigration—to Palestine or elsewhere—by schemes to ease and facilitate the transfer of assets. The responsible sections in the government and party were troubled only by the presence of indigent Jews who were unable to pay either the costs of travel or present the necessary "minimum funds" required for being given a visa and who, should they remain in Germany, would become a burden for the welfare services. Consequently, the Altreu was utilized by the German authorities "to obtain profit for the Reich using the subterfuge of assistance for indigent Jewish emigrants."[108] Emigrants had to pay in a certain sum (up to RM 50,000 for a family of three, up to RM 30,000 for individuals). Upon emigration, they received a cash sum that averaged RM 1,800 per person in foreign exchange. The largest proportion was retained by the Gold Discount Bank, that is, the German Reichsbank. A small portion of the money went to the Reichsvertretung to establish a special Altreu Fund, which provided loans of up to RM 900 in foreign exchange to destitute emigrants. By February 1939, 1,657 such Altreu loans were distributed; these made possible the emigration of nearly three thousand destitute Jews, mainly bound for South America. It is not clear from the sources how much the emigrated Jewish "capitalist" had had to pay for all this.[109]

The negotiations that Hjalmar Schacht conducted at the end of 1938 with George Rublee, director of the Intergovernmental Committee that had been set up in Evian, should also be viewed in this context. The topic for discussion, in which representatives of Jewish relief organizations from England and the United States also participated, was a plan of Schacht's to make possible the emigration of some four hundred thousand Jews in the course of three to five years by means of an agreement with the government on transfer of assets.[110] Schacht himself made the following remarks on his plan in a letter written in April 1959:

> After the desecration of synagogues on November 9, 1938, I developed a plan for facilitating Jewish emigration, and received permission from

> Hitler for its implementation. According to the plan, I wanted to place all Jewish assets in Germany, estimated at the time to be RM 6 billion, under the administration of a trustee committee . . . [which was supposed to] be responsible for its proper handling. In addition, the assets were to serve as security for a loan . . . of approximately RM 1.5 billion. . . . Every Jew who wished to emigrate was to be given an amount of financial assistance to be determined by the committee and paid out in foreign exchange from this loan fund—in order to be enabled to build a new life abroad. . . . I discussed . . . this plan in December 1938 and January 1939 in London with the representative of the American Jewish aid committee, Mr. Rublee. I obtained their agreement, although the Zionist Jewish group had come out against the plan.

Schacht's description contains several inaccuracies. Rublee was the director of an international institution that had been set up by the conference in Evian to find ways for German Jews to emigrate and be accepted as immigrants. Moreover, Schacht remains silent about the less attractive facets of his plan, which emerge clearly from his detailed explanation submitted on January 16, 1939 to the Foreign Office:

> Jewish assets in Germany are to be gathered together. Approximately 25 percent of this wealth is to be placed in a trust. The assets of this trust are to be converted gradually into cash and transferred only if the foreign exchange situation in Germany permits, or even before this in the event of a possibility for additional exports. The remaining 75 percent of Jewish assets are to remain at the disposal of Germany, insofar as they are not required for support for Jews until their emigration, or for assistance to the aged and to Jews not suited for emigration until they expire.

The description by Schacht, along with Hitler's endorsement, is in any event documented by other sources—as are the reservations voiced by Jewish organizations abroad, which were by no means limited solely to the "Zionist group." Thus, for example, the plan was sharply criticized in a memorandum of the Jewish Central Information Office in Amsterdam, an organization of German-Jewish emigrants that had close ties with the Centralverein:

> German governmental offices are sparing no effort to utilize the monies pilfered from the Jews to . . . expand German export trade and reduce German foreign debts. . . . The plans which Herr Schacht has recently been circulating in London suggest that the method of exporting German Jews in exchange for foreign currency is to be further developed. . . . It is of the greatest importance that other countries, in full knowledge of

the German policy of plunder, voice their resolute opposition to such policies.

Schacht's initiative may have been motivated at the least by a certain modicum of "good will." Such "good will" is a virtue one is prepared to attribute to Schacht, especially in contrast with the attitudes prevalent in the Nazi top echelons. Apparently, the Jewish representatives negotiating with him saw this in a similar light, despite all of the reservations they may have had. Although an agreement in the sense of Schacht's proposals would have been tantamount to an official Jewish renunciation of any claim to 75 percent of the assets of Jews still living in Germany, those suggestions met with the basic acceptance of the Jewish relief organizations in America and Great Britain. The negotiations were continued, with Hitler's permission, even after the dismissal of Schacht from his post on January 20, 1939. However, they ultimately ended in failure, probably for two reasons: first, the Foreign Office refused to initial the agreement with Rublee; second, it turned out that "international Jewish high finance" had been unable to raise the required amount of $600 million. The entire budgetary income of the "Joint" for 1938 amounted only to some $8 million.

It is no longer possible to determine exactly how much money German Jews succeeded in transferring abroad illegally. Surprisingly, the otherwise copious files of the Gestapo, insofar as they have been preserved, note only a small number of isolated cases. It is likely that the German Jews, educated in strict respect for the law, were unwilling even at this juncture to act in violation of the Nazi laws. Or perhaps they were simply afraid. Maybe most of those who did nonetheless dare to violate those laws were not found out—at least one would like to hope so.

In any event, there was no lack of efforts by the authorities to close even the smallest loophole and to pursue every possible statement by informers for this purpose. In February 1938, the border authorities were advised that, among Jews, there were signs of a greater inclination to sell their businesses, and payment in cash was often demanded. In addition, attention was called to the various methods to smuggle assets abroad that had been uncovered by the authorities. For example, the NSDAP district office in Recklinghausen learned from an informer in June 1938 that "since the proclamation of Göring's law regarding declaration of Jewish assets, large amounts of platinum, gold and silver in the form of painted auto license plates had been smuggled over the border into Holland." This was followed by an instruction sent by the tax office director in Düsseldorf to pay special attention to all license plates.[111]

The constantly rising level of Jewish unemployment as a product of "Aryanizations" was certainly one of the reasons for the enormous increase in the number of participants in courses on *hachshara* teaching farms and in other occupational retraining programs. By 1937, there was already too little funding available for the expansion of such institutions. Yet the level of interest in participating in such courses was low in 1937, especially as regards retraining courses for older workers. The budget controller of the Reichsvertretung had thus suggested, with a certain justification, that two *hachshara* farms be closed and their trainees be divided up among other farms.[112] But the pressure of events was inexorable: By the end of 1938, there were a record number of 5,520 trainees in occupational retraining courses in the various centers, including many new trainees who had taken the places of those deported from the *hachshara* farms to Poland. The Reichsvertretung had a budget in 1938 of RM 1.3 million for maintaining the system of *hachshara* farms and retraining centers; this was more than a quarter of its entire annual budget. As in 1933, the number of adult retrainees rose again significantly.[113] Many hoped to be able to improve their emigration chances with a partial, or even pretended, agricultural training course: Numerous countries gave preference to immigrants who had agricultural or artisan craft occupations. The Gestapo, in fact, requested the corresponding offices to register the preferred occupations in passports and other identification papers of Jewish emigrants even after a short period of training.[114]

Despite this, it was not possible at this point for more than 10 to 15 percent of those in the fifteen to twenty-five age bracket, still living in Germany, to be trained in organized *hachshara* and artisan crafts courses. It was likewise very difficult to assist the approximately thirty thousand nonclassifiable older unemployed persons. The officials active in vocational training and occupational retraining were left with no other alternative than to repeatedly bemoan the constant lack of funds.[115]

Jewish unemployment also began to be a "source of concern" to the German authorities toward the end of 1938 because in accordance with laws still valid, the Jewish indigent had to be supported by public welfare, at least in part. Thus, on December 20, 1938, the head of the Reich Employment Office and Bureau for Unemployment Insurance, Dr. Syrup, stated: "The state has no interest in allowing the labor power of able-bodied Jews to go unutilized and to support such individuals if necessary from public funds, without any contribution in return. Accelerated attempts must be made to employ all unemployed, able-bodied Jews. . . . They will be assigned to factories, plant sections, on construction sites, renovation and improvement, etc., segregated from the rest of the work crew."[116] This then was the beginning of the practice of *Arbeitseinsatz* (conscripted labor) for indigent Jews. During the war, it was expanded to include all ablebodied Jews—and those less able to work—for obligatory forced labor.

By 1937–1938, it was possible to employ only an extremely small proportion of unemployed Jews within the Jewish economic sector. Even before the forced "Aryanization" of 1938, only a negligible number of Jewish firms remained in existence, and these too were forced to lay off more and more Jewish workers under pressure from the party and the DAF.[117] The constantly swelling administrative bureaucracy of the Jewish *Gemeinden* and organizations was able to provide only minor relief. Thus, the Jewish *Gemeinde* in Berlin had a staff the end of 1937 numbering some thirteen hundred, including teachers and religious officials.[118] We have no reliable figures on the total number of those employed with Jewish organizations. Based on estimates, it must have been a maximum of five thousand—a minute figure in comparison with the ranks of the unemployed.

The contraction of the Jewish economic sector also restricted the field of activity of the credit associations. By October 1938, the number of loans awarded had declined by 30 percent, the total amount of credit by 24 percent. This too is testimony to the advanced state of the liquidation process. By this point there was no longer any hope whatsoever of providing constructive financial assistance by means of the loans. They were given without any security or collateral as "liquidation or emergency loans." The 1938 annual report of the Reichsvertretung wistfully summed up the activity of this institution, which at the beginning of 1938 had still encompassed a total of forty-five loan bureaus in the *Altreich*: "The basis for productive economic assistance no longer existed . . . in the wake of the total exclusion of Jews from economic life. Although up until then . . . it had been possible, to a quite appreciable extent, to contribute to helping people survive and make a new start in Germany by means of social loan assistance, now all possibility for making use of such loans evaporated. An important branch of Jewish social relief aid in Germany had to close its doors." On January 1, 1939, the credit associations officially ceased all activity on the order of the Reich Commissioner for Loans and Credit. Of their total capital assets, some RM 420,000, which had been provided by the "Joint," were transferred to the Reichsvertretung "to promote emigration."[119]

The other Jewish credit institutions, such as cooperative commercial or private banks, substantially reduced their volume in the course of 1938; this resulted in mounting financial difficulties for Jewish firms still in business. Even a respected textile concern like F. V. Grünfeld found it impossible to get credit. After the management had applied for a loan to one of the still existing Jewish private banks, the bank president expressed his regrets:

> . . . I do hope that you can appreciate why we are today unable to decide favorably on your request for a new loan. Even if there is no risk associated

The face of despair: a crowd at the welfare office of the Jewish community in Vienna after the occupation, March 18, 1938.

> with such a loan, it could possibly entail an investment of bank capital which might become problematical for us in our own situation. You will probably ask, and with good right: so what then are bankers for? To which I can only reply: I no longer know the answer to that question either.[120]

By the middle of 1938, most German Jews had been reduced to paupers, but there were still several hundred who were quite wealthy. Although Jewish economic activity had largely come to a halt, they still had sizable reserves, savings that had been accumulated over generations. The figures published in the German press about the numerous "Jewish millionaires"[121] were doubtless much exaggerated and designed principally to dampen any feelings of sympathy that may have arisen in the population in the wake of the November pogrom. Nonetheless, the mere fact that the Jewish community in Germany—even in 1938—was still capable of bearing almost completely by itself the heavy burden of the drastically increased expenses for the welfare support of its needy members is ample proof that there were still substantial amounts of money in Jewish hands.

A government decree of November 19, 1938, stipulated that Jews in need of assistance "should be referred" to the Jewish welfare system.

However, the possibility was still open, "to the extent that [system] was unable to provide assistance," to turn to public welfare.[122] As a result of this decree, an endless process of applications and denials developed at the local level, involving haggling over every mark of assistance and which welfare office was responsible for what. Even before the decree, there had been no uniformity of approach among the local authorities. Each welfare office had had the prerogative, largely on its own, of determining the criteria for indigency and the amount of payment. After the decree of November 19, the situation had become totally confusing:

> The various public welfare offices handle this question, of decisive import for the financial burden born by the Jewish free welfare system and its supporters, in quite different ways. . . . While public welfare frequently refuses to be involved in any way, thus placing the entire burden on the Jewish welfare offices, there are various diverse arrangements and practices at local level in different Gemeinden, with every conceivable division of costs, according to a numerical key or depending on the type of aid. . . . Assuming that total welfare expenditures for the Jewish indigent in the Altreich amount to an annual figure of approximately RM 36 million, there can be no doubt whatsoever that a sum of this magnitude cannot be mobilized by the Jewish welfare system—even by total and ruthless exploitation of all possible sources for funding.[123]

By 1938, the expenditures for welfare were already consuming almost half of the total annual budget of the Reichsvertretung. The Jewish *Gemeinden* generally needed to expend an even higher percentage of their resources. Some relief was provided by gifts from emigrants, who donated the funds they still had in Germany sitting in blocked accounts. This proved to be an important source of income as long as the German authorities "upon application, generally released the full value of the marks in blocked accounts for promoting the emigration of needy Jews from Germany. In this way, . . . funds at 100 percent value were transferred to the Reichsvertretung. For the now emigrated previous owner, these would have only been convertible at a rate between 6 and 10 percent of their value."[124]

In addition to this, there were substantial proceeds from the liquidation of Jewish communal property and assets: the sale of real estate, synagogues, schools, and even cemeteries, which now were no longer needed. Even prior to the November pogrom, the view had gained gradual acceptance that

> [one] had a right to proceed with the material liquidation of Jewish life in Germany. This means that all Jewish institutions, associations, soci-

eties, foundations, etc. should utilize their assets systematically in order to provide at least partial relief for the financial distress of the Jewish Gemeinden by means of the funds available. However, its realization must keep pace with the reduction in the numbers of Jewish residents and not fall behind, because what is involved here is Jewish survival and material aid for Jewish individuals.[125]

4

1939–1943
The Last Chapter

In the aftermath of the pogrom, the leadership and officials of the Reichsvertretung, slowly recovering from the shock, found themselves confronting an altered situation. They soon realized that their organization was now increasingly responsible for the task not only of offering advice and various services to the remaining Jews in Germany but also particularly of assisting them with sheer physical survival.[1] Most Jewish *Gemeinden* were no longer in existence or were in an advanced stage of dissolution. Their duties had been transferred to the central office in Berlin or to the various regional offices. The latitude for Jewish self-help became ever more circumscribed as a result of a tightening of control by the Gestapo. In early 1939, the Gestapo established the Central Authority for Jewish Emigration on the top floor of the Jewish *Gemeinde* center in Berlin located on Oranienburger Strasse, based on experience that Adolf Eichmann had gathered in the autumn of 1938 in Vienna. Emigrating Jews were processed here in a rapid procedure that brought together all concerned authorities:

> In practice, the emigrating Jew was fleeced, totally and completely, in the manner of an assembly line. As he entered the hall, he found himself facing a long row of tables with ten or twelve booths, a Gestapo official sitting at each one. When he entered, he was still a German citizen, the owner of an apartment, perhaps a business, a bank account and some savings. As he went—or better, was pushed—from booth to booth, one possession after the next was taken from him. So that by the time he got to the other end of the hall and left, he had been reduced to the status of a stateless beggar with the only thing he possessed clutched in his hand: an exit visa. At the first window, he had to present his entry visa for a foreign country, at another . . . the "emigration fee" had to be paid. At still another window, the "Aryanization" of his business or his other real estate was finalized. Then he had to prove he was not leaving behind any unpaid debts, take care of any outstanding taxes, transfer his house or

apartment and pay the gas and electric bill. Not until the very last window did he get his exit visa, approved and authorized.[2]

Nonetheless, no one had any doubts that those who had managed to get out of Germany had been more fortunate than their co-religionists remaining behind. None could foresee what the future held in store for them, yet there was a vague and ominous premonition of approaching disaster.

By the beginning of 1939, the measures for "*Entjudung* of the German economy," long in preparation, were, for all practical purposes, now complete. The bulk of businesses demolished in the November pogrom remained closed until some of them were later transferred to "Aryan hands." The Jews were almost totally excluded from any kind of active, gainful economic activity, aside from certain services performed by and for Jews. Social isolation was given its clearest expression in the ordinance that went into force on January 1, 1939: All Jews were required to add the name "Israel" (for males) or "Sara" (for females) to their first names if their own names did not appear in a special official list of "typically Jewish" names issued by the interior minister.[3] The Jews were increasingly at the mercy of the Gestapo, now officially responsible for them (beginning in 1939, Jewish institutions referred to it euphemistically as the *Aufsichtsbehörde* or "control agency," in order to avoid direct mention of the Gestapo). The Gestapo proceeded to order the concentration of all remaining Jewish assets; arranged for the "utilization" of Jewish labor, the distribution of the most necessary food staples, and the gathering together of Jews in so-called *Judenhäuser*; and ultimately organized their transport to the concentration camps in the East.

Demographic and Social Developments

At the time of the November 1938 pogrom, there were still some three hundred thousand "Jews by religion" (*Glaubensjuden*) resident in the *Altreich*. The May 1939 census gave the figure of 214,000 Jews living in Germany; by the outbreak of the war in September, that number had dropped to only approximately 185,000.[4] According to these statistics, an estimated 115,000 Jews had managed to leave Germany in the period from mid-November 1938 to September 1, 1939. Another twenty-five thousand Jews were able to emigrate—until emigration was officially prohibited in October 1941.[5] Of the 214,000 Jews included in the May 1939 census, 70 percent lived in a total of twenty-four cities, more than 75,000, better than one-third, resident in Berlin alone. Such figures are not surprising if one takes the heavy internal migration movement of the previous years

Table 4.1. Age Distribution of the Jewish Population, 1933–1939[8]

Age Group	1933	1939
Up to 14	15.9%	7.5%
14–30	19.8%	11.3%
30–65	53.8%	59.9%
Over 65	10.5%	21.3%

into account. Rather, what is astonishing is that almost a third of all remaining Jews were still living in smaller localities.[6]

The demographic and social structure of the German-Jewish population had undergone a massive change in the period from 1933 to 1939. The proportion of females now stood at 57.5 percent, as compared with 52.2 percent in 1933, a tendency that was to increase as time progressed, and 22.7 percent of all women were widowed. The percentage of divorced men and women had risen from 1.6 to 3.1 percent, apparently a by-product of the spate of divorces resulting from introduction of the Nuremberg racial legislation.[7]

The striking degree of overaging in comparison to the population as a whole and to the earlier Jewish demographic structure, even in 1933, had increased markedly over the ensuing six-year period (see Table 4.1).

The results of the May 1939 census substantiate the degree of success Nazis had already achieved in forcing Jews to leave active economic life. In 1933, 48.1 percent of all Jewish residents had been gainfully employed; by May 1939, that figure had plummeted to 15.6 percent. A total of 107, 850 Jews were classified as "self-employed without occupation," a figure amounting to nearly 71 percent of all Jews over the age of 14. This group was subcategorized as shown in Table 4.2.[9]

Only some thirty-four thousand persons—22.3 percent of all Jews between the ages of fourteen and sixty-five—were still active in any gainful economic pursuit in 1939. The occupational distribution of this negligible remaining fraction of former Jewish economic activity thus reveals very little about the actual social structure of the Jews still left in Germany at this time. It is nonetheless instructive to compare these data with figures for the year 1933 (see Table 4.3).

Aside from the "self-employed without occupation," these statistics document a "process of normalization"—an adaptation to the general occupational structure surpassing the wildest expectations of even the

Table 4.2. "Self-employed without Occupation" Subcategories

Subcategory	Percentage
Rentiers living on their own funds	41.0
Recipients of pensions for widows, the disabled, and other categories; retired pensioners	45.9
Patients in homes for the incurably ill, prison convicts, etc.	5.3
Others	7.8

Table 4.3. Occupational Structure of German Jews, 1933–1939

Economic fields	1933	1939
Agriculture	1.7%	8.9%
Crafts and industry	23.1%	33.8%
Trade and transport	61.3%	18.9%
Private and public services and free professions	12.5%	25.3%
Domestics	1.4%	13.1%

most avid adherents of a "productivization" of Jewish occupational activity. The category "trade and transport" had accounted in 1933 for 61.3 percent of gainfully employed Jews; by 1939, that figure had shrunk to only 18.9 percent. It should be remembered, however, that by 1939 more than two thirds of all German Jews had no source of gainful employment. Already the remaining Jews, almost totally destitute, were engaged in conscripted labor, a preliminary stage of the later scheme of forced labor introduced for all ablebodied Jews during the war economy.

Scraping By from Day to Day

How did these individuals live, what did they survive on in the few years that remained to them before deportation to the extermination camps? The available source material provides a clear answer to this question: Most lived off of their savings from earlier years (and earlier generations), in the form of capital investments and the proceeds of liquidations they still possessed, even if these were largely deposited in blocked accounts controlled by the Gestapo. It was permitted to withdraw fixed monthly amounts, as determined by the "control agency." Those who had no such account were kept alive and above water by assistance from the Jewish welfare system. Its funds—derived from proceeds stemming from the liquidation of Jewish communal property and, increasingly, from Jewish private assets—were temporarily channeled by the Gestapo into the accounts of the Reichsvereinigung der Juden in Deutschland. The starvation wages doled out to those working in conscripted labor now constituted almost the sole remuneration Jews were still receiving for any economic activity.

From mid-1939 on, Jews were permitted to pursue economic activity only if it was for other Jews within the framework of the "Jewish sector." This had to be with the express authorization and under the strict supervision of the Gestapo. Some 600 Jewish firms had still been listed for the city of Munich at the end of 1938, though most were reported to be "in the process of transfer," but only 162 were registered by March 17, 1939. By the end of that year, the figure had withered to a total of twenty-seven "firms," involved mainly in renting out rooms—naturally only for Jewish tenants. The situation in other localities was probably quite similar to that in Munich, for which we happen to have detailed information.[10]

Permission to engage in economic activity was given only in a very circumscribed number of occupations and then exclusively for a Jewish clientele. Along with the Jewish *Krankenbehandler* and *Konsulenten,* a small number of barbers, operators of "lunchrooms" in their private homes, persons renting out rooms, and gravediggers were allowed to continue to pursue some form of gainful employment.[11] Other remunerative activities were permitted only by rare exception. For example, the local Gestapo office in Essen was criticized by its superiors in July 1941 for having approved an "exceptional permit" issued by the office of the district governor for the Jewish craftsman K. "for tailoring services, with the express restriction that such be limited to Jewish customers." In its defense, the Essen Gestapo stated an investigation had indicated that "several hundred Jews are employed in Essen in underground construction work and the like. This activity involves a greater degree of wear-and-tear of clothing. K. mends the damaged and torn articles of clothing. For this reason, I see a need for his activities, especially since these Jews do not have a ration card for clothing." This argument finally convinced the Gestapo superiors in the Düsseldorf office.[12]

Here and there, Jews attempted to earn a bit of extra cash by "illegal work" in their former professions. This was fraught with danger and ventured by only a small few. A typical example is the case of the former Düsseldorf leather merchant M., arrested in April 1941 because he had been making leather ornamentation at home for shoes for the new owner who had purchased his business (liquidated in November 1938). The seventy-five-year-old man was released after a lengthy stay in jail, given a sharp reprimand, and sent home with the warning that he could expect "the state police would take measures leading to compulsory internment in a camp, should any violations be discovered." The "Aryan" proprietor who had placed the order also was reprimanded, but, through the "services" of the Gestapo, he was able to purchase the goods and equipment of the Jew at a low price, "in order to render it impossible for M. to continue to practice his trade, even as a worker at home."[13]

Under such conditions, the "official" Jewish economic sector—that is, the administrative bureaucracy of the Jewish organizations—took on an even greater importance as employer. The Reichsvertretung was not officially replaced as a "legal association" by the Reichsvereinigung der Juden in Deutschland until issuance of the Tenth Ordinance of the Reich Citizenship Law of July 4, 1939.[14] In actual fact, however, talks had already taken place in Jewish organizations pertaining to a reorganization of the Reichsvertretung and the Jewish *Gemeinden*. It had been recognized that the existing institutions were no longer capable of dealing with the mortal threat to German Jewry posed by the Nazi dictatorship. In particular, the law effective March 28, 1938, rescinding the legal status of "Jewish religious organizations and their associations" (i.e., the Jewish *Gemeinden*) as recognized public bodies had made it necessary to restructure their relationship to the central Jewish representative body. In this connection, it is immaterial whether the Reichsvereinigung arose as the result of Jewish initiatives—as a direct continuation of the Reichsvertretung, which had already been reorganized in February 1939—or whether it was forced on the Jews by the Nazi authorities. What was decisive was that the situation and living conditions of the Jewish community had been fundamentally transformed. Thus, the tasks and sphere of activity of Jewish organizations had to be redefined.

A strict centralization of functions was undertaken at organizational level. The still existing *Gemeinden*, designated by the term *Kultusvereinigung* in the wake of the March 1938 law rescinding their status as autonomous incorporated bodies, functioned now as local branches of the Reichsvereinigung. The system of Jewish welfare and education was also placed under the control of the Reichsvereinigung. All disbanded Jewish organizations, foundations, youth leagues, and the like were incorporated into the Reichsvereinigung if they had not as yet been fully liquidated. The Reichsvereinigung also took over their remaining assets and debts. In this way, the Reichsvereinigung became—along with the Jüdischer Kulturbund, not officially disbanded until September 1941—the only recognized Jewish organization in the Reich. Under constant supervision of the Gestapo, the Reichsvereinigung not only coordinated all spheres of Jewish life but increasingly also directed all activity within the Jewish sector and provided for its financing. With the expansion of the scope of its tasks, the staff of the Reichsvereinigung and its district and local branches throughout the Reich was substantially enlarged. Employment in this "official" Jewish sector not only provided many individuals with jobs but also protected them for a time from forced labor and deportation.

No data are available on the total number of Jews employed by the Reichsvereinigung. The Jewish *Gemeinde* in Berlin alone had over four thousand employees in 1940.[15] As late as the middle of 1941, it was still operating a 450-bed hospital and an outpatient clinic with a total staff of 230 doctors, 80 dentists, and numerous additional personnel. In the Jewish educational system, there were at that time five elementary schools and two junior high schools with some 2,500 pupils and a teaching staff of 103. For Christian "non-Aryans," the Reichsvereinigung operated two additional schools with approximately one hundred pupils. There was also a school for housekeeping and domestic science with 290 Jewish girls, as well as a trade school, until early 1941, with an enrollment of 700. Even a privately supported conservatory was able to operate for some time, without financial assistance from the Reichsvereinigung.

In May 1941, an order was issued by the "control agency" (i.e., the *Judendezernat* of the Gestapo in the RSHA) to effect a substantial reduction in the administrative bureaucracy of the Reichsvereinigung and its branches.[16] This move was justified by reference to economy measures and the intended release of all workers who could be spared for the purpose of general conscripted labor in the broader war economy. Probably in reaction, the Reichsvereinigung instructed its branches to add a note, where applicable, to the names of the employees to be dismissed, advising that they were not capable of performing even the lightest types of physical labor and would now have to be supported by Jewish welfare. Simultaneously, a decree was handed down stipulating an immediate halt to all expenditures for religious purposes.[17] Synagogues and other religious institutions had in future to rely solely on voluntary financial contributions from their members for support. In Berlin at that time, there were still eleven synagogues and several prayer rooms, largely for religious services in homes for the aged. Rabbis and other religious officials, whose salaries until then had been financed out of the budget of the Reichsvereinigung, had to be paid from that point on from voluntary contributions. However, such contributions were not deductible from the prescribed taxes and other payments to the Reichsvereinigung.

On May 28, a new "Salary Schedule for the Reichsvereinigung" was issued,[18] valid for all persons employed by the Jewish *Gemeinden*. Previous salaries and wages were drastically cut. The scale provided for seven salary groups, ranging between RM 311 and RM 57 monthly. Married employees received an RM 15 bonus but no child allowance. A salary of RM 57 monthly was roughly equivalent to the "wages" of those Jews working in forced labor. Even the term "starvation wages" fails to do justice to this amount.

From *Arbeitseinsatz* to Forced Labor

As mentioned, on December 20, 1938, the president of the Reich Institute for Employment and Labor Insurance issued a secret order to the employment offices to put jobless Jews to work in special groups, segregated from the rest of the work force, in private and public enterprises. These groups were recruited to perform specially chosen dirty and difficult menial tasks.[19] Over the course of time, especially after the outbreak of the war, more and more Jews were obligated to report for such labor duties. According to the sources, the implementation of the decrees and the treatment of those mobilized for labor varied considerably from place to place and even from firm to firm. The local employment offices, under the supervision of the Gestapo, were given enough latitude for their own initiatives.

In addition, however, central actions were ordered from time to time. In October 1940, the Reichsvereinigung issued a directive to all branches in the Reich to release a "substantial number" of workers for construction of the autobahn. In order to determine the obligatory quotas for each locality, the local branches had to telegraph figures on the number of men between the ages of eighteen and fifty-five who were not as yet in conscripted labor. They were also asked for the number of ablebodied *Gemeinde* employees who could be replaced by others, along with the number of pupils in vocational training courses and the number of men (no age limit specified) who were already on the job in "intensified Jewish conscripted labor."[20] According to various sources, thirty thousand (or even fifty thousand) Jewish men were working in autobahn construction or at other heavy menial manual labor at the beginning of 1941.[21]

It was already clear by the end of 1940 that the war would not be over soon and that there would be a step-up in the war economy. Preparations for mobilizing all available Jewish labor power also began at this point and were concluded by February or March 1941. Forced labor was supposed to encompass all Jews in any way still able to work: youth, men, and women, quite apart from their level of income or wealth, previous employment, or family status. The circular issued by the Jewish *Gemeinde* in Munich on February 20, 1941, detailed the following instructions:[22]

> We declare it to be the duty of all Jewish women to accept the employment assigned to them by the Municipal Employment Office without giving any consideration to their own personal wishes. The physical condition of those summoned to work will be examined by the staff doctor of the Employment Office. Half-time offers of employment are not permissible. . . . Consideration can be given to a planned emigration only if the proposed emigré can show that the date for emigration has been officially fixed, and this is confirmed by us in writing. In general, responsibility for relatives in need of care is not a sufficient reason to be released from the obligation to accept the employment assigned. . . . Jews summoned to the Employment Office must limit their replies to questions asked and avoid any irrelevant comments or explanations. . . . In accordance with the directives of the authorities, we expect all able-bodied Jewish women to be aware of the necessity for engaging in conscripted labor, both in their own interest and the general interest of the Jewish community. Whoever attempts, in a purely selfish manner, to avoid the duty of assigned work does himself harm, and bears partial responsibility for any possible consequences arising for the Jewish community as a whole due to the refusal of certain individuals to work.

When the war broke out, there were already many thousands of Jewish workers employed in "voluntary" conscripted labor who had been compelled to accept such work by application of all sorts of intimidations, threats, and pressure.[23] In Berlin alone, there were some twenty thousand Jews engaged within segregated groups working in road and street construction, as well as in unskilled jobs on construction sites and in earth removal. In the summer of 1940, a large number of Jewish workers were employed under particularly degrading circumstances in the motor manufacturing firm of Siemens & Schuckert. These workers were prohibited from using the general toilets and canteen facilities and were identifiable by a special emblem on their work clothing. The mayor of Leipzig proudly announced that he had been able to put a large number of Jewish men and women to work in street and shelter construction, as well as in "especially dirty" menial labor. Naturally, the Jews were not issued the usual clothing allowances and special bonuses for such work.

Until March 1941, conscripted labor was officially binding only for the unemployed on welfare. For this reason, local employment offices exerted various kinds of pressure via the Gestapo and offices of the Reichsvereinigung to secure a larger pool of Jewish workers. The tone of instructions from the Reichsvereinigung left no doubt about the true character of the "well-meaning suggestions" of the Gestapo. These were more than enough to motivate Jews to report to their local employment office to be assigned a job for which they would receive practically nothing in the way of remuneration.[24]

Munich can again serve as an example. In the spring of 1941, a barracks camp was set up as a "community settlement" for Munich Jews in Milbertshofen. The work had been given to a private construction firm but was supposed to be done exclusively by "Jewish helpers" without payment of any kind.

> The District Party Headquarters was of the opinion that the planned camp would have to be built in the interest of the Jewish community, and therefore no recompense should be offered. . . . Every Jewish helper was . . . compelled to sign a draft contract in which he expressly renounced any wages and stated that he was participating voluntarily [!] and at his own risk in the work. . . . The reply to a refusal to sign was the terse comment that there was still a lot of room in the Dachau concentration camp. Thus, in the period from March 25 to October 11, 1941, some 450 Jews were employed in the construction of their own ghetto.[25]

On March 4, 1941, the Reich labor minister ordered the compulsory employment of all ablebodied Jews on the basis of a secret decree by Göring. They had to work in groups segregated from the rest of the work force and be housed in camps to reduce contact with the population to a minimum.[26] In this way, what previously had appeared to be a supposedly voluntary labor conscription was now transformed into genuine forced labor. The regulation requiring Jews to wear a Star of David for identificational purposes, which went into effect in September 1941,[27] completed and facilitated the implementation of these orders. The Jews were now singled out and marked for the deportations soon to follow.

According to the sources, the number of Jews employed in all types of conscripted labor increased substantially as a result of the introduction of forced labor. Robert Prochnik, an official of the Jewish *Gemeinde* sent to Berlin from Vienna in July 1941, reported that there were forty thousand forced laborers in Berlin, nearly the total number of Jews of working age. Prochnik said that this had been preceded by orders of the Gestapo, which had led to a considerable thinning of the ranks in the administrative bureaucracy of the Jewish *Gemeinde* and the Reichsvereinigung.[28] At the end of 1941, after the first wave of deportation, 21,000 out of a total of some 33,450 "wearers of the star" under the age of sixty-five were employed in forced labor, according to the figures of the Reichsvereinigung in Berlin, and 2,000 were working in the Jewish administrative bureaucracy. The remaining number were either children, the sick or permanently disabled, or living in "privileged mixed marriages," for whom there was no obligation to work at forced labor.[29]

Until October 1941, there do not appear to have been any fixed guidelines for payment and working conditions of Jewish forced laborers, and arbitrary decisions were made in various individual localities and places of employment. The only order generally adhered to was the one stipulating that Jews be kept separate and segregated on the job. In larger factories, Jewish workers were permitted to communicate with the plant management only via a specially designated "spokesperson."[30] There were nine to ten working hours a day, and the work week was occasionally extended to include Sundays. In addition, there was the distance to and from work, which, beginning in September 1941, generally had to be traversed on foot. Only those living more than seven kilometers from their place of work were still allowed to use public transportation after this time. In November 1941, Jews were prohibited from owning or using bicycles, and forced laborers were allowed a bicycle only in exceptional cases.

Not until October 1941 were special guidelines issued on payment for Jewish forced laborers.[31] The existing regulations and pay schedules served as the basis, but these were restricted and substantially cut: child allowances and other special benefits were excluded, and Jews could no longer be given special wages for overtime, work on Sundays and holidays, and so forth. In addition, a "renunciation of any claims" was declared permissible and payment of full wages made dependent on "full performance." These restrictions sufficed for all practical purposes in giving the employers a free hand when it came to determining wages.

Jews by definition were always placed in the highest tax bracket and were obliged, from the end of 1940, to pay an additional "social compensation tax" (*Sozialausgleichsabgabe*) of 15 percent of their income; therefore, not much remained of their fixed "wages." In actual fact, the Jewish forced laborer often received a pay envelope that contained less than half—and sometimes only a third—of the wages of comparably employed "Aryan" workers. According to H. Eschwege, Jews working in Siemens received average weekly wages of RM 16 to RM 20 whereas "Aryans" in comparable work averaged RM 42. (By way of comparison: the minimum taxable weekly wage at the time was RM 54.[32]) But the wages at Siemens were still relatively high. Else Rosenfeld reports that she worked on a flax farm and took home RM 11.70 a week for a ten-hour day of hard manual labor. A Jewish construction worker in Essen was taking home RM 36 a month![33]

Elisabeth Freund has described the working conditions and pay in a large Berlin laundry:[34]

> We were not told when we were hired how much we were going to be paid. We are doing forced labor and should be happy if we get anything

at all. When our first pay-day arrived, then we finally knew: about 12.50 marks for a married female worker. The unmarried workers get a little more because there's no deduction for "double wages." Still, they also don't make much more than 14 marks at the most. From this then, you have to subtract the 1.80 a week for the streetcar, along with nearly three hours unpaid for most workers spent getting to and from the job . . . 12-and-a-half marks! We get about half of what an unskilled Aryan female worker earns. . . . A housecleaner in Berlin asks 50 pfennig an hour and meals thrown in as well!

Some of us don't get any money paid out directly to us. We have a "security account." The Aryan forewoman wants to know what the heck that is. She can't understand how somebody should work and not get a pfennig for it. Well, it's really no simple matter trying to explain this to her. We are not allowed to dispose freely of our money. Our bank accounts are blocked. Each month, we're allowed to withdraw only a fixed amount . . . and we are not permitted to take any cash payments directly. . . . But you can't make it on 12 to 14 marks a week. What with the high price of food. . . . Yet that is precisely the intention: . . . that Jewish workers won't be able to make ends meet on their wages. They are supposed to use up the last of their savings, if they have any. And those who don't have anything saved up can apply to the welfare office of the Jewish Gemeinde. Which is always supposed to take care of everything.

Elisabeth Freund, who later managed to emigrate, wrote this report in December 1941 in Cuba, her memories of the ordeal still fresh in mind, under the title "Forced Labor for Hitler." The authenticity of her description is confirmed by a large number of other sources. Thus, Alfred Wiener recorded statements in London during the war, according to which Jewish women up to the age of fifty-five and Jewish men up to sixty were forced in Breslau to work for a mark a day shoveling snow and collecting garbage.[35] The situation described by Elisabeth Freund regarding security accounts—namely, the fact that Jews with such accounts were forced to work for practically no wages whatsoever—is also confirmed by numerous other sources. The monthly "permissible amount" that Jews were allowed to withdraw from these accounts for their living expenses was RM 150 per family, no matter what wages or other income they had and independent of the number of family members.

The exhibition "Jewish Labor," put on in the summer of 1941 by the Reichsvereinigung, gave expression under these circumstances to a renewed defiant Jewish sense of self. Perhaps the intention was to show that Jewish labor was far more than the humiliation and slavery of this conscripted labor. It was a "relatively extensive exhibition . . . for which the various vocational retraining programs of the Reichsvereinigung had furnished copious material, particularly in respect to crafts. The Hechalutz [the Zionist Youth Federation] had a large booth for itself, replete with models of the various hachshara-kibbutzim and a series of select and beautiful pictures of Palestine."[36]

The introduction of general forced labor also led to significant changes for the still existing *hachshara* training farms. In 1939, there were still twenty such training farms with more than fifteen hundred participants, along with a number of urban day courses in crafts. Since they were designed to prepare those enrolled for emigration, they were tolerated by the Gestapo. Until March 1941, and in some instances even later, these *hachshara* centers ran their own farming operations, within which the young people worked at various jobs. They lived there in almost total isolation, in a youthful enclave of communitarian sharing, cut off in a strange, almost bizarre way from the urban Jewish misery and the general events of the war; there they learned Hebrew, sang the old songs, and discussed ideological problems and their future life in Palestine.

Ezra Ben-Gershom, under the pen name of Joel König, has vividly and impressively described the atmosphere of this youth community and the changes caused by the ordinance on forced labor:

> We lived so secluded from everything! A broad belt of fields and forests separated the farm from the surrounding villages. You would hardly meet anybody walking down the sandy path that led to the farm. . . . In the midst of a Germany bristling with uniforms and weapons, here was a peaceful enclave where neither police nor SA could be seen. An enclave without block wardens, without air wardens. And we were allowed to live there. . . .
>
> Among the educational objectives of the training camps for Palestine was the promotion of the spirit of community. One attempted diligently to imitate the Palestinian kibbutz. . . . The Hebrew word for the members of a community was "*chaverim*" [sing., '*chaver*'], and this is what the young men and women called each other on the farm. . . . Democratic self-management was an essential aspect of the form of kibbutz life. So this was also put into practice. Once or twice . . . a meeting of all members was convened. All sorts of different questions were discussed: how much in private funds should each chaver be allowed to have? Should a chaver share a food package sent him by his parents with his roommates, or should he hand it over to the kitchen? A passionate debate was sparked by the question: should we continue to sing German songs, or Hebrew songs only? The majority wished to go on singing German songs. . . .
>
> The general meeting of all chaverim had to elect a five-man committee which, under the chairmanship of the youth counselor, took care of internal organization. The committee assigned work tasks, divided the

> community into study groups and appointed the course heads. But its most important task was to select the candidates for emigration to Palestine.

Emigration to Palestine at that time, due to the British restrictions, was only possible illegally. The Gestapo tolerated this and even actively supported it. Organized groups, especially members of the Zionist youth leagues, were brought on chartered ships to Palestine from various Mediterranean and Black Sea ports and then secretly set ashore along the coast.[37]

The *hachshara* teaching farms were allowed to continue with their farming operations largely unhindered, though under strict Gestapo supervision, until the spring of 1941. The agricultural products had to be handed over to the authorities. Gestapo supervision not only involved the agricultural operations of the *hachshara* farms and checks on the participants; occasionally, there were bizarrely grotesque checks on whether the cultural activities schedule was being adhered to or the manner in which Hebrew was being taught.

All of this changed after the introduction of forced labor. During the course of 1941, most of the *hachshara* farms were disbanded, and the remaining young trainees were concentrated on three farms, called from then on Communes for Jewish Forced Laborers. One of these was located near Paderborn and was probably the last to be disbanded in 1943. Two contracts concluded with the town of Paderborn serve to illustrate the fundamental change that had occurred: After the first contract, signed in July 1939, the town of Paderborn provided the land cost-free for the purpose of vocational retraining and preparation for emigration. In return, all the *hachshara* had to provide to the town were a few persons to help out in gardening work. The same contract in June 1941 designated the site as a camp "for housing Jews in conscripted labor." Sixty workers had to be placed daily at the disposal of the municipality, the others delegated to the employment office.[38]

Another of the three still existing farms was that in Steckelsdorf, described by Ezra Ben-Gershom. As with other farms, both young and older people, now required to do forced labor in the surrounding agricultural and industrial enterprises, had been assembled and concentrated there from various other localities. Ben-Gershom comments on the changed situation:

> The transformation of the training school for Palestine into a work camp required considerable efforts on our part. The work no longer had anything educational about it. . . . Whoever was working outside the camp got some malt coffee, plus four thin slices of the inferior, spongy bread

> which the village baker supplied the Jews. This was our food until dinner. Two farmers several chaverim were working for voluntarily gave their emaciated helpers milk and eggs. These were laudable exceptions. . . . Not only were we plagued by hunger; our clothing and shoes were wearing out faster too. There was no replacement for these. Jews did not receive clothing cards. We also had much less free time now. Many of us spent more than an hour travelling to and from our place of work.

At the end of 1942, almost the entire group from the farm in Steckelsdorf was taken to Berlin and then "resettled" at Auschwitz. Nothing more was ever heard of that group. We have only a report from Ora Borinski noting that she found articles of clothing with the name of the leader of the Steckelsdorf group in the SS laundry in Auschwitz.

In the spring of 1943, the last *hachshara* in Paderborn was shut down, and these young people also disappeared together in the extermination camps in the East. It was during this period that an end to Jewish forced labor appeared in the offing—and with it the end of the existence of German Jewry. In light of the decision taken by the Nazis in mid-1941 to implement the total and final destruction of the Jews, the "Final Solution," economic considerations and exigencies, such as the labor shortage in the armaments industry, remained secondary in the framework of this overriding goal.

The unmistakable sign marking the beginning of this last phase was the "factory action" of February 27, 1943, in Berlin: Jewish workers who had been spared deportation up to then and were working in plants crucial to the war effort were taken from their factories directly to assembly camps. Other Jews were arrested in their homes or on the street. On April 28, 1943, there was a secret decree of the Gestapo "to remove all Jews still working in jobs crucial for the war from their 'situation of employment' and to register them, insofar as they can be considered for evacuation to the East or for a 'change of residence' to Theresienstadt. In order to avoid escape, Jews to be transported must be kept under lock and key." For the few remaining in Germany, an order was issued for "closed conscription labor, revocable at any time."[39] In the following weeks, almost all Jews living in Germany were ferreted out and deported. Those remaining were a few thousand *Mischlinge,* Jews living in "privileged mixed marriages" (in which the children were being brought up as Christians), or Jews who had gone into hiding. It was these persons who managed to survive the Third Reich. Individuals still fit in any way for physical labor continued, under heavy guard, to be mobilized for use in clearing rubble and for other dangerous jobs.

Pauperization in the Ghetto without Walls

As was noted, consideration had been given to the possibility of a ghettoization of German Jews even before the November 1938 pogrom. Hitler had ordered Jews to be accommodated in houses belonging to Jewish owners in connection with the "Aryanization" of land and real estate. On April 30, 1939, the Law on Renting Arrangements with Jews went into effect.[40] It initiated efforts to concentrate Jews in *Judenhäuser.* Non-Jewish landlords were freed from the obligations of laws for the protection of tenants if they rented to Jews; they would give such tenants immediate notice of eviction if the municipal authorities gave them a certificate saying that "the tenant is assured of accommodations elsewhere." From this point on, Jews were allowed to rent empty or soon-to-be-vacated rooms only on receipt of permission from the municipal authorities, and they were required to allow other Jews to share the room or apartment if the authorities so demanded.

The formulation "accommodations elsewhere" in the law was interpreted in various ways. A letter from the Reichsvereinigung to the Reich Labor Ministry, dated July 17, 1939,[41] listed cases in which "even a makeshift accommodation along the lines of emergency shelter for the homeless is regarded as sufficient. Thus, for example, there is a plan to house Jews in Kolberg in barracks located about an hour from town. These have been used up to now for housing the homeless." The Reichsvereinigung, in contrast, argued that "to implement the planned resettlement of Jews, the law considered . . . only normal living space, whose availability was limited." It referred in this connection to the official commentary on the law of April 30, 1939, which stated that "Jewish use of German living space could be eliminated [by] . . . assuring that space available to Jews in Jewish houses is utilized by accommodating additional Jewish families."

Until 1941, the various plans to concentrate Jews in ghettos had not materialized, although Jews were gradually gathered together in the *Judenhäuser.* The implementation of the measure was the prerogative of the municipal authorities. The Jewish *Gemeinden,* now functioning as branches of the Reichsvereinigung, had to provide for emergency accommodations for evicted Jews as tenants or roomers in the apartments of other Jews. This was handled by special "housing offices" set up by the local Jewish *Gemeinden.* In accordance with a supposedly announced "prohibition against ghettoization," it was necessary to avoid wherever possible setting up several "houses for Jews" adjacent to one another. If need be, Jews could be required to relocate to another town, but this was to be done quietly, without making a stir.[42]

The available source material does not indicate how many such relocations were actually carried out or the number of Jews affected. The success of such actions probably differed from locality to locality and was dependent on the number of Jewish house and apartment owners. Once again, Munich was a bit ahead of general developments elsewhere. After a new ordinance on renting to Jews[43] in September 1940 had "freed" the city of Munich, along with Berlin and Vienna, from all limitations specified in the Tenant Protection Code as applied to Jewish tenants, 450 Jewish forced laborers began construction of a barracks camp in Milbertshofen in February 1941. After its completion in October, almost all Jews in Munich were assigned living quarters there or in the monastery Berg am Laim near Munich.[44]

The Munich initiative was soon followed by others. When the mass deportations of Jews from the area of the Reich began in October 1941, the "vacated" Jewish apartments made it possible finally to concentrate those Jews who had not yet been "deported." Camps such as Milbertshofen or Berg am Laim became assembly points for subsequent deportation. In order to facilitate the concentration and deportation of Jews, special identification of Jewish apartments was ordered in March 1942.[45] By the beginning of 1943 at the latest, all Jews or *Mischlinge* still left in Germany were housed in camps or *Judenhäuser.* A very small number were able to survive the war in hospitals and old age homes under the strict supervision of the Gestapo.[46]

The freedom of movement of Jews had been curtailed for the first time shortly after the November 1938 pogrom. An ordinance of November 28, 1938, empowered the state and provincial governors to place "spatial and temporal restrictions" on Jews. Such restrictions prohibited under penalty entry into certain districts or going out in public at certain times of the day.[47] One day later, an order issued by Himmler prohibited Jews from going out in public on December 3, 1938, the "Day of National Solidarity," "which Jews have no part in."[48] Right after the outbreak of the war, Jewish *Gemeinden* were given a secret order forbidding Jews from leaving their homes between 8 P.M. and 6 A.M. When this was reported on the foreign press, a confidential note to the German press confirmed the existence of the instruction, indicating as a reason that there had been "frequent incidents where Jews had made use of the cover of darkness to molest Aryan women."[49] The curfew remained in effect, but it was not until the introduction of the compulsory identification of Jews (wearing of the yellow star) in September 1941 that there could be any effective check on this. At the same time, Jews were prohibited from leaving their town of residence and from using public transportation. Only in urgent cases was it possible to submit a request for an exception permit to the police.[50]

The regulations limiting Jews to certain times for the purchase of rationed foods should also be counted among the restrictions on freedom of movement. Fixing the period for making such purchases in the afternoon hours, initially locally ordered, was explained by the statement that otherwise Jews would "grab up" the best and freshest produce and foods. After introduction of rationing cards at the start of the war, the Agriculture Ministry ordered cuts in rationed items (less meat and butter, no cocoa, chocolate, or rice, etc.) for Jews.[51] The ration cards for Jews were stamped *J,* and the ration stamps for these items were removed when the card was issued. Although the non-Jewish population received the ration cards in the mail, Jews were required to pick up their cards in person. In the larger cities, the Jewish *Gemeinden* were given the task of issuing ration cards. In the *Gemeinde* in Munich, for example, twelve persons were employed just in handling the mechanics of issuance.

In the meantime, the Reichsvereinigung and its branches had become arms for implementation of Gestapo directives: they had to announce and carry out Gestapo orders. Announcements were made in the official newspaper, *Jüdisches Nachrichtenblatt,* published by the Reichsvereinigung, the only Jewish publication still permitted. Mimeographed and personally delivered newsletters put out by the individual *Gemeinden* also served this purpose. Information that was supposed to remain confidential was passed only by word of mouth. This orally transmitted news, mixed with rumors of varying veracity, now constituted the main source of information for Jews. This network soon was dubbed the "Jewish mouth-radio."

Over the course of time, food rations for Jews were subject to ever greater restrictions. Noodles and butter were more and more rare, and special extra allowances for children and the sick were canceled. In September 1942, Jews were finally deprived of rations for meat, dairy products, eggs, and a number of other food items. Under these conditions, it became more and more difficult, even for those who still had a little money, to obtain sufficient food for survival. Naturally, people tried in every way they could to obtain additional provisions. Non-Jewish acquaintances or former suppliers also provided help in a number of instances. Just how dangerous this could be for the "Aryans" who assisted is demonstrated by one of many cases recorded in the files of the Düsseldorf Gestapo: In August 1941, the Jew X, aged sixty-five, was arrested for having purchased thirty kilos of beans. The Gestapo had received information from an informer that the farmer in question had set aside the beans for the Jew on the morning of the market day before opening its stand for customers. Although beans were not rationed and could be freely sold, both the Jew and the farmer were taken into custody. As the file indicates, the Jew was not "released" until November and was then deported to the ghetto in Łódź. The farmer got off with a lighter penalty:

at the request of the party headquarters in his local town, he was released after two weeks with a warning.[52]

Things were even worse when it came to procuring clothing or shoes. Not only were Jews not allotted any clothing, they were even deprived of the greater part of what they still owned.[53] In January 1942, the Reichsvereinigung was ordered, via its branches, to collect fur coats, or pieces of fur such as fur sleeves and collars, from all Jews. Likewise, any warm woolen clothing, ski suits, and warm winter shoes had to be handed in as well. A few woollen articles were allowed to be kept for personal use, but the collection points were instructed to "exercise strict criteria" in this regard. In June of that same year, there was a similar collection. The order this time stipulated that it be carried out in "Jewish institutions, in particular hospitals, old age homes, homes for the chronically ill and children's homes":

> The following are to be handed in: articles of clothing . . . no longer absolutely necessary for one's personal use in accordance with a modest style of life, including [new and old] men's and women's apparel, suits, coats, hats and caps, dresses, blouses, women's suits, skirts and coats, aprons and work smocks, old textile goods, such as underwear, stockings, neckties, towels and scarfs. In addition, rags, all types of cloth, remnants of yarn and thread.[54]

This announcement contained in the newsletter of the Nuremberg Jewish *Gemeinde* is pervaded by a sense of overanxious zeal not to leave out anything from the list. The item "coats" is even mentioned twice. Everything had to be handed over four days later at the cemetery central building "in a clean condition. Socks and gloves should be tied together in pairs. Any identifying marks or labels should be removed, especially anything indicating the former owner." Thus, the "yellow star" had to be assiduously removed!

On July 27, 1942, this same *Gemeinde* informed its members of the Nuremberg Gestapo order "to surrender to the authorities all fur items still in Jewish possession, including the smallest fur articles, as well as collars and fur trimming, even if the article of clothing is made unwearable by removal of the fur. . . . We expect members to check their closets and wardrobes carefully to make sure that even the smallest fur article has been removed. Non-compliance will be punished by the *severest* measures of the state police."[55] The word *severest* is underlined twice in the original, and the hint was understood by each and every Jew at this point.

Prohibitions and orders to hand in clothing now were issued with great frequency and bore the features of open, sadistic harassment, at times without any attempt being made, even for the purpose of appearances, to justify such measures in rational terms.[56] Thus, for example, Jews had been required to hand in the radios in 1939, specifically on Yom Kippur, the Day of Atonement and holiest day of the year in the Jewish calendar. In November 1941, they had to surrender all bicycles, typewriters, and optical goods, with the exception of eyeglasses. In February 1942, Jews were prohibited from buying newspapers or magazines. That previous August, an order had been issued barring them from using lending libraries. In the summer of 1940, all phones of Jewish subscribers had been taken back by the phone company; the only exceptions were phones for *Krankenbehandler* and *Konsulenten* or for the leading officials of the Reichsvereinigung. In December 1941, *Sternträger* (wearers of the star) were also enjoined from using public telephones. Beginning in February 1942, Jews were prohibited from having pets or caged birds; a month later, they were forbidden to buy flowers. Everything was aimed at rendering even the short remaining period of their lives as unbearable as possible for the outlawed, socially isolated Jews. The reason often advanced in earlier years, that such measures were designed to make them "amenable to the notion of emigration," had long since lost any validity.

The persons inundated by this flood of prohibitions, orders, and humiliating restrictions were impoverished, frightened, largely older Jews, who were now dependent more and more on relief assistance from the Jewish *Gemeinden*. In 1940–1941, only a fourth to a third of them were still living on what was left of their own assets.[57] Aside from employees of the *Gemeinden* and the Reichsvereinigung, only those who had been inducted into forced labor had any income.

Strangely enough, there were also a few persons receiving pensions who had been missed by the otherwise painstakingly thorough bureaucracy. Widows of soldiers and disabled World War I veterans still received small monthly payments. Some former civil servants were also still getting a pension. Perhaps the respect of the bureaucracy for the special status of the German civil service still played a certain role in this. In the summer of 1942, an inquiry was directed from Bonn to the Gemeindetag (German National Association of Municipalities), followed by a lengthy investigation indicating that there was no clear legal regulation on which to base cancellation of pension payments to the Jews affected. The Berlin municipality reported that it had long since ceased payments of pensions to Jews. However, the legal advisors of the Gemeindetag decided this could not be regarded as a precedent. The Bonn mayor would, it was ruled, have to decide on his own in accordance with the circumstances.[58] Viewed in this context, it is possible to comprehend the fact that individual Jews received pension payments down to the very end of the Third Reich and that in certain attested cases pensions were even forwarded to people in the Łódź ghetto.[59]

The preponderant majority of Jews were supported by the welfare departments of the *Gemeinden*. Ordinances of November 1938 and July 1939, on the occasion of the official establishment of the Reichsvereinigung,[60] had directed needy Jews to Jewish welfare services. Even without any legal order, at that point Jews were receiving little assistance from official public welfare. In 1941, the Reichsvereinigung spent RM 18 million, more than half of its annual budget, for welfare purposes.[61] Beginning in June of that year, it was no longer permissible for synagogues and other religious institutions to receive financial support from the funds of the Reichsvereinigung. Rabbis and other religious officials had to be paid out of voluntary contributions from *Gemeinde* members, which could not be deducted from the obligatory membership fees. In June 1942, the few remaining Jewish schools also had to be closed down.[62] By this point at the latest, the expense budget of the Reichsvereinigung and the *Gemeinden* included only administrative costs and expenditures on welfare, along with payment of taxes. The bulk of expenditures on welfare went for maintenance of childrens' homes and homes for the aged and the chronically ill. In mid-1941, before the mass deportations of German Jews began, there were still over fifty institutions, along with a large number of day-care homes and soup-kitchens. There were clothing supply departments in all of the *Gemeinden*; such departments had become an increasingly important source of mutual assistance ever since Jews had been prohibited from purchasing clothing and textiles.[63]

The expense budget of the Reichsvereinigung for 1941 was approximately seven times as large as the entire budget of the predecessor organization, the Reichsvertretung, had been in 1938. This comparison alone makes clear how very different the character and tasks of these two institutions were, although one had evolved from the other and there was a high degree of continuity in personnel. Expenditures had soared, although the number of Jews remaining in Germany had declined substantially. Income, especially from abroad, had also dwindled. According to various estimates, some 40 percent of expenses were still being covered in 1941 by income from membership fees. These members now also included, by compulsory regulation, *Mischlinge* and persons who had officially disaffiliated from the Jewish religious community.[64]

The Reichsvereinigung and the *Gemeinden,* functioning as local branches, now collected the prescribed "contributions" in place of the former *Gemeinde* taxes. This was done in accordance with the orders of the Gestapo and under their strict supervision. The 1941 membership fee regulations issued by the Gestapo fixed the compulsory amount to be paid uniformly at 30 percent of income tax. For most Jews, however, the rates for tax on property and assets would have been more relevant at this time. Annually, they were from 0.25 to 5 percent of total assets reported in April 1938.

This did not include the *Sühneleistung* and other payments and taxes or the loss of value as a result of "Aryanizations" and liquidations. Thus, in actual fact, the property tax rate was much higher. Added to this were compulsory payments during the six winter months for JWH; during the summer months, there were similar payments of an equal amount to a scheme known as *Jüdische Pflicht*. A notice contained in the newsletter of the Munich *Gemeinde* makes it clear that these were no longer voluntary contributions for welfare but rather additional taxes levied by the Gestapo: The newsletter reminded readers once again that "a number of members have still not paid in their contributions for *Jüdische Winterhilfe*. We request that you remedy this oversight immediately, since we are obligated to report the names of any members partially or completely in arrears by April 5, 1941. We wish to spare our members the consequences resulting from such a report."[65] The content and tone of this short notice also provide a vivid picture of the *Gemeinden* and the Reichsvereinigung as an organization for implementation of orders and communication between their members and the Gestapo as "control agency."

A more important source of income was probably the "emigration tax" (*Auswanderungsabgabe*), imposed on all Jewish emigrants as early as February 1939 by a secret order of the Gestapo. The reason given at the time was the possibility of financing emigration for indigent Jews by means of a tax on wealthier emigrating Jews. We have no reliable total estimate of the amount of money robbed from the Jews by this punitive tax, but it is likely that a considerable sum was involved. According to the 1939 annual report of the Reichsvereinigung, the "emigration fund," a separate category in the account books, already had a total of RM 23 million in mid-1939. This tax, like the property and wealth tax, was levied based on the amount of reported assets in April 1938. Until the beginning of 1941, it was 1 to 10 percent of reported personal wealth; after that time, it soared as high as 60 percent! In practical terms, emigrants were left nothing, not even in their blocked accounts.[66]

The confiscation of the remaining property of the Jewish *Gemeinden* yielded further income. The actual total value of these properties is difficult to estimate. Results of a 1947 survey of surviving officials of 1,050 former *Gemeinden* indicated total assets before the November pogrom to be an estimated RM 250 million.[67] In October 1941, after a large proportion of the buildings and land holdings had probably already been sold—undoubtedly at far below true market value—the Reichsvereinigung reported a total wealth of RM 101.5 million, 62 million of this in currency.[68] The documents shed no light on the relative proportions of individual income sources or on what other assets were still in the formal possession of the synagogues.

All of this income was funneled into a total fund of the Jewish community. Jews, who had been stripped of their rights and now were expropriated and left without any income, had to survive with the aid of this fund without becoming a burden for the "Aryan folk economy." Social differences disappeared swiftly. Even persons who still had money deposited in security, or blocked, accounts, in some instances sizable amounts, were allowed to withdraw only a monthly fixed amount. The introduction of forced labor for all ablebodied Jews, the standardized living arrangements, and the rationing of foods also blurred the differences in everyday living conditions as the process of ghettoization picked up momentum. Forced on the Jews by Nazi fiat, a process of social leveling and equalization now took place during this last phase of the existence of German Jewry. Persons who for a long time had not belonged in any way to the Jewish community found themselves affected: *Rassejuden* of Christian faith, dissidents, nonbelievers, *Mischlinge* of various degrees, and those living in "non-privileged" mixed marriages. They had now become a part of the Jewish community of fate and, almost completely equal in their privation, were allowed for a brief time to eke out a miserable existence in Germany. What awaited them all was the common fate of deportation to the East.

"Emigration tax," "membership fees," and other compulsory payments, which had to be collected by the Reichsvereinigung at the order of the Gestapo, prepared the ground for the final stage in state expropriation of Jewish private and communal assets. First, all assets were transferred step by step to the account of the Reichsvereinigung. This enabled the Gestapo to concentrate and supervise all remaining Jewish assets in a single place. Even the smallest amount could be spent only with the express permission of the Gestapo. All that remained in the hands of the Jewish employees and officials were direct payments and the keeping of the account books. In this way, preparations were made for the final seizure of the remainder of Jewish assets as a prelude to future deportations.

The *Entjudung* of Assets

> Wherever it is a question of something as morally despicable as collective hate, the redemptive character of "redeeming" murder harmonizes well with the redemptive character of "redeeming" robbery. Not simply is the money that has been taken away from Jews without any stink—it is also money that has been "redeemed," which is not liberated from the grip of the power of evil, so to speak, until it rests in the robber's sack—whether that be the state or someone else.[69]

According to the ideology of National Socialism, the "folk economy"

(*Volkswirtschaft*), as a romantic-organic concept, stood above "private economy" and the "world economy." Private property was considered necessary and "natural" but was also regarded as a kind of fief or usufruct deriving from communal property, over which the *Volk* had ultimate jurisdiction and control.[70] Since Jews did not belong to the German *Volk* according to the basic principles of the party program and had been "legally" excluded as well on the basis of the Nuremberg Laws, they had no right to any portion of the "folk wealth" (*Volksvermögen*) in the eyes of Nazi ideology. Whatever they owned was considered to be fraudulent, pilfered and "exploitative" capital, that now had been returned to its legal owners—namely, the *Volk,* or the *Volksgenossen* by proxy.

In this sense, the "redemption" of Jewish assets had already begun with the first "Aryanizations." The fact that many *Volksgenossen* gained personally made them accomplices—whether they wished so or not—who then continued to benefit from further Nazi crimes: Only after the previous owners and their heirs had been murdered could they be absolutely certain of their spoils. Using devices such as the *Sühneleistung,* special taxes, and expropriations for the benefit of the Reich and the individual states, additional amounts of Jewish assets had been seized by orderly administrative procedure. The last phase in the "redemption" of Jewish assets began in the autumn of 1941 with the first mass deportations. The well-oiled bureaucratic machinery now made sure that all Jewish holdings in currency and real estate were totally expropriated and "utilized" (*verwertet*).

The mass deportations began the end of October 1941 with the deportation of some twenty thousand Jews from the *Altreich,* Vienna, and the Czech "Protectorate" to the Łódź ghetto. This was followed shortly thereafter by further transports of Jews to the conquered Soviet areas: Riga, Minsk, Kovna, and other places. Approximately one third of all Jews living in the *Altreich* in 1933 were murdered as a result of these transports—some immediately, some after brief or protracted periods of stay in ghettos and concentration camps.[71]

Even before October 1941, there had been cases of expulsions of Jews, based on local initiatives but with the express approval of the top echelon of the state. In February 1940, some twelve hundred Jews were deported from Stettin and the surrounding towns to the area of Lublin, where they were taken in by local Jews.[72] In October of that year, more than seven thousand Jews were deported from Baden and the Saar-Palatinate to non-occupied France; they were interned in camps near the Spanish border, principally in Gurs. In the wake of these deportations, the authorities had been faced with the problem of what to do with the property of those who had been deported. The Jews in Stettin and Scheidenmühl were required to renounce in writing any claim to the property they had left behind. The SS confiscated valuables and cash before the transport got underway. This procedure led to a lengthy dispute between the SS and the Reich Finance Ministry regarding whom the abandoned and confiscated property should be handed over to. In Baden and the Palatinate, the properties left behind by deported Jews were appropriated by the state via a decree after the fact issued by the Baden interior minister on April 7, 1941. In this instance too, the Gestapo lodged a protest: In their view, the property should have been seized as "property hostile to the Volk and the Reich" on the basis of the emergency ordinance of February 28, 1933. The guidelines issued by Himmler on November 9, 1940, called for "administration by a trusteeship" and the setting up of a special blocked account.[73]

A decree by the Führer in May 1941 then provided the basis for "appropriation of property hostile to the Volk and the Reich" by the state; it empowered the Reich interior minister to transfer the properties, or a portion thereof, to "autonomous bodies in the various areas" for their purposes and tasks.[74] It would appear that the Gestapo, which was formally a part of the Interior Ministry and the only authorized official *"Aufsichtsbehörde"* for Jews, saw this as the "legal" basis for "transferring" the property of those deported to the Reichsvereinigung.

But the finance minister had other notions. With the beginning of the mass deportations, he issued exact regulations on November 4, 1941, regarding the appropriation of property belonging to "Jews to be deported . . . in the coming months to a city in the eastern territories."[75] According to these regulations, the appropriation orders were to be issued by the local district governors or the Reich governors, and in Berlin by the Gestapo; they would then be "officially handed over to Jews by marshals of the court before their transport to the East." The finance minister assigned the directors of the regional offices of the Finance Ministry the task of "administration and utilization of the appropriated properties." They had "to take receipt of the lists of property and appropriation orders from the local responsible state police offices, and then to take possession of all property. It is especially necessary to make sure that there are no appropriation orders issued for these properties by other offices." This is followed by detailed instructions regarding the implementation and clear and well-arranged registration of the appropriated property.

The responsible bureaucracy—that is, the Reich finance administration and its staff—were to get a share of the spoils. Thus, for example, the finance minister requested that "the possibility be explored as to whether a portion of the apartments so acquired might be obtained from the authorities responsible for their maintenance for the purposes of welfare service for civil servants." He also requested that "before the furniture in the apartment is put to another use, one should check what objects might be of use to the Reich finance administration officials. Office furnishings of interest include . . . desks, bookcases, armchairs, carpets, pictures, etc.; as furnishings for vacation homes and schools of the finance administration: bedroom sets, beds, musical instruments and, in particular, sheets and pillow cases, table clothes, hand towels, etc." Only "objects not needed for purposes of the finance administration" should be handed over, "in return for reasonable payment," to the National Socialist *Volkswohlfahrt* (Folk Welfare) or to municipal authorities for "providing furniture and household goods to citizens who have suffered losses due to the air raids." Securities and bank accounts were supposed to be handed over to the Reich Main Treasury in Berlin.

The Eleventh Ordinance of the Reich Citizenship Law was issued on November 25, 1941.[76] It stipulated that the property belonging to Jews "whose usual place of residence is abroad . . . should pass to the ownership of the Reich upon loss of citizenship." The ordinance became law with the date of its publication for all Jews already "located abroad." For Jews not yet deported, it became valid "with the transfer of their place of residence abroad." According to a supplementary circular from the finance minister on December 3, 1941, the term "abroad" also included the "territories occupied by German troops or under German administration . . . especially the Generalgouvernement and the Reich 'Commissariats' of Ostland and the Ukraine."[77]

The Finance Ministry then announced "procedural changes in the deportation of Jews" in a letter dated December 9, 1941. Since their property "falls to the German Reich" according to the Eleventh Ordinance of the Citizenship Law, it would no longer be appropriated.[78] The orders of November were to remain unchanged. At first glance, this new order appears to have been nothing more than a matter of procedure: The previous "appropriation" required notarized statements; this had been taken care of by special personnel from the judiciary assigned to the assembly points for the transports. Now the "forfeiture" was automatic and did not require any special procedural step. However, in actuality, this was an attempt to avoid confiscation of the property by the Gestapo. The "responsible offices of the state police" were supposed to be instructed by "the head of the security police and the SD" to give the director of the regional office of the Finance Ministry "lists dealing with the Jews deported," thus creating the "conditions for a forfeiture of property." In order to make this even clearer, it was emphasized in the text of the decree that "what was decisive for forfeiture of property . . . [was] not the determination . . . by the chief of the security police and the SD, but rather the fact that the Jew maintains his regular place of residence abroad." In the view of the Finance Ministry, this fact was sufficient to assign administration of the properties "of Jews who had been deported from their districts" to the responsible director of the regional Finance Ministry office.

As is clear from a decree issued by Bormann on January 3, 1942,[79] the Gestapo was not satisfied with this solution. The head of the party chancellery determined that "the property of the Jewish Gemeinden and of the Reichsvereinigung should not be viewed as Jewish, but rather as property serving the purposes of the Reich." The "Central Authority for Jewish Emigration" (i.e., the Gestapo) was expressly mentioned as the authorized agency. This tug of war between the Gestapo and the Finance Ministry continued throughout the entire year. On April 2, 1942, Heydrich issued a decree to all offices of the state police, according to which, "more than anything else, the property of the Reichsvereinigung serves the Final Solution of the question of European Jewry . . . so that funds of the Reich do not have to be utilized for this purpose. For that reason, this property should no longer be viewed simply as Jewish property, but rather, in the final analysis, as property already earmarked for purposes of the German Reich. Therefore, it would constitute interference in the powers vested in me as special appointed officer of the Reichsmarschall for the Final Solution of the European Jewish question if other agencies and offices should upset . . . our plans in this area by confiscations, etc."[80]

The expert in the Finance Ministry responsible for Jewish affairs, Dr. Mädel, quoted Heydrich's decree in a detailed report on the "Financing of Measures for the Solution of the Jewish Question" dated December 14, 1942. In the introduction, the role of the Reichsvereinigung was explained: "The head of the security police and the SD makes use principally of the 'Reichsvereinigung der Juden in Deutschland' for implementation of its measures. . . . The financing of the measures, extremely costly in part, has been handled to date without the use of budgetary funds. Money has been procured by various means."

This was followed by an exact list of various "taxes," "contributions," "(old-age) home purchase contracts," and so on, which are described in greater detail below. The expert then stated the following regarding the disposition and utilization of the funds concentrated in the accounts of the Reichsvereinigung in this manner:

> There is no doubt that the transport costs and other expenses associated with deportation are covered by funds from contributions. The offices of the state police are not entitled to control these monies from contributions. However, it can be gathered from occasional conversations with representatives of the RSHA that the offices of the state police in actual fact have considerable influence on the utilization of the funds (payment for transport costs, etc.). Yet no direct proof for this can be presented. . . . There are no legal objections to this procedure. However, property

> in the hands of the Jew shortly before his deportation is, in this way, removed from the grasp of the Reich. It is impossible to estimate the magnitude of assets which in this way elude an appropriation by or forfeiture to the Reich. Yet there can be no doubt that the sums involved are considerable. . . . It must be decided whether the procedure of self-financing initiated by the Reichsfuhrer of the SS should be agreed to implicitly, or whether an attempt should be made to direct the *entire* sum of assets involved to the Treasury, and accordingly to include the expenses in the regular budget. The question has already been broached on occasion with representatives of the RSHA. There is apparently no inclination to deviate from practices. The way of obtaining approved funding via the budget is viewed as too complicated. The objection has been voiced that the solution of the tasks to be completed could be impeded if the present method of financing, highly flexible and adapted to requirements, were to be given up.

In conclusion, Mädel recommended that "the assets appropriated earlier for the Reich should also be placed at the disposal of the Gestapo . . . because the new method of the head of the security police and the SD had then not as yet been perfected." Apparently there was no longer any hope at this point that the Finance Ministry was chary about locking horns with the Gestapo. In view of the practical methods in use since the beginning of 1939, these attempts had little chance for success. The methods of "self-financing" and of pseudo-autonomous "self-administration" of Jewish assets had already been effectively applied before being utilized in the final phase for covering the costs of deportation.

Ordinances issued relatively early in the process had facilitated the concentration and supervision of Jewish assets. Since December 1938, the securities accounts (and since August 1939 the bank accounts as well) were open only to limited disposition by their owners as supervised security accounts. On the basis of these accounts and additional information, the Gestapo had set up a detailed catalog of file cards covering all Jewish assets. In October 1940, this was updated with the help of the Reichsvereinigung.[81] The final point was an eight-page questionnaire in which all assets and property had to be listed before deportation, down to the smallest item: from furniture, jewelry, and art objects, ordered according to the rooms they were located in, to books, cutlery, and single individual articles of clothing and underwear and bed linen.[82]

One day before Göring gave Heydrich the order, on July 31, 1941, to make preparations for the "total solution of the Jewish question,"[83] the banks at which Jews had security accounts were asked to supply the Economy Ministry with detailed lists of these accounts and their contents by August 20.[84] On August 21, all *Gemeinden* were instructed by the Reichsvereinigung in Berlin to begin with an exact inventory of the homes and apartments of their members. In this connection, Jewish residents should be warned that any unauthorized sale, gift, or other disposition of the objects in their possession would result in arrest.[85]

All sources mentioned and many others, such as those quoted by H. G. Adler in detail in his comprehensive study, prove the intention of the Gestapo to assure itself sole right to the disposition of and control over the entire sum of Jewish property and assets, both private and communal. Even the smallest possession was not to elude its grasp. And neither private individuals, local party offices, nor the state finance office should have access to Jewish assets, at least until the conclusion of the process of *Entjudung*. After the Gestapo had succeeded in excluding the assets of the Reichsvereinigung and the Jewish *Gemeinden* associated with it from the regulations on appropriation and forfeiture as "non-Jewish property," it was now of utmost importance to find ways to direct as much as possible of Jewish private assets into the coffers of the Reichsvereinigung. The more the process of deportation took hold, the more inventive their methods became.

On November 12, 1941, the officer for questions of property law in Section IV B4 of the RSHA, Fredrich Suhr, issued an order through the Reichsvereinigung that all money still owed to the organization in the form of "fees" or "voluntary contributions" should be excluded from appropriation or forfeiture in the case of deportation. Jews should transfer these outstanding sums by their own signatures to the offices of the Reichsvereinigung before being deported, preferably even before they reached the assembly point. These amounts of money should not be listed in the declaration of assets that had to be made in writing and presented at deportation. In the case of any difficulties, persons should be referred to "our control agency."[86]

The procedure had been perfected in the first few months of mass deportation to the point that practically the entire liquid private assets of the Jews—cash, valuables, money in security accounts, and bonds were transferred to the Reichsvereinigung even before deportation. Starting in March 1942, deported Jews were obliged to pay a "special tax" in addition to fees due for the entire year and payments for JWH and *Jüdische Pflicht*. This was calculated as a surcharge of 150 percent on previously assessed fees but was supposed to amount to at least 25 percent of remaining liquid assets. In addition, Jews not yet indigent were required to pay a sum of RM 6,000 (or the remainder of their assets) for "covering the cost of transport." From this "fee for transport expenses," the RM 50 per person should also be paid. This payment of RM 50 was given to the transport managers who then passed it on after arrival to cover initial maintenance costs for the deportees. In the case of the first transports to the Łódź ghetto, on which RM 100 per person was taken, there is documentary attestation that this money was indeed passed on to the ghetto administration.[87] If anything was left over, the deportees were "encouraged," at the order of the Gestapo, to transfer the rest of their assets to the Reichsvereinigung as a "contribution." Apparently most people did just this and not just because they were frightened. They were familiar with the stipulations of the Eleventh Ordinance of the Citizenship Law and probably preferred to leave their assets to the Reichsvereinigung rather than to the Reich, where it would be "forfeited." They may well have believed that in this way it might be of potential use, at least in part, for fellow Jews who had been left behind, which was indeed true for the short time still remaining.

All sums of money gathered in this way had to be deposited in a "special account W" of the Reichsvereinigung or the *Gemeinden*. Naturally, this account was only formally at the disposal of Jewish implementation organizations. Any withdrawal had to have the approval of the Gestapo as control agency, and the monthly balance statement had to be presented to the Gestapo as well. However, there is also evidence that withdrawals for the running expenses of the Reichsvereinigung and its branches were also approved from these accounts.[88]

Another procedure was chosen for the transports being sent beginning in June 1942 to the "old age ghetto Theresienstadt." Use was made of the "home purchase contracts" that had been common in earlier years in connection with admission to a Jewish home for the chronically ill or an old people's home. But in place of the purchase fee and the monthly maintenance charges, the deportees sent to Theresienstadt had to transfer their entire liquid assets to the Reichsvereinigung, including outstanding debts and life insurance claims. In return, the Reichsvereinigung "obliged itself" to support the "contract partner" for the rest of his or her life, supplying everything needed. Since the deportation was, in "legal terms," not emigration but rather a mere "change in place of residence," the Gestapo demanded reimbursement of the already paid Reich Flight Tax from the finance administration via the Reichsvereinigung. Such persons, who in any case had to hand over their entire assets "in accordance with contract," were exempted from payment of the other customary fees and special fees. The transferred assets were administered by the Reichsvereinigung in a "special account H," which was supposed to cover the maintenance costs for the "old age ghetto." It is not known just how much money was seized in this manner, but there are indications that at least a part of it actually found its way to the *Judenältesten* in Theresienstadt. According to other sources, this money was transferred to the "emigration center" of the Gestapo in Prague.[89]

Not only the Reichsvereinigung but the banks as well were dragged by the Gestapo into the continuing, albeit veiled dispute with the Reich tax authorities regarding ultimate competence. The economic group "Private Banking" informed its members once more, in a circular dated October 9, 1942, of the regulations for "handling Jewish assets." There was a special reference in this regard to the regulations of the Eleventh Ordinance, according to which dispositions by Jews for the benefit of the Reichsvereinigung "are only possible as long as there has been no forfeiture of the property, or effective appropriation." Since property forfeiture was automatic as soon as one crossed the borders of the Reich, bank orders by the deportees that had not as yet been executed could be carried out only "with the approval of the director of the regional Finance Ministry office responsible for the area in which the last residence of the Jew in the country was located." For this reason, the RSHA instructed the district offices of the Reichsvereinigung to make a note on the bank orders of the Jews, such as "migration to the East (abroad) will not occur until one week after the date of the bank order." This would allow the banks enough time to carry out the orders without approval by the director of the regional Finance Ministry office. Immediately thereafter, on October 17, 1942, the Reichsvereinigung issued the order to include the identically formulated note on "each bank order . . . underneath the date, without making any reference to the actual date of migration."[90] In factual terms, this was nothing other than the complicity (ordered by the Gestapo) of the banks and the Reichsvereinigung in circumventing the "legal" power of disposition of the tax authorities.

Another document proves that the Gestapo took certain liberties with the laws and that genuine attempts at tax evasion were at least given some consideration. In a lengthy memorandum of August 28, 1942, the head of the Tax and Transactions Office of the Reichsvereinigung called the attention of the RSHA to the fact that funds deposited in the special accounts "W" and "H," which "can only be disposed of upon instruction of the control agency," could be "subject to corporate, sales and gift tax." He included a "request for advisement . . . as to whether a corresponding report for the tax office should be submitted."[91] The reply of the RSHA has not been preserved, but the inquiry alone proves that the author of the memorandum did not absolutely rule out the possibility of tax evasion.

> The RSHA . . . soon seized upon the notion of removing from the grasp of the Finance Minister, at least temporarily, a portion of Jewish assets far exceeding the transport costs of deportation. The idea was to do this by means of the special account "W." In the process, the RSHA made use of the Reichsvereinigung for reasons of moral cover vis-á-vis other German agencies, in a mixture of sleight-of-hand and deception as the official "control agency." The Reichsvereinigung as an organization was

> not only . . . under the jurisdiction of the RSHA, but was also totally powerless financially, and merely the nominal owner of any assets.[92]

Our presentation above basically confirms the view advanced by H. G. Adler. Nonetheless, the status of the Reichsvereinigung at that time should be seen more differentially. This is not the place to analyze in detail the development of Jewish representative organizations and leadership boards, from the Jewish *Gemeinden* through the Reichsvertretung founded in 1933 and on to the Reichsvereinigung, which was in the main directed from the outside in the final phase of existence of German Jewry. But even amid the horror of deportations east to the extermination camps, the leaders and functionaries of the Reichsvereinigung and the *Gemeinden* did not function simply as passive tools in the hands of the Gestapo.

As long as Jews were still living in Germany, Jewish representatives considered it their duty to provide services for them. Since 1939, that had encompassed almost all spheres of life, from education and religion to vocational training and emigration, as long as that option was still feasible. Indeed, such services went all the way to providing for the basic necessities of everyday life. In the process, Jewish functionaries, either knowingly or unawares, were implicated by the Gestapo—with satanically inventive design—in the National Socialist policies of *Entjudung* and extermination. H. G. Adler has accurately analyzed this creeping policy:

> There was a close and solid entanglement of the Berlin executive board of the Reichsvereinigung der Juden in Deutschland with the RSHA IV B4. Likewise, the various Jewish offices were closely linked with the Gestapo in the Altreich and with the "Central Offices" in Austria and Bohemia-Moravia. These links had undoubtedly become routine operation long before the beginning of general deportations. So when the process of deportation did commence in earnest, especially out in the German provincial areas, there could not even be any thought of a forceful refusal to comply. The leading officials were totally paralyzed and unable to make decisions. Basically, they no longer knew what they were doing, indeed had not known for a long time.[93]

Even if, in connection with deportations, they were forced to act as accomplices for the Gestapo, most of these "leading officials" were motivated by the best of intentions. They sincerely believed, rightly or wrongly, that they could ameliorate the suffering of Jews and prevent worse things from happening. In this they may have been mistaken, but who today has the right to stand in judgment and condemn them for that error? Even after the beginning of deportations in October 1941, there were still 150,000 Jews living in the *Altreich*. These individuals had to be provided for and given the most basic essentials for daily survival. Financial means were necessary for this, and they were provided by the Gestapo in the manner described. The Jewish functionaries had only a limited, temporary, and strictly supervised power to dispose of these funds. They had to account for every pfennig spent and obtain approval for each expenditure from their superiors. Nonetheless, they were probably justifiably apprehensive that "forfeiture" of Jewish assets to the state treasury would have completely blocked any possibility for them to utilize at least a portion of this capital to help provide for the daily survival of Jews still remaining in Germany. Any attempt to obtain funds from the tax and welfare offices would have certainly proved a great deal more complicated, with far fewer prospects for success, than the familiar routine of working together with the "control agency." Quite aside from the fact that they had no say in the matter, the Jewish functionaries definitely had an interest in channeling Jewish assets into the accounts of the Reichsvereinigung. It was probably clear to everyone by this time that these assets were now lost as far as the original Jewish owners were concerned. What reason would the Jewish officials have had to prefer a "legal" transaction at the hands of the directors of the regional offices of the Finance Ministry to the manipulations of the Gestapo?

Even today, it is not completely clear what happened in the end to the monies still on deposit in the special accounts and to the funds of the Reichsvereinigung. The Reichsvereinigung was officially disbanded in June 1943, and the regional tax office directors were instructed to take over the assets of the organization.[94] In contrast, a circular dated August 3, 1943, from the tax office was in express contradiction with the earlier decree:

> The assets are the property of the Reichsvereinigung. The Reichsvereinigung still exists. It has not been disbanded. Accordingly, the Reich finance bureaucracy will initially assume only the administration of these assets. . . . Taking over the administration of the assets of the Reichsvereinigung includes neither the administration of the assets of second parties, handled up to now by the Reichsvereinigung, nor the running of any enterprises still being maintained for Jews, such as hospitals, old age homes and the like. Such institutions will continue to be operated by the Reichsvereinigung. . . . Likewise, the administration of the assets of the Reichsvereinigung does not include the implementation of welfare measures for Jews, such as payment of relief aid. There are contact persons for these purposes, and Jews can turn to them.[95]

There is no doubt that this decree was referring to the "Rump-Reichsvereinigung," which existed from the summer of 1943 to the end of the war and had its offices in the Jewish Hospital on Iranische Strasse in Berlin. It was led by the former head of the medical department in Berlin police headquarters, Dr. Walter Lustig. Lustig was director of the health section of the Reichsvereinigung until 1943. Because he lived in a "privileged" mixed marriage, he was the only member of the executive board of the Reichsvereinigung who was not deported. Lustig was appointed by the Gestapo to head the residual hulk of the Reichsvereinigung. According to all that is known about him, he was a willing tool of the Gestapo. For this reason, he was executed by the Russians in 1945.[96] This residual Reichsvereinigung, which provided services for only a few thousand Jews, generally *Mischlinge* or in some way "privileged" by Nazi law, cannot be considered the Jewish successor organization to the Reichsvereinigung. There are no documents regarding the funds available to it, but they can have been only a small remainder of the former assets of the Reichsvereinigung proper.

How much this total sum amounted to after the conclusion of the mass deportations in the summer of 1943 is not known. H. G. Adler, in a voluminous and carefully documented chapter on the "material exploitation of deportation," has attempted to investigate the transactions concerning these assets conducted between the Gestapo and the Reich finance bureaucracy. There is no need to reiterate his conclusions here. However, future research will probably confirm Adler's general finding:

> [The RSHA] . . . or, a formally less accurate but objectively more apt description—Himmler's SS bureaucracy . . . in contrast with all other offices or other institutions of the state and the Party, had, after 1938, the but barely restricted and jealously guarded privilege of exercising direct power [and terror] over Jews. So that it was easy for this bureaucracy, at its discretion, to extort money and other valuables from the persecuted. And, in any event, to pocket whatever was necessary for "all purposes connected with the solution of the Jewish question."[97]

It is completely pointless in the framework of this study to examine what portion of Jewish property and capital remained to line the pockets of the Gestapo and its industrious individual officials and how much was forfeited and reverted "legally" to the treasury of the Nazi state. In any case, what was involved was only a fraction of the assets that German Jews had originally owned in 1933. The far larger proportion had ended up in the hands of the German *Volksgemeinschaft* in the earlier stages, always legitimated by the state authorities. Numerous *Volksgenossen* had been able to reap personal gains as a result of the "Aryanizations." The Reich Flight Tax revenues, *Sühneleistung* payments, and other special taxes had channeled a further portion into the state coffers. The party and its various formations, including the SA and SS, who ran the concentration camps, had also gotten their share of the spoils.

From the small remainder that had not been stolen from them, Jews—under the harsh supervision of the Gestapo—had been able to eke out a meager existence. After their deportation to the extermination camps, everything could then be finally incorporated, with diabolical consistency, into the body of the German *Volksvermögen*. Now this not only encompassed the movable possessions or real estate of the Jews, their money, houses, and businesses but their shoes and suitcases as well, their eyeglasses and gold teeth. And even their hair, supplied to the German "*Volk* economy" by the SS Main Office of Economy and Administration as part of *Werteerfassung,* the "inventorying of utilizable materials."

Conclusion

> They took away their professions, stole their possessions. They were no longer allowed to inherit or bequeath. They were forbidden from sitting on park benches, or keeping a pet canary. They weren't allowed to use public transportation, or go to restaurants, movie houses, theaters or concerts. Special racial laws were introduced for them, they were stripped of all civil rights and freedom of movement. Their human rights and human dignity were trampled under. Until their final deportation to the gas chambers. . . . In order to carry out this program of annihilation, based on racial insanity and rapacious greed, an enormous bureaucracy was built up within the government service, the NSDAP and the various occupational organizations. . . . This bureaucracy of annihilation spread like a cancer, gradually engulfing all sections of the entire state bureaucracy. Its creators and executive organs were obsessed with the idea of legitimation. They believed they were not murderers—if they could but camouflage their crimes against Jewish citizens in the cloak of "legality," packaging every misdeed against Jews in the form of ordinances, decrees, legal orders and the like.[1]

In these few short sentences, Robert Kempner, with unsurpassed conciseness, has placed the complex of anti-Jewish measures in Germany within the broader historical context of the mass murder of Jews during World War II. In 1933, there were just under half a million Jews living in Germany, only a fraction over 5 percent of European Jewry. Nearly one third of them were murdered during the war, amounting to something in excess of 2 percent of all Jews exterminated. The possessions stolen from the German Jews were only a small portion of the spoils pilfered in a monstrous predatory campaign. This spoliation included the expropriation of Jewish assets, the exploitation of Jewish labor, and finally, the "extraction of their ultimate utility" in the work and extermination camps. However, even if their numbers are small in comparison to the magnitude of the total number exterminated, the fate of the German Jews, as in earlier periods in modern Jewish history, had a far greater significance. They served as in a laboratory, the objects on which to test and develop the necessary methods and train the "experts" in their use. Without these methods, the ultimate implementation of the genocidal murder of the Jews, so perfected and precise in administrative terms, would not have been possible.

Yet it was not only the "bureaucracy of annihilation" and its "legal" framework that were created in Germany between 1933 and 1939. In addition, "some one million German speakers, who were directly involved with the extermination of the Jews—not counting their relatives," as Rudolf Augstein wrote in 1986,[2] were also "preprogrammed" for the future atrocities. The economic measures aimed at exclusion and displacement described in this study likewise contributed to such a programming of the population. Like the massive social and human discrimination inflicted on them, the gradual but systematic and consistent economic despoliation of Jews took place in public—before the eyes of millions of Germans from all social classes and involving their lucrative complicity. As a result, the special status of Jews was gradually fixed in "*Volk* consciousness" and the "*Volk* morality" was liberated from traditional moral compunctions. Not until after the Jews had been expelled from the all-embracing and all-justifying *Volksgemeinschaft* and had been duly labeled "enemies of the people" did it become possible to exclude them from the human community as well. Placed on a level with rats and vermin, they were then subjected to the corresponding *Sonderbehandlung*. From the ranks of those "frolicsome schoolkids out for a holiday romp" who enlivened the boycott against the Jews on German streets in the summer of 1933 came the later recruits, burdened by so few hesitations or scruples, for the execution squads of the Einsatzgruppen storming through the East.

NOTES

See Bibliography for full reference citations and expansions of abbreviations.

Introduction

1. See Toury, *Geschichte,* p. 69ff. and passim; Prinz, passim.
2. Silbergleit, p. 61f.
3. Schmelz, p. 37f. According to the 1910 census, there were 615,000 Jews within the borders of the Reich at that time, including some 34,700 in Alsace-Lorraine and 40,500 in Posen–West Prussia. The increase that continued until 1925 can be accounted for in part by the internal migration to the center of the Reich, a population shift that had gotten underway even before World War I.
4. See Lowenstein, "Modernisation," p. 41ff.; idem, "Rural Community," p. 218ff. Monika Richarz is currently preparing a detailed study on rural Jews in Baden-Württemberg, focusing on cattle trade and the agrarian crisis.
5. *RV/Arb.* 1937, p. 4; see also Birnbaum, p. 88f.
6. See Barkai, "Weimar," p. 331ff.; Barkai, *Aspekte,* p. 248f.
7. Schmelz, p. 56; Silbergleit, p. 61.
8. *DR/Stat.* 451/5, p. 9. The cities: Berlin, Frankfurt am Main, Breslau, Hamburg, Cologne, Leipzig, Munich, Dresden, Essen, and Dortmund.
9. Official census and occupational survey data as calculated by Kahn, "Schichtung," p. 57. Bennathan (p. 104) arrived at somewhat different estimates for the area of the Reich on the basis of the figures for Prussia and Saxony. The calculation made by Herbert Kahn in the framework of the Statistics Office of the Reichsvertretung in 1936 are the only figures that gather together the scattered results of the 1925 census for the entire Reich.
10. Kahn, "Handwerk," p. 3.
11. Genschel, p. 283 (statistical appendix, based on official census and occupational survey data).
12. Schmelz, p. 66.
13. Bennathan, p. 126.
14. See, e.g., Lestschinsky, *Schicksal,* p. 130.
15. Genschel, p. 283; Schmelz, p. 66. On the rise in the number of Jewish working women, see also Lestschinsky, *Schicksal,* p. 134; Richarz, vol. 3, p. 19; Kaplan, 176ff.
16. Marcus, "Lage," p. 26ff. Marcus advanced the same view, though less ada-

mantly, in his 1931 book (see Marcus, *Krise*). See also Niewyk, *Weimar,* p. 20ff. Margalioth, "Occupational Restructuring," p. 101ff.; Bermann, passim.

17. Schmelz, p. 64.
18. *DR/Stat.* 451/5, p. 25f.
19. In the German census of occupations and enterprises, all independent commercial units—ranging from banks to the independent practice of a physician or attorney to the itinerant business of the peddler or that of independent salesmen and agents—were classified as an "enterprise" (*Betrieb*). The 1925 occupational census listed 132,000 Jewish self-employed, more than 90 percent of which were defined as "proprietors and leaseholders." Taking into consideration a certain number of partnerships and corporations, I consider the estimate of approximately 100,000 to be accurate.
20. See Menes, *JWSP,* vol. 3 (1932), p. 87ff. and the discussion on p. 298ff. and 421ff.
21. Niewyk, "Impact," p. 20. See also the commentary by G. D. Feldmann, ibid., p. 38f.
22. Ibid., p. 24.
23. *JWSP,* vol. 3 (1932), p. 153f.
24. Niewyk, "Impact," p. 30; *JWSP,* vol. 3 (1932), p. 62.
25. Calculations based on figures in the *Allgemeine Viehhandelszeitung,* 1929/30. I am grateful to Dr. Monika Richarz for this reference.
26. In detail in Marcus, *Krise.*
27. All figures according to Kahn, "Einzelhandel." This investigation, based on a survey in 69 large communities, was issued by the Statistics Office of the Reichsvertretung in mimeographed form in February 1934. The author had been director of the Commerce Research Section until 1933 and was familiar with the material. The survey design and statistical evaluation are highly professional, and the findings have been confirmed by other sources. A copy of this rare document can be found in the library of Yad Vashem, Jerusalem.
28. See Barkai, "Industrialisation," p. 143f.
29. To mention only two examples: K. Zielenziger, *Juden in der deutschen Wirtschaft: Vom Ghettohändler zum Wirtschaftsführer* (Berlin, 1930); D. Bernstein in S. Katznelson, ed. *Juden im deutschen Kulturbereich* (Berlin, 1958), pp. 720–797. The latter is a "survey of accomplishments" of prominent German Jews from all spheres of endeavor; it was published in early 1933 but had been confiscated by the Gestapo. It was expanded by the editor and republished in Jerusalem 25 years later.
30. See Marcus, *Krise,* passim; Toury, *Textilunternehmer,* passim; E. Landsberg, "Die Beteiligung der Juden an der Montanindustrie," *Der Morgen* 3(1927); 201ff.; idem, "Die Juden in der Textilindustrie," ibid., p. 99ff.; G. Buer, "Die Beteiligung der Juden an der Eisen- und Metallwirtschaft," ibid., p. 86ff.
31. S. Friedländer in E. Jackel, J. Rohwer, eds., *Der Mord an den Juden im Zweiten Weltkrieg* (Stuttgart, 1985), p. 48.
32. Hitler, *Mein Kampf,* 291st to 295th printing (Munich, 1938), p. 344.
33. Ibid., p. 54.

34. G. Feder, *Die Juden* (Munich, 1933), p. 7.
35. G. Feder, *Das Programm der NSDAP und seine weltanschaulichen Grundgedanken* (Munich, 1932), p. 45.
36. *Mein Kampf,* p. 209ff. See Barkai, *Wirtschaftssystem,* p. 26f.
37. For the early period, see especially M. H. Kater, "Zur Soziographie der frühen NSDAP," *VfZ* 19(1971): 139f.
38. Ibid., p. 136.
39. See H. A. Winkler in W. Schieder, ed., *Faschismus als soziale Bewegung* (Hamburg, 1976), p. 97ff.
40. Kater, in Schieder, op. cit., p. 27.
41. R. F. Hamilton, *Who Voted for Hitler?* (Princeton, N.J., 1982) demonstrates in particular the influx of voters from the bourgeois middle classes. J. W. Falter, "Wer verhalf Hitler zum Sieg," in *Aus Politik und Zeitgeschichte,* vols. 28 and 29 (1979), notes a similar development among the working classes.
42. T. Childers, *The Nazi Voter: The Social Foundations of Fascism in Germany 1919–1933* (Chapel Hill, N.C., and London, 1983) expands on this view, using statistical analyses that are somewhat difficult to follow. His presentation of the NSDAP election propaganda aimed at the occupational interests of various voter strata is convincing; see p. 11 and passim.
43. Winkler, op. cit., p. 99.
44. Falter, op. cit., p. 19. Likewise, Winkler, op. cit., p. 98f. and W. S. Allen, *Central European History,* 12(1984); Special Issue: Who Voted for Hitler?, p. 54ff.

CHAPTER I
1933: Consolidation of Power and Boycott of the Jews

1. See S. Adler-Rudel, *Ostjuden in Deutschland 1880–1940* (Tübingen, 1959). For the Nazi period, see especially Maurer, p. 190ff., which emphasizes the difference between the "legal" considerations regarding the foreign status of the Eastern Jews and everyday bureaucratic practice.
2. Affidavit, Julius Rosenfeld, in Knipping, p. 25f.
3. Buchloh, p. 131. See similar descriptions from other localities in Drobisch, p. 78f.; Krausnick, p. 311f.; Düwell, p. 83f.
4. See Barkai, *Wirtschaftssystem,* p. 87ff. On the Kampfbund für den gewerblichen Mittelstand, see entry for "NS-HAGO" in glossary.
5. Adam, p. 47f.
6. Ball-Kaduri, p. 49f.
7. H. A. Winkler, in Martin-Schulin, p. 283.
8. B. Martin, in Martin-Schulin, p. 299.
9. HStaA Düsseldorf, Reg. Aachen, 211/23883.
10. Uhlig, p. 52f., 115ff.
11. Order of the Party direction of the NSDAP, dated March 28, 1933; in Scheffler, p. 69f.
12. Ibid., p. 69. See also Schleunes, p. 75f.; *Wiener Library Bulletin* 14(1960): 14; Bauer, p. 104f.

13. *Berliner Börsen-Zeitung,* 31 March 1933.
14. *Frankfurter Zeitung,* 1 April 1933, in *Das Schwarzbuch: Tatsachen und Dokumente* (Paris, 1934), p. 305f.
15. Drobisch, p. 85f.; Knipping, p. 30; Buchloh, p. 135. For Berlin, the personal recollections of the author. See also K. Sabatzky, in Richarz, vol. 3, p. 293; Genschel, p. 52f.
16. Ball-Kaduri, p. 86.
17. Richarz, vol. 3, p. 104.
18. Schleunes, p. 70ff.
19. Adam, p. 61.
20. Herzfeld, in Ball-Kaduri, p. 81f.
21. *Jüdische Rundschau,* 17 March 1933 and 28 March 1933: Kundgebungen der Zionistischen Vereinigung für Deutschland (ZVfD); ibid., 28 March 1933, and *C.V. Zeitung,* 30 March 1933; Kundgebungen des Centralvereins deutscher Staatsbürger jüdischen Glaubens (C.V.). See also Genschel, p. 47f.
22. Contrasting with this is the tendentious and speculative description by the American journalist Edwin Black in a recent publication. He claims that a well-organized, worldwide Jewish boycott of German goods would have toppled the Hitler government before the winter of 1933 but that such a boycott was prevented by the Zionists for political considerations. See Black, especially p. 380f.
23. Barkai, *Wirtschaftssystem,* p. 135ff.
24. Krausnick, p. 315f.
25. Genschel, pp. 51, 54.
26. BAK, R 43 II, no. 600, p. 63f.
27. Adam, p. 17.
28. See A. Barkai, "The 'Führer-State': Myth and Reality," *Studies in Contemporary Jewry* 2(1986): 291–298.
29. Herzfeld, p. 8.
30. Walk, I/38. Laws and ordinances are generally cited according to the collection edited by Josef Walk et al. The interested reader will find details there on the original and complete publication of the various individual laws, etc.
31. See Adam, p. 51ff.
32. The individual laws and ordinances in Walk; lawyers and patent attorneys: I/66; doctors in state-supported health insurance programs: I/71; pharmacists: I/72; government employees lacking civil-service status: I/74, 86, 98; university teachers, schoolteachers, notaries public: I/90.
33. Statement by Ludwig Ruge, quoted in Ball-Kaduri, p. 93. See also Herzfeld, and statement by W. Callmann, YVA, 01/142.
34. Conrad Kaiser, YV, 01/25; Ball-Kaduri, p. 97f.
35. Walk, I/20.
36. Ibid., I/35, I/37.
37. ALBI/Jm, no. 11b, *Statistischer Bericht des Zentralausschusses für Hilfe und Aufbau,* no. 516, May 12, 1933. The Central Committee was formed even before the establishment of the Reichsvertretung der deutschen Juden (after 1935: Reichsvertretung der Juden in Deutschland, cited hereafter as Reichsvertre-

tung). After the Reichsvertretung was established, the Central Committee became, for all practical purposes, a section within the Reichsvertretung. Nevertheless, annual reports and other publications in the first few years continued to appear in part under its letterhead. These will generally be quoted as publications of the Reichsvertretung.

38. *RV/Arb.* 1933, p. 32f.; *C.V. Zeitung,* 10 August 1933.
39. Walk, I/90.
40. Blau, "Vierzehn Jahre," p. 23f. (on the biography of Bruno Blau, see Richarz, vol. 3, p. 459); Herzfeld, p. 5f.
41. Blau, "Vierzehn Jahre," p. 26.
42. ALBI/Jm, B 11, 11a, Statist. Abteilung der Reichsvertretung. According to the census of June 16, 1933, there were still 5,557 Jewish doctors in Germany, amounting to just under 11 percent of all doctors in the area of the Reich. See Bennathan, p. 111.
43. See Z. Zofka, "Der KZ-Arzt Josef Mengele: Zur Typologie eines NS-Verbrechers," *VfZ* 34(1986), especially p. 250ff.; M. Kater, "Doctor Leonardo Conti and His Nemesis," *Central European History* 18(1985): 299–325.
44. S. Ostrowski, YVA, 01/16; Ball-Kaduri, p. 45ff.
45. Walk, I/71.
46. Ibid., I/20, I/24; Adam, pp. 49, 67ff.; StA Duisburg, Best. 500, no. 307.
47. *RV/Arb.* 1933, p. 34f.; Adler-Rudel, p. 139.
48. Adler-Rudel, p. 137; *RV/Arb.* 1933, p. 35f.
49. Walk, I/248.
50. Ibid., I/264.
51. Adam, p. 77f.; Genschel, p. 283.
52. The preceding, unless otherwise indicated, according to Bennathan and Schaeffer, principally file No. 26, which contains statistical data and internal material of the Reichsvertretung, along with personal information.
53. Verdict of the Reich Labor Court; Sabatzky, in Richarz, vol. 3, p. 294.
54. *DR/Stat.* 451/5, p. 27.
55. Quoted in Genschel, p. 82.
56. Walk, I/173; GStaA Dahlem, Rep. 151, no. 3576.
57. Thus, for example, in the case of a firm in Essen, which was "Aryanized" in 1937 with the aid of the Gestapo (see pp. 74–75).
58. StA Duisburg, Best. 500, no. 136. In detail in H. Zimmermann, "Untersuchungen zur Geschichte der Duisburger Judengemeinde 1933–1945," unpublished graduate thesis (Staatsexamen), 1969, p. 16ff. (copy in StA Duisburg).
59. Buchloh, p. 108; Genschel, p. 81f.
60. StaA Münster, Reg. Arnsberg, IG/572.
61. Knipping, p. 33f.; similarly in Munich: Hanke, p. 100ff.
62. Herbert Strauss regards these differences as so pronounced that he speaks about "the existence of 'two Jewish economies'" and "the 'two economies' characteristic of the Jews of the period"; see Strauss 1980, p. 345.
63. Margalioth, "Rescue," p. 247f.; Rosenstock, p. 377; Strauss 1981, p. 348f.
64. Knipping, p. 161ff.

65. StaA Münster, Reg. Arnsberg, IG/573.
66. Lestschinsky, *Schicksal,* p. 63. On the Prussian State Association, see Birnbaum, passim.
67. On the activities of the Zentralwohlfahrtsstelle, see its publication *Jüdische Wohlfahrtspflege und Sozialpolitik* (*JWSP*; until 1930: *Zeitschrift für jüdische Wohlfahrtspflege*). The volumes of this journal are an indispensable source of information for all social-historical research in this area.
68. *Gemeindeblatt der Jüdischen Gemeinde zu Berlin* 23(1933), no. 4. Elbogen's essay in *C. V. Zeitung,* 4 April 1933, quoted here according to *Jüdische Emigration,* p. 42.
69. See Ball-Kaduri, p. 136ff.; Herzfeld, p. 11ff.; Max Gruenewald, "The Beginning of the 'Reichsvertretung,'" *YLBI* 1(1956): 57–67.
70. Gruenewald, op. cit.
71. On the first organizational efforts, see Adler-Rudel, p. 10ff.; *Haavara-Transfer,* pp. 11, 15f.
72. *Gemeindeblatt der jüdischen Gemeinde zu Berlin* 23(1933), no. 5 (May).
73. *C.V. Zeitung,* 15 September 1933.
74. Richarz, vol. 3, p. 222f.
75. Szanto, *Erinnerungen,* p. 133f.
76. Richarz, vol. 3, p. 247f.
77. Leibfried, p. 20ff.
78. Adler-Rudel, p. 139ff.
79. *RV/Arb.* 1933, p. 21f.
80. *JWSP,* 1933/34, pp. 123ff., 215ff.
81. Ibid., p. 113.
82. Szanto, *Erinnerungen,* p. 153f.
83. Schaeffer, file no. 26.
84. Ibid., Szanto, *Erinnerungen,* p. 150ff.
85. *C.V. Zeitung,* 15 September 1933.
86. Wirtschaftshilfe der jüdischen Gemeinde Berlin, Wiener Library, Tel Aviv, PC3/4, no. 4. The official exchange rate of the reichsmark was pegged early during the Nazi period at an overvalued RM 2.5 to the U.S. dollar (instead of the long-standing rate of 4.2 to the dollar) but was manipulated in an extremely complex manner, resulting in a panoply of multiple rates, depending on type of transaction. Cf. Howard S. Ellis, *Exchange Control in Central Europe* (Cambridge, Mass., 1941), especially pp. 233–242. Also Gustav Stolper et al., *The Germany Economy: 1870 to the Present* (New York, 1967), especially p. 329 (chart).
87. See Barkai, *Wirtschaftssystem,* p. 136f.
88. Rosenstock, p. 378f.; Strauss 1980, p. 345; Strauss 1981, p. 348f.
89. HStaA Düsseldorf, Gestapo-Akten (RW 58), no. 23 201.
90. CZA, L51/527.
91. The Hebrew word for "transfer" (*haavara*) was also the official term in the German documents.
92. *Haavara-Transfer,* p. 21ff.
93. Ibid., pp. 19, 51. A detailed discussion of the Haavara Agreement in the

Jewish public and press abroad preceded the Zionist Congress decision. One of the initiators, the head of the Political Department of the Jewish Agency, Haim Arlosoroff, was murdered in June 1933, a case that has never been fully cleared up. Within the Jewish public, his murder was associated, most probably incorrectly, with the negotiations on Haavara. In any event, these public debates and discussions, as well as the later literature, prove just how misleading the subtitle of Black's book (*The Untold Story of the Secret Agreement . . .*) is. It is just as untrue that the story was "untold" as that the Haavara Agreement was "secret" in nature. Therefore, it remains astonishing that a reputable publisher engaged in such a sensationalist promotion campaign for the book and indeed stooped to publish the volume at all.

94. *Haavara-Transfer,* p. 26.
95. Ibid., p. 22.

CHAPTER 2
1934–1937: The Illusion of a "Grace Period"

1. *RV/Arb.* 1937, p. 4; Rosenstock, p. 377; Strauss 1980, p. 326.
2. The figures are based on calculations by Phiebig 1936, pp. 23–28; *DR/Stat.* 1939, p. 85; Joint 1936, pp. 5, 36.
3. BAK, R 58, no. 994.
4. Walk, I/354.
5. Ibid., I/391.
6. Ibid., I/517. See also World Jewish Congress 1937, p. 37; Genschel, pp. 90, 116ff.
7. For example, see Genschel, p. 108f.; Adam, p. 114f.
8. Walk, I/636.
9. Ibid., II/46; 140.
10. On this and the following, see Genschel, p. 108ff.; Hanke, p. 127f.; Knipping, p. 51f.
11. Quoted in Knipping, p. 54f. The "NS-Hago (Nationalsozialistische Handwerks-, Handels- und Gewerbeorganisation), which replaced the Kampfbund für den gewerblichen Mittelstand after its official disbandment in August 1933, was the most militant instigator of the middle-class anti-Jewish boycott.
12. Ibid., p. 55.
13. Quoted in Hanke, p. 139, on which this presentation is largely based.
14. Ibid., p. 130.
15. Adam, p. 172f.
16. W. A. Boelcke, *Die deutsche Wirtschaft 1930–1945* (Düsseldorf, 1983), p. 210.
17. *IMT,* vol. 12, p. 490f. See also Genschel, p. 106; Pätzold, *Faschismus,* p. 229ff.
18. *IMT,* vol. 12, p. 491f., quoted in Genschel, p. 106.
19. Genschel, p. 106, n. 4.
20. Hjalmar Schacht, *76 Jahre meines Lebens* (Bad Wörishofen, 1953), p. 450.
21. Genschel, p. 105ff.
22. See Adam, p. 122ff.

23. *IMT*, vol. 12, p. 638. The presentation by Genschel, p. 112ff., is also based on the Nuremberg documents, especially NG 4067, nos. I and II.
24. Transcription of B. Lösener, *Rassereferent* (racial expert) in the Interior Ministry, quoted in *Jüdische Emigration*, p. 71f.
25. Hanke, p. 157.
26. Heinz Pentzlin, *Hjalmar Schacht: Leben und Wirken einer umstrittenen Persönlichkeit* (Berlin, 1980), p. 250. The memorandum of May 3, 1935, is also quoted according to this book (p. 180). My thanks to Professor Carl L. Holtfrerich for this reference.
27. Barkai, *Wirtschaftssystem*, p. 39f. Especially useful data on the role of the district economic advisors in ousting Jews from the economy and Aryanizations can be found in the extensive files in the State Archives of North-Rhine Westphalia, Münster.
28. *Westfälische Landeszeitung*, 3 May 1936; *Frankfurter Zeitung*, 17 April 1936.
29. Muellerheim, p. 14.
30. Ibid.; World Jewish Congress 1937, p. 80; *Rheinisch-Westfälische Zeitung*, 3 October 1935.
31. StaA Münster, Reg. Arnsberg, no. 679; 11059.
32. Ibid., IG/573 no. 2428.
33. Ibid., IG/574 no. 1106.
34. Ibid.; for 1935–36: IG/572; for 1937: IG/574.
35. Forschungsstelle für die Geschichte des Nationalsozialismus in Hamburg, A/6263; also YVA, JM 2245.
36. See Genschel, p. 139f.; Adam, p. 359f.
37. *RV/Arb.* 1936, p. 120f.; Wiener Library, Jewish Central Information Office, Amsterdam: Keine jüdischen Rechtsanwälte mehr in Deutschland (PC 3/61).
38. Walk, II/82; Muellerheim, p. 13.
39. HStaA Düsseldorf, RW 58, no. 51003.
40. *RV*, annual reports, 1934–1936; Adler-Rudel, p. 137; YVA, 01/25.
41. Adam, p. 132; *Frankfurter Zeitung*, 24 September 1935.
42. World Jewish Congress 1937, p. 31; Adler-Rudel, p. 132.
43. Representative of many press reports: *Israelitisches Familienblatt*, 26 March 1936; *Frankfurter Zeitung*, 17 September 1936, 20 October 1936; *Germania*, 18 October 1936; *Der Gemeindetag*, 5 January 1937; *JWSP*, 1933/34, p. 219ff.
44. Walk I/172, 198.
45. Maurer, p. 195ff.
46. My estimate is based on the census and occupational survey of June 1933, data in Bennathan, Marcus, *Krise* (1931), and the figures calculated in the Statistics Office of the Reichsvertretung; and in particular the studies cited by Herbert Kahn on retail trade (1934) and Jewish crafts (1936).
47. Quoted in Genschel, p. 125; see also *Jüdische Rundschau*, 1 November 1935.
48. Walk, II/453.
49. HStaA Düsseldorf, RW 58, no. 38379.
50. *Israelitisches Familienblatt*, 24 December 1936.
51. Ibid., 12 February 1936.
52. BAK, NS 10, no. 172, fol. 72; quoted in Pätzold, *Verfolgung*, p. 98.

53. On secret collections: Wiener Library, PC 3/54, for 1934. Likewise, openly discussed recommendations somewhat later: *Deutsche Allgemeine Zeitung,* 25 September 1935; *Frankfuter Zeitung,* 3 November 1935. On the close cooperation between the DEAs and the administrative offices in keeping Jewish enterprises under common observation: StaA Münster, Gauwirtschaftsberater, no. 788; see also Lestschinsky, *Zusammenbruch,* p. 21ff.; Schleunes, p. 143ff.
54. The fifth department store chain, Karstadt AG, had also belonged in part to Jewish stockowners. However, the majority stock holdings had passed to the banks, to which the firm was heavily indebted, during the economic crisis. The previous Jewish director, Schoendorff, had only 12 percent of the stock left in his hands, and he apparently sold this fairly early. This data is from an informative newspaper article: "Wem gehören die Warenhäuser?," *Danziger Vorposten,* 8 September 1936. See also Uhlig, *Die Warenhäuser im Dritten Reich* (Cologne, 1956), p. 210f. On Schocken, see Moses, p. 85f.
55. On Erfurt: Wiener Library, no. 542; on Duisburg: HStaA Düsseldorf, RW 58, no. 53782.
56. Toury, *Textilunternehmer,* p. 241ff.; on Berlin, see U. Westphal, "Der 'eigene deutsche Stil' und deutsche Traditionen," *Tageszeitung* (Berlin), 14 August 1985.
57. Details in Genschel, p. 99f.
58. Ibid., p. 103.
59. On Hamburg: Genschel, p. 99ff.; on Essen: HStaA Düsseldorf, RW 58, nos. 27548, 55028, 61516.
60. Nürnberger Dokumente, NI 3254; see Hilberg, p. 76ff.; Drobisch, p. 166.
61. Details in Genschel, p. 218.
62. Lestschinsky, *Zusammenbruch*; detailed in "Vom grossen Raubzug," *Neue Welt,* Vienna, 8 September 1936.
63. *Kölnische Zeitung,* 13 October 1935.
64. See H. D. Kirchholtes, *Jüdische Privatbanken in Frankfurt a. M.* (Frankfurt, 1966), p. 69ff.
65. YVA, 01/137; *Israelitisches Familienblatt,* 13 February 1936; *Jüdische Rundschau,* 3 December 1935.
66. Rosenbaum, p. 121ff.; Sherman, p. 170f.
67. The worry of the party offices was manifested in the exchange of the district leadership in North Westphalia; StaA Münster, nos. 10 (1935), 25 (1937). On the true situation of the Jewish representatives, see *Israelitisches Familienblatt,* 5 March 1936.
68. *C.V. Zeitung,* 19 December 1936; *Israelitisches Familienblatt,* 14 November 1935.
69. Sabatzky, in Richarz, vol. 3, p. 293; see also Weil, ibid., p. 271.
70. *RV/Arb.* 1936, p. 103; see also Adler-Rudel, p. 121ff.; Szanto, "Economic Aid," p. 208f.; Szanto and Löwenberg, in Richarz, vol. 3, pp. 221, 246f.
71. This presentation based on the following: Margalioth, "Tendencies," p. 345f.; Szanto, *Erinnerungen,* p. 134; Adler-Rudel, p. 124f.; *C.V. Zeitung,* 7 November 1935; *RV/Inf.,* no. 12, December 1936, p. 127f.; Bauer, p. 130f. Likewise, the information sheets and annual reports of the Reichsvertretung generally, 1934 to 1937.

72. *C.V. Zeitung,* 23 April 1936.
73. German name: Gesellschaft zur Förderung wirtschaflicher Interessen von in Deutschland wohnhaften oder wohnhaft gewesenen Juden m.b.H. See the following: *RV/Arb.* 1935; *RV/Inf.,* no. 3–4 (1936); YVA, 01/273.
74. Council, 1937, p. 7.
75. Margalioth, "Tendencies," p. 348f.
76. *RV/Arb.* 1934–37; see Poppel, *Salman Schocken and the Schocken Verlag, YLBI* 17(1972): 93ff.; M. T. Edelheim-Mühsam, "The Jewish Press in Germany," *YLBI* 1(1956): 163ff.; E. Simon, "Jewish Adult Education in Germany as Spiritual Resistance," *YLBI* 1(1956): 68ff.
77. "Die jüdische Presse als Wirtschaftsspiegel," *Israelitisches Familienblatt,* 2 April 1937.
78. *RV/Arb.* 1934, p. 59f.; 1936, p. 102f.; Adler-Rudel, p. 133ff.; Szanto, *Erinnerungen,* p. 137f.; idem, "Economic Aid," p. 221f.
79. *C.V. Zeitung,* 24 April 1936, 11 June 1936, 25 June 1936, 6 August 1936, 7 May 1937: *Jüdische Rundschau,* 25 June 1937.
80. Jüdische Gemeinde Berlin, *Verwaltungsbericht für das Jahr 1937,* p. 24.
81. Moses, p. 81; H. G. Reissner, "The Histories of 'Kaufhaus N. Israel' and of Wilfried Israel," *YLBI,* 3(1958): 247f.
82. *RV/Arb.* 1935, p. 105f.; *RV/Arb.* 1936, p. 117f.; *JWSP,* 1937, p. 7ff.
83. *Israelitisches Familienblatt,* 23 April 1936.
84. Kaplan, p. 182ff.; *RV/Arb.* 1935, p. 108f.; *RV/Arb.* 1936, p. 121f.; *C.V. Zeitung,* 10 October 1935, 23 April 1936; *Israelitisches Familienblatt,* 9 January 1936.
85. *C.V. Zeitung,* 5 December 1935, 19 December 1935.
86. *Jüdische Rundschau,* 26 May 1936; *Israelitisches Familienblatt,* 24 December 1936.
87. Walk, II/42.
88. *JWSP,* 1937, p. 1ff.
89. Walk, I/323; see also *RV/Inf.,* 2 September 1934.
90. Walk, I/473.
91. Adler-Rudel, p. 50; *RV/Arb.* 1934/II, p. 61; *C.V. Zeitung,* 5 July 1934, 19 July 1934.
92. *Israelitisches Familienblatt,* 3 December 1936, 17 June 1937; *C.V. Zeitung,* 8 October 1936, 17 December 1936.
93. *RV/Inf.* no. 1–2 (Jan.–Feb.) 1936.
94. Adler-Rudel, p. 147f.
95. *Aliyah,* Hebrew for "ascent," is the Zionist term for immigration to the land of Israel.
96. Szanto and Löwenberg, in Richarz, vol. 3, pp. 224f., 249f.; Szanto, *Erinnerungen,* p. 157f.; *Jüdische Rundschau,* 20 September 1935.
97. *RV/Arb.* 1935, p. 142f.; 1936, p. 144f.
98. *RV/Richtlinien für die Berufsausbildung* (ab 1.1.1937 gültig), p. 13f.
99. *RV/Arb.* 1937, Finanzbericht (Anlage), pp. 37, 91; *RV/Arb.* 1938, p. 37.
100. G. van Tijn, "Werkdorp Nieuwesluis," *YLBI,* 14(1969): 182–199.
101. N. Bentwich, *They Found Refuge* (London, 1956), p. 91; quoted in Adler-Rudel, p. 71.

102. Richarz, vol. 3, p. 250 (Löwenberg): *Jüdische Rundschau,* 20 July 1937.
103. Wollheim (transcription), p. 2; *RV/Arb.* 1935, p. 124f.; *RV/Arb.* 1936, p. 146f.; *RV/Arb.* 1937, p. 87f.; Szanto, *Erinnerungen,* p. 155f.
104. *RV/Inf.* 1936, nos. 10–11, 12; *RV/Inf.* 1937, no. 1–2; *Israelitisches Familienblatt,* 27 February 1936; 1 April 1937.
105. Calculated according to *RV/Inf.* 1938, no. 5–6; Adler-Rudel, p. 48.
106. *DR/Stat.* 451/5, p. 17.
107. Phiebig 1938, p. 138; *RV/Arb.* 1938, p. 37.
108. *JWSP,* 1938, p. 7.
109. Szanto, in Richarz, vol. 3, p. 226f.; see also Barkai, "Weimar," p. 336.
110. See Angress, *Jüdische Jugend,* especially p. 55ff.
111. Szanto, in Richarz, vol. 3, p. 225ff.; *JWSP,* 1937, p. 173f.
112. *JWSP,* 1937, p. 55.
113. Angress, *Gross-Breesen,* p. 185; idem, *Jüdische Jugend,* p. 64ff.
114. An order in this connection was not issued until after the November 1938 pogrom (Walk, III/20). On the previously customary procedures, see *RV/Arb.* 1935, p. 45; Hanke, p. 263f.; Adler-Rudel, p. 159f.
115. Hanke, p. 263f.
116. Adam, pp. 133, 191ff.
117. Strauss 1980, p. 342; Adler-Rudel, p. 161f.; Bauer, p. 125; *RV/Arb.* 1935, p. 49.
118. Adler-Rudel, p. 166f.
119. Calculations based on the annual reports of the Reichsvertretung. See also A. Kober, "Jewish Communities in Germany from the Age of the Enlightenment to Their Destruction by the Nazis," *Jewish Social Studies* 9(1947): 227.
120. Adler-Rudel, p. 168.
121. Figures for 1932: G. Lotan (G. Lubinsky), "The Zentralwohlfahrtsstelle," *YLBI* 4(1959): 198; for 1937: Phiebig 1938.
122. Walk I/636.
123. *RV/Inf.* 1935, no. 10–11, p. 94.
124. *Frankfurter Israelitisches Gemeindeblatt,* 14(2) (November 1935).
125. Adler-Rudel, p. 164f.; Strauss 1980, p. 341; G. Lotan, in Strauss 1980, p. 205f.; Hamburg, Wiener Library, PC 3/9.
126. *Israelitisches Familienblatt,* 7 October 1936; see also Maurer, p. 202f.
127. Adler-Rudel, p. 42ff.; *RV/Inf.* 1938, no. 5–6; *C.V. Zeitung,* 16 April 1936, 26 August 1937; *Israelitisches Familienblatt,* 27 May 1937.
128. *Israelitisches Familienblatt,* 29 April 1937, 14 October 1937; *C.V. Zeitung,* 23 January 1936; *Jüdische Rundschau,* 21 January 1936.
129. *Israelitisches Familienblatt,* 8 April 1937; see also *RV/Arb.* 1936, p. 63f.; 1937, p. 43f.
130. The following account of the Flight Tax is based mainly on official data and their evaluation by Hilberg, p. 90f., and by Feilchenfeld, Michaelis, and Pinner, *Haavara-Transfer.* According to the *Frankfurter Zeitung,* 15 June 1937, a total of RM 173 million was collected in Flight Tax revenues to the end of 1936.

131. BAK, R 18, no. 5514, pp. 199–211; quoted in *Jüdische Emigration,* p. 211.
132. IfZ, F71/3, Fasz. 5, fol. 229ff., quoted in *Jüdische Emigration,* p. 213.
133. *Jüdische Emigration,* p. 214; IfZ, F71/3, Fasz. 5, fol. 228f.; quoted ibid.
134. *Bericht über Palästina-Ägypten-Reise, Eichmann und Hagen,* 4 November 1937, quoted ibid., pp. 219f.
135. *Haavara-Transfer,* p. 74f.
136. CZA, p. 25/9810.
137. *Haavara-Transfer,* p. 44f.
138. Margalioth, "Reaction," p. 81f.; Bauer, p. 182f.
139. *Haavara-Transfer,* p. 79f.; Herzfeld, p. 30 and appendix.
140. Council 1936, p. 10f.; *Haavara-Transfer,* p. 61ff.
141. Angress, Gross-Breesen, p. 181f.; M. H. Mayer, *Ein Frankfurter Rechtsanwalt wird Kaffeepflanzer im Urwald Brasiliens: Bericht eines Emigranten, 1938–1975* (Frankfurt am Main, 1975); personal communication from Dr. Geert Koch-Weser to Dr. A. Margalioth, October 15, 1985.
142. *Haavara-Transfer,* p. 93. The maximum estimate for 1933 is from Ludwig Pinner, "Vermögenstransfer nach Palästina 1933–1934, in *In Zwei Welten: Siegfried Moses zum 75. Geburtstag* (Tel Aviv, 1962), p. 166. Herbert Strauss quotes an informed estimate of total Jewish assets in 1933 at "10 billion RM and probably considerably more," which he believes is too low; see Strauss, 1980, p. 342, n. 58.
143. BAK, R2/4863.
144. Walk, II/468.
145. *New York Times,* 19 August 1936, 9 September 1936.
146. *RV/Arb.* 1937, p. 66f.; ALBI/Jm, Adler-Rudel Collection, G/16, p. 5; *Israelitisches Familienblatt,* 2 April 1936, 29 October 1936.
147. Joint 1937; Budget, Reichsvertretung, 1938; *RV/Arb.* 1936, p. 101.
148. Walk, II/138; 374; ALBI/Jm, Adler-Rudel Collection, G/6, p. 2f.
149. *Westdeutscher Beobachter,* 30 October 1935.
150. *Reichspost,* Vienna, 1 December 1935.
151. Quoted in Bauer, p. 136f.
152. Lestschinsky, *Zusammenbruch,* p. 31.

CHAPTER 3
1938: The "Fateful Year"

1. *RV/Arb.* 1938, p. 1f.
2. Ibid., p. 2.
3. The annual report of the Reichsvertretung for 1937 gives a figure of approximately 350,000. I believe the estimate by Strauss of 365,000 is more accurate. See Strauss 1980, p. 326.
4. A. Krüger, *Die Lösung der Judenfrage in der Wirtschaft: Kommentar zur Judengesetzgebung* (Berlin, 1940), p. 44. Genschel lists this source, but nonetheless estimates that only 25 percent of the businesses and a much smaller percentage of manufacturing enterprises had been "Aryanized" by the autumn of 1937 (p. 136). It is possible that the liquidated Jewish firms have not been included.

5. *Textil-Zeitung,* 3 December 1938; *Berliner Morgenpost,* 25 November 1938.
6. The following quotations and figures from StaA Münster, Gauwirtschaftsberater Westfalen-Süd, no. 165.
7. Ibid., no. 703.
8. Walk, II/457; 458.
9. GStaA Dahlem, Rep. 151 no. 1658a, RWM, III/Jd. 8910/38, 28 November 1938.
10. See chap. 2, n. 141.
11. W. Treue, "Hitlers Denkschrift zum Vierjahresplan," *VfZ* 3(1955): 210.
12. BAK, R 2, no. 31097. On February 2, 1936, David Frankfurter shot and killed the head of the NSDAP in Switzerland, Wilhelm Gustloff. A Swiss court sentenced Frankfurter to 18 years in prison, but he was pardoned in 1945.
13. BAK, ibid.
14. BAK, R 18, no. 5514, fol. 199–211.
15. Genschel, p. 141.
16. Ibid., p. 144.
17. See Hitler's speech of November 5, 1937, in the well-known "Hossbach Protocol," *IMT,* 25, PS-386.
18. Along with the comprehensive collection of "special legislation" compiled by Walk et al., which gives a brief summary of the content of the various laws, the full texts of the laws as published by Bruno Blau, *Ausnahmegesetzgebung,* and URO are on occasion indispensable. See also Scheffler, p. 27ff.; Genschel, p. 143ff.; Adam, p. 172ff.
19. Walk, II/441, 442, 450, 455.
20. *RV/Arb.* 1938, p. 19f.
21. Walk, II/416, 420, 424, 426.
22. Walk, II/454.
23. *Salzburger Volksblatt,* 25 April 1938.
24. Walk, II/457, Blau, *Ausnahmegesetzgebung,* p. 43ff.
25. Walk, II/458.
26. BAK, R 18, no. 5519, fol. 153–163.
27. Auswärtiges Amt, Bonn, no. 32/179, Akten betr. Judenfrage, 1935–1940, Inland IIg, 169, pp. D520 322–329.
28. BAK, p. 155.
29. GStaA Dahlem, ibid. (see note 9, above).
30. An original copy of the questionnaire can be found in the Wiener Library, Tel Aviv, under PC 3/51.
31. *Foreign Relations of the United States; Diplomatic Papers 1938,* vol. 2, p. 366.
32. Herzfeld, p. 43.
33. Walk, II/487.
34. Walk, II/503.
35. Wiener Library, PC 3/57.
36. Walk, II/500.
37. *Der Aufbau,* 1 January 1938.
38. Walk, II/510.

39. Adam, p. 188.
40. Leibfried, p. 11.
41. Walk, II/547.
42. Wiener Library, PC 3/61.
43. Walk, II/572.
44. Herzfeld, p. 42f.
45. StaA Münster, Gauwirtschaftsberater Westfalen-Süd, no. 778; Walk, II/382, 385.
46. StaA Münster, ibid., no. 139; Hanke, p. 144, 199f.
47. *Schleswig-Holsteinische Landeszeitung,* 25 February 1938; *Neue Freie Presse,* Vienna, 10 March 1938.
48. *NS-Rechtsspiegel,* 8 September 1938. *Rechtswahrer* was a Nazi term introduced for "attorney."
49. BAK, R 58, no. 956: Sicherheitsdienst des RFSS, SD Hauptamt II/112, Zum Judenproblem, January 1937, fol. 9f.
50. Genschel, p. 144f.
51. *Foreign Relations of the United States: Diplomatic Papers 1938,* vol. 2, p. 382.
52. StaA Münster, Gauwirtschaftsberater Westfalen-Süd, no. 681, 682, 788.
53. Ibid., no. 648; Toury, *Textilunternehmer,* p. 250f.; Wiener Library, PC 3/55.
54. *Fränkische Tageszeitung,* 17 September 1938.
55. *National-Zeitung* (Essen), 30 March 1938.
56. Figure for 1935: Kahn, "Handwerk," p. 1; for 1938: *RV/Arb.* 1938, p. 15f.
57. Calculations based on Bennathan, p. 106.
58. Kahn, "Handwerk," p. 1f.
59. *RV/Arb.* 1938, p. 15f.
60. Genschel, p. 218.
61. Ibid., p. 173ff.
62. *RV/Arb.* 1938, p. 15ff.
63. Genschel, p. 247.
64. StaA Münster, Gauwirtschaftsberater Westfalen-Süd, nos. 682, 707; examples in Knipping, p. 74ff.
65. StaA Münster, ibid., no. 707.
66. Communication dated April 16, 1938, to IHK, Munich, quoted in Hanke, p. 154f.
67. Hanke, p. 224.
68. *Fränkische Tageszeitung,* 3 September 1938.
69. StaA Münster, Gauwirtschaftsberater Westfalen-Süd, no. 485.
70. *IMT,* vol. 37, PS-1816.
71. GStaA Dahlem, Rep. 151, no. 1658, p. 58, RWM III Jd., I/2082/39, February 6, 1939.
72. BAK, R 18, no. 3746a: Beauftragter für den Vierjahresplan, St.M.Dev. 1763g, December 28, 1938.
73. YVA, 08/17; pp. 16, 22, 29, 32, 36.
74. *RV/Arb.* 1938, p. 15.
75. S. Milton, "The Expulsion of Polish Jews from Germany: October 1938 to July 1939—Documentation," *YLBI* 29(1984): 169–199.

76. Telegram, signed Heydrich, November 10, 1938, *IMT,* vol. 27, p. 491; see also Scheffler, p. 73ff.
77. *IMT,* vol. 37, PS-1816; Kochan, pp. 107, 131f.
78. Jochen Klepper, *Unter den Schatten Deiner Flügel. Aus den Tagebüchern der Jahre 1932–1942* (Stuttgart, 1956), p. 675f.
79. General Consul Bell, November 14, 1938, in *Papers concerning the Treatment of German Nationals in Germany 1938–39* (London, H.M.S.O., 1939), p. 17.
80. *Berliner Börsen-Zeitung,* November 19, 1938.
81. *IMT,* vol. 37, PS-1301, session of October 14, 1938.
82. Circular, October 28, 1938, published in Adam, p. 183.
83. HStaA Düsseldorf, OFD Düsseldorf, Br. 1026/276, RWM, express letter, August 19, 1938.
84. YVA, 01/249; Scheffler, p. 28f.; Kochan, p. 34.
85. Walk, III/7, 13; Drobisch, p. 602; *IMT,* vol. 37, PS-1301, session of October 14, 1938.
86. "Erste Verordnung zur Ausschaltung der Juden aus dem deutschen Wirtschaftsleben." Cf. Walk, III/8.
87. Walk, III/21; full text in GStaA Dahlem, Rep. 151, no. 2193.
88. Walk, IV/23; GstaA Dahlem, ibid.
89. Hilberg, p. 92.
90. BAK, NS1, Vorl. 430, published in Pätzold, *Verfolgung,* p. 193ff.
91. "Verordnung über den Einsatz des jüdischen Vermögens." Cf. Walk, III/46.
92. Walk, III/132; full text in GStaA Dahlem, Rep. 151, no. 1658a, RWM, III Jd./1/2082/39.
93. Strauss 1980, p. 326; Rosenstock, p. 377.
94. E. Kogon, *Der SS-Staat. Das System der deutschen Konzentrationslager* (Frankfurt am Main, 1965), p. 193f.
95. Call of the Reichsvertretung, quoted according to *RV/Arb.* 1937, p. 109f.
96. *Jüdische Rundschau,* 14 January 1938.
97. *Manchester Guardian,* 28 January 1938; *Die Stimme* (Vienna), 19 January 1938.
98. *Israelitisches Familienblatt,* 14 July 1938, 21 July 1938, 29 September 1938, 27 October 1938; *C.V. Zeitung,* 22 September 1938. See also the warning issued by the Hilfsverein on November 2, 1938, in *Jüdische Emigration,* p. 348; see Toury, *Judenaustreibungen,* p. 171f. on the private initiative of the Gestapo and individual Gestapo officials to smuggle Jews across the "green border" in return for a fee.
99. A. Margalioth, "Emigration," p. 308 and passim.
100. H. Winterfeldt, in Richarz, vol. 3, p. 339f.
101. Friedrich Brodnitz at the conference of the Leo Baeck Institute in Berlin, session of October 29, 1985, afternoon; tape transcript. See also idem, "Memories of the Reichsvertretung: A Personal Report," *YLBI* 31(1986): 276f.
102. Das Neue Tagebuch (Paris) 6(1938): 705f., quoted in *Jüdische Emigration,* p. 207.
103. W. Rosenstock, "Die subjektive Judenfrage," in *Der Morgen,* 13, 516f.
104. *Haavara-Transfer,* p. 90.

105. Rosenstock, p. 386ff.; Strauss 1981, p. 359ff.
106. *Jüdische Emigration,* p. 189ff.
107. *Haavara-Transfer,* pp. 45f., 75.
108. *Jüdische Emigration,* p. 187.
109. Ibid.
110. On the Schacht plant, see Schacht to Dr. Hans Lamm, April 2, 1959, YVA, 01/321; *Akten zur auswärtigen Politik 1918–1945,* series D, vol. 5 (Baden-Baden, 1953), p. 775f.; Jewish Central Information Office, Amsterdam, Memorandum on the Expropriation of German Jewry, January 29, 1939, Wiener Library, PC 116/7. In general on this topic, see Bauer, p. 273ff.; *Jüdische Emigration,* p. 207ff.
111. HStaA Düsseldorf, OFD Düsseldorf, Br. 1026, no. 276.
112. ALBI/NY, Coll. Nationalsozialismus, AR 221.
113. *RV/Arb.* 1938, p. 41f.
114. Düwell, p. 129; BAK, R 58, no. 276, RMI, January 21, 1939; YVA, 08/104b.
115. *Israelitisches Familienblatt,* June 9, 1938.
116. BAK, R 18, no. 3746a, circular letter, December 20, 1938; Walk, III/82.
117. For example, "Jews Disregard Labor Laws," *Völkischer Beobachter,* March 3, 1938.
118. Jüdische Gemeinde, Berlin, *Verwaltungsbericht für das Jahr 1937,* p. 5.
119. *RV/Arb.* 1938, p. 33f.
120. ALBI/NY, Ar-C 1445/3659, letter to Grünfeld, June 21, 1938.
121. For example, "Still 199 Jewish Millionaires in Berlin," *Berliner Nachtausgabe,* November 15, 1938.
122. Walk, III/20.
123. *RV/Arb.* 1938, p. 17f.; *RV/Inf.* 1938, no. 3–4, p. 26.
124. *RV/Arb.* 1938, p. 43ff.; *JWSP,* 1938, p. 17.
125. *Israelitisches Familienblatt,* August 25, 1938.

CHAPTER 4
1939–1943: The Last Chapter

1. *RV/Arb.* 1938, p. 18.
2. Szanto, *Erinnerungen,* p. 221.
3. Walk, II/524, 526.
4. *RV/Arb.* 1938, p. 48ff. The census of May 17, 1939, listed the figure of 233,676 *Rassejuden*; of these 213,930 were classified as *Glaubensjuden* (*DR/Stat.* 1939, p. 84f.); data for September 1939 from an interview with Otto Hirsch, *Jüdisches Nachrichtenblatt,* November 10, 1939. The later figures issued by the Reichsvereinigung are always based on its membership, which necessarily included Christian *Rassejuden* as well as a number of *Mischlinge.* Generally, only the category of *Glaubensjuden* can be used for comparative purposes, but this sometimes results in inaccuracies.
5. According to data of the Reichsvereinigung, YVA, JM/2828, no. 231; Walk, IV/256.

6. Blau, *Juden in Deutschland,* p. 271.
7. Ibid., p. 278.
8. Figures for 1939: Blau, ibid.; figures for 1933: *DR/Stat.* 451/5, p. 17. See Genschel, p. 263.
9. All of the following figures based on Blau, *Juden in Deutschland,* p. 280f.; Genschel, pp. 209, 278f.; Lamm, "Entwicklung," p. 118f.
10. Hanke, pp. 224, 232.
11. Walk, III/228, YVA, 08/106.
12. HStaA Düsseldorf, RW 58, no. 49549.
13. Ibid., no. 13589.
14. Walk, III/211.
15. Following data from Prochnik, pp. 13f., 21f., 24ff.; also Weiss Collection, ALBI/NY, which contains many original circular letters and other original material from the Munich *Gemeinde,* here mainly folder no. 4.
16. Circular letter of the Reichsvereinigung, District Office Bavaria, dated May 26, 1941, Wiener Library, MF (microfilm) 7213. The designation of the offices responsible for executing policy toward the Jews changed from time to time. To avoid confusion, those designations will not be introduced here. In point of fact, it was always the Gestapo that implemented policy.
17. Circular letter, May 14, 1941, ibid.
18. Gehaltsordnung der Reichsvereinigung, May 15, 1941. My thanks to Mr. Efraim Frank, who placed this document at my disposal.
19. Adam, pp. 202, 210f.; Genschel, p. 216f.; Walk, III/82.
20. Circular letter of the Reichsvereinigung, October 20, 1940, ALBI/NY, Weiss Collection, folder no. 4.
21. NG-1143, quoted in Hilberg, p. 98; World Jewish Congress 1943, p. 27.
22. ALBI/Jm, D 29. For Nuremberg, see YVA, 08/23; for Offenbach, YVA, 08/16; for Mainz, YVA, 08/4.
23. The following is based on Drobisch, p. 248ff.; Eschwege, p. 171f.
24. It is clear from the minutes of the meeting of the executive of the Reichsvereinigung on April 8, 1940, that already "conscripted labor via the employment office" was no longer voluntary.
25. Hanke, p. 282ff.
26. Walk, IV/174.
27. Walk, IV/229.
28. Prochnik, p. 2f.
29. Report of the Reichsvereinigung, late January 1942, YVA, JM/2828, p. 152.
30. Following presentation based on Eschwege, p. 171ff.; Rosenfeld, p. 104ff.; E. Freund, in Richarz, vol. 3, p. 374ff.
31. Walk, IV/264.
32. Reichssteuerblatt 1940, no. 85, p. 873.
33. HStaA Düsseldorf, RW 58, no. 5360.
34. Freund, p. 25ff.
35. Wiener Library, P.IIIa, no. 613, 619.
36. Borinski, p. 9. On the *hachshara* teaching farms during the war years, see in particular the description and comments by Ezra Ben-Gerschom (Joel König) quoted on pp. 111–199.

37. On illegal immigration and its support until 1940, see J. Rohwer, "Jüdische Flüchtlingsschiffe im Schwarzen Meer 1933–1944," in U. Büttner, ed., *Das Unrechtsregime: Festschrift für Werner Jochmann,* vol. 2 (Hamburg, 1986), especially pp. 203f., 216ff., 221ff.
38. Efraim Frank was kind enough to place the Paderborn contracts at my disposal. On the *hachshara,* see also Ehud Growald, YVA, 01/241.
39. Walk, IV/481.
40. Walk, III/190; *IMT,* vol. 25, p. 131ff.; Adam, p. 218.
41. YVA, 08/13, p. 100f.
42. Adler, p. 43ff.
43. Walk, IV/122.
44. Hanke, p. 278ff.; Lamm, *Gedenkbuch,* p. 354ff.; Rosenfeld, p. 115ff.
45. Walk, IV/316.
46. Hanke, p. 293f.; Adler, p. 54; Hamburg 1942, p. 112ff.; Blau, in Richarz, vol. 3, p. 470ff.
47. Walk, III/34.
48. Walk, III/37, 43; Adler, p. 42f.
49. Walk, IV/1, 12.
50. Walk, IV/229, 240, 249.
51. On food rations for Jews, see Walk, IV/47, 182, 186, 220, 374, 426, 501; BAK, R 14, no. 274, 159; YVA, 08/13; Prochnik, p. 15f.; ALBI/NY, Weiss Collection, folder no. 2.
52. HStaA Düsseldorf, RW 58, no. 3804, 64554.
53. On clothing restrictions, see Walk, IV/48, 67, 295, 296, 365; YVA, 08/28; ALBI/Jm, D 42.
54. Israelitische Kultusgemeinde, Nüremberg e.V., Wichtige Mitteilungen, no. 9/42, June 18, 1942, YVA, 08/23, p. 30.
55. Ibid., p. 34.
56. On the following prohibitions, see Walk, IV/4, 24, 115, 117, 219, 264, 265, 287, 308, 310, 321, 368, 373, 437; Adler, p. 43f.
57. Prochnik, p. 2f; Hamburg 1941, p. 37; YVA, 08/15; ibid., JM/2828, no. 70–75.
58. YVA, 08/104b, letter dated August 28, 1942.
59. Barkai, "Lodz," p. 302f.
60. Walk, III/20, 211.
61. ALBI/NY, Weiss Collection, Mitteilungen der Jüdischen Kultusgemeinde München, June 22, 1941; Prochnik, p. 9.
62. Walk, IV/376, 386.
63. YVA, 08/24a+b, 08/13; Drobisch, p. 318; Prochnik, p. 17f.
64. Jüdische Kultusgemeinde Berlin, Finanzbericht, December 31, 1941, Wiener Library, W/1b.
65. ALBI/NY, Weiss Collection, Wichtige Mitteilungen Munich, March 28, 1941.
66. Reichsvereinigung, Arbeitsbericht 1939 (probably the last such annual report in this form), Finanzbericht (Anhang) and p. 8; YVA, 08/24b, 08/11; Walk, IV/53.

67. American Federation of Jews from Central Europe Former Communal Property in Germany, A Questionnaire (n.d.).
68. YVA, JM/2828, p. 70ff.
69. Adler, p. 451.
70. Barkai, *Wirtschaftssystem,* pp. 62f., 82ff.
71. Blau, "Last Days," p. 198ff.; Adler, 176ff.; A. Barkai, "German-Speaking Jews in Eastern European Ghettos," *YLBI* 34(1989); 247–266; cf. also Barkai, "Lodz," passim.
72. Toury, "Austreibungsbefehl," p. 439ff.; idem, *Judenaustreibungen*; E. Rosenfeld and G. Luckner, eds., *Lebenszeichen aus Piaski: Briefe Deportierter aus dem Distrikt Lublin 1940–1943* (Munich, 1968).
73. Decree, Interior Minister, Baden, in *Bodensee Rundschau,* April 7, 1941. See also Adler, p. 145ff.; Düwell, p. 260ff.
74. Adler, p. 511.
75. Walk, IV/261; full text: BAK, R 2, appendix 17.
76. Walk, IV/272.
77. Walk, IV/279.
78. Express letter, RFM, December 9, 1941 (0505-98 VI), in URO, p. 277f.
79. Walk, IV/294; Adler, p. 512.
80. Quoted in the memorandum of Mädel cited in detail below, Finanzierung der Massnahmen zur Lösung der Judenfrage, December 14, 1942, BAK, R 2, no. 12222, p. 226ff.
81. Walk, III/46, 227; URO, p. 197; M. Plaut, "Die Juden in Deutschland von 1939 bis 1941," in YVA, 01/53, p. 12f.
82. Copy of an original declaration of assets filled out in April 1942 and in the possession of the author.
83. *IMT,* vol. 26, p. 266f., PS-710.
84. Walk, IV/216.
85. ALBI/Jm, D 33.
86. Adler, p. 524ff.
87. *Jüdisches Nachrichtenblatt,* 5 December 1941, 20 March 1942, 3 April 1942; YVA, 08/24a; Barkai, "Lodz," p. 289.
88. Note of Paul Epstein on conversation in the RHSA, April 27 and 28, 1942, YVA, JM/2828. On transport costs: HStaA Düsseldorf, OFD, Br. 1026/276; BAK, R 139 II/110; Adler, p. 562f.
89. Hamburg 1942, p. 16f.; YVA, 08/17; original copy of a contract to purchase a place in a home, ALBI/NY, AR-C 1676/4185.
90. YVA, JM/2829.
91. Ibid., p. 64ff.
92. Adler, p. 563.
93. Ibid., p. 355.
94. Walk, IV/487.
95. Walk, IV/495; full text: circular RMF, August 3, 1943 (05210–350 VI), URO, p. 337f.
96. See Richarz, vol. 3, p. 441f. (nn. 8, 13); Blau, "Last Days," p. 461f.
97. Adler, p. 630.

Conclusion

1. Walk, I/13.
2. *Der Spiegel,* no. 41, 6 October 1986.

GLOSSARY

ALTREU Allgemeine Treuhandgesellschaft (General Trusteeship Corporation). Special company for capital transfer abroad to countries other than Palestine.

BERUFSBEAMTENGESETZ Civil Service Law, proclaimed in April 1933 as the legal basis for the expulsion of Jewish civil servants, academics, and other professionals.

C.V. Centralverein deutscher Staatsbürger jüdischen Glaubens (Central Association of German Citizens of the Jewish Faith). Large assimilationist organization, its official organ the *C.V. Zeitung*.

DAF Deutsche Arbeitsfront (German Labor Front). Replaced all previous unions. Compulsory membership of all employed personnel. No admittance to Jews.

DEA Cf. Gauwirtschaftsberater.

DER STÜRMER Malicious and vulgar antisemitic weekly edited by Julius Streicher, until 1940 Gauleiter of Franconia.

DEUTSCHNATIONAL German-National, connected with the right-wing, conservative Deutschnationale Volkspartei, part of the first coalition government under Hitler in 1933.

GAULEITER District leader of the NSDAP.

GAUWIRTSCHAFTSBERATER District economic adviser (DEA) of the Gauleiter. Leading Nazi Party official in anti-Jewish economic measures.

GEMEINDE Autonomous, incorporated Jewish local community, to which every Jew who did not officially declare his withdrawal automatically belonged and paid taxes (*Gemeindesteuer*).

HAAVARA Hebrew for "transfer." Scheme for capital transfer to Palestine.

HACHSHARA Hebrew for "training." Agricultural training farm of the Zionist movement.

HILFSVEREIN Hilfsverein der Deutschen Juden (Aid Society for German Jews). Founded in 1901 to provide financial assistance for Jews abroad and transient Jewish migrants. After 1933, its main activity was aiding needy emigrants.

JUDENÄLTESTER Head Jewish functionary in Nazi ghetto, such as Theresienstadt.

JUDENDEZERNAT Department for Jewish Affairs.

JUDENREFERENT Official in charge of Jewish affairs.

JÜDISCHER KULTURBUND Jewish Cultural League. Established in March 1933 in various cities, active until September 1941.

JWH Jüdische Winterhilfe (Jewish Winter Relief).

MISCHLINGE Jews from "mixed marriages" in first or second generation.

NSBO Nationalsozialistische Betriebszellen-Organisation (National Socialist Organization of Factory Cells). Independent Nazi union before 1933, afterward incorporated into DAF.

NSDAP Nationalsozialistische Deutsche Arbeiterpartei (National Socialist German Workers' Party). The full official name of the Nazi party from its founding in 1919.

NS-HAGO Nationalsozialistische Handwerks-, Handels- und Gewerbe-Organisation (National Socialist Organization of Crafts, Commerce and Industry). Main Nazi middle-class interest group, successor of the pre-1933 Kampfbund für den gewerblichen Mittelstand. Incorporated into the DAF in 1933. Most militant instigator of middle-class anti-Jewish boycott activity.

PALTREU Palästina-Treuhandgesellschaft (Palestine Trusteeship Corporation). For capital transfer to Palestine.

RASSENSCHANDE "Racial defilement." Sexual relations between Jews and "Aryans," a penal offense under the Nuremberg Laws of September 1935.

REICHSBÜRGERGESETZ Reich Citizenship Law. Proclaimed in Nuremberg in September 1936, defining the inferior civil status of Jews of German nationality. Most later anti-Jewish legislation was issued in the form of *Verordnungen* (Ordinances) to this law.

REICHSFLUCHTSTEUER Reich Flight Tax. Proclaimed 1931 under the Brüning government to prevent flight of capital from Germany. Implemented by the Nazi government as a means to pilfer the property and assets of emigrating Jews.

REICHSVEREINIGUNG Reichsvereinigung der Juden in Deutschland (Reich Association of Jews in Germany). Compulsory organization of all "Jews by race" (*Rassejuden*), established in February 1939 as successor to the Reichsvertretung and supervised by the Gestapo.

REICHSVERTRETUNG Reichsvertretung der Juden in Deutschland (Reich Representation of German Jews). Organization representing all German Jews, established in the autumn of 1933.

RSHA Reichssicherheitshauptamt. Reich Main Security Office, founded in 1939. Its departments included the IV B4 (specializing in Jewish affairs), the Gestapo, the Criminal Police, and the SD.

SD Sicherheitsdienst (Security Service), unit of the SS, incorporated in 1939 into the RSHA. Its section II/112, which dealt with Jewish affairs, was succeeded by IV B4.

SONDERBEHANDLUNG "Special treatment." The officially used euphemism for extermination of European Jews.

SÜHNELEISTUNG Atonement contribution. Levied as a penalty on all German Jews after the November 1938 pogrom.

WIRTSCHAFTSHILFE Zentralstelle für Jüdische Wirtschaftshilfe (Central Office for Jewish Economic Assistance). Founded in early April 1933 in Berlin.

ZENTRALAUSSCHUSS Zentralausschuss für Hilfe und Aufbau (Central Committee for Relief and Rehabilitation), established early in 1933, and later incorporated into the Reichsvertretung as the main agency for Jewish self-help.

BIBLIOGRAPHY

ADAM: U. D. Adam. *Judenpolitik im Dritten Reich*. Düsseldorf, 1972.

ADLER: H. G. Adler. *Der verwaltete Mensch. Studien zur Deportation der Juden aus Deutschland*. Tübingen, 1974.

ADLER-RUDEL: S. Adler-Rudel. *Jüdische Selbsthilfe unter dem Nazi-Regime 1933–1939*. Tübingen, 1974.

ALBI/JM: Archive, Leo Baeck Institute, Jerusalem.

ALBI/NY: Archive, Leo Baeck Institute, New York.

ANGRESS, *Gross-Breesen:* W. T. Angress. "Auswandererlehrgut Gross-Breesen," *YBLI* 10(1965): 168–187.

ANGRESS, *Jüdische Jugend:* W. T. Angress. *Generation zwischen Furcht und Hoffnung: Jüdische Jugend im Dritten Reich*. Hamburg, 1985.

BAK: Bundesarchiv Koblenz (Federal Archives, Koblenz).

BALL-KADURI: K. J. Ball-Kaduri. *Das Leben der Juden in Deutschland im Jahre 1933: Ein Zeitbericht*. Frankfurt am Main, 1963.

BARKAI, *Aspekte:* A. Barkai. "Sozialgeschichtliche Aspekte der deutschen Judenheit in der Zeit der Industrialisierung." *Jahrbuch des Instituts für deutsche Geschichte* (Tel Aviv) 11(1982): 237–260.

BARKAI, "Industrialisation": A. Barkai. "The German Jews at the Start of Industrialisation—Structural Change and Mobility, 1835–1860." In *Revolution and Evolution: 1848 in German-Jewish History,* edited by W. E. Mosse, A. Paucker, and R. Rürup, Tübingen, 1981.

BARKAI, "Lodz": A. Barkai. "Between East and West: Jews from Germany in the Lodz Ghetto." *Yad Vashem Studies* 16(1984): 271–332.

BARKAI, "Weimar": A. Barkai. "Die Juden als sozio-ökonomische Minderheitsgruppe in der Weimarer Republik." In *Juden in der Weimar Republik,* Beiheft 9, *Jahrbuch des Instituts für deutsche Geschichte,* edited by W. Grab and J. H. Schoeps, 330–346. Stuttgart and Bonn, 1986.

BARKAI, *Wirtschaftssystem:* A. Barkai. *Das Wirtschaftssystem des Nationalsozialismus: Der historische und ideologische Hintergrund 1933–1936*. Cologne, 1977.

BAUER: Y. Bauer. *My Brother's Keeper: A History of the American Joint Distribution Committee 1929–1939*. Philadelphia, 1974.

BENNATHAN: E. Bennathan. "Die demographische und wirtschaftliche Struktur der Juden." In *Entscheidungsjahr 1932: Zur Judenfrage in der Endphase der Weimarer Republik,* edited by W. E. Mosse and A. Paucker, 87–131. Tübingen, 1965.

BERMANN: T. Bermann. *Produktivierungsmythen und Antisemitismus: Eine soziologische Studie*. Vienna, 1973.

BIRNBAUM: M. Birnbaum. *Staat und Synagoge 1918–1938: Eine Geschichte des Preussischen Landesverbandes jüdischer Gemeinden*. Tübingen, 1981.

BLACK: E. Black. *The Transfer Agreement: The Untold Story of the Secret Agreement between the Third Reich and Jewish Palestine*. New York, 1984.

BLAU, *Ausnahmegesetzgebung:* B. Blau. *Die Ausnahmegesetzgebung für die Juden in Deutschland 1933–1945*. Düsseldorf, 1954.

BLAU, *Juden in Deutschland:* B. Blau. "Die Juden in Deutschland von 1939 bis 1945." *Judaica* 7(1951): 270–284.

BLAU, "Last Days": B. Blau. "The Last Days of German Jewry in the Third Reich." *Yivo Annual* 8(1953): 197–204.

BLAU, "Vierzehn Jahre": B. Blau. "Vierzehn Jahre Not und Schrecken." Manuscript in YIVO Institute, New York. Excerpts published in Richarz, 3: 459–475.

BORINSKI: O. Borinski. "Erinnerungen 1940–1943." Yad Vashem Archive, 01/174.

BUCHLOH: I. Buchloh. *Die Nationalsozialistische Machtergreifung in Duisburg*. Duisburg, 1980.

COUNCIL: Council for German Jewry, London. Reports 1935, 1937, 1938.

CZA: Central Zionist Archive, Jerusalem.

DR/STAT. 451/5: *Die Glaubensjuden im Deutschen Reich: Statistik des Deutschen Reichs*. Vol. 451, no. 5, *Die Volks- und Berufszählung vom 16.5.1933*.

DR/STAT. *1939: "Die Juden und jüdischen Mischlinge im Deutschen Reich: Vorläufiges Ergebnis der Volkszählung vom 17.5.1939." Wirtschaft und Statistik* 20 (1940): 84–87.

DROBISCH: K. Drobisch, R. Goguel, and W. Müller. *Juden unterm Hakenkreuz: Verfolgung und Ausrottung der deutschen Juden*. Frankfurt am Main, 1973.

DÜWELL: K. Düwell. *Die Rheingebiete in der Judenpolitik des Nationalsozialismus vor 1942*. Bonn, 1967.

ESCHWEGE: H. Eschwege. "Resistance of German Jews against the Nazi Regime." *YLBI,* 15(1970): 143–180.

FREUND: E. Freund. "Zwangsarbeit für Hitler." Manuscript in ALBI/NY. Published in part in Richarz, vol. 3, pp. 374–386.

GENSCHEL: H. Genschel. *Die Verdrängung der Juden aus der Wirtschaft im Dritten Reich*. Göttingen, 1966.

GSTAA DAHLEM: Geheimes Staatsarchiv (Secret State Archive), Dahlem, Preussischer Kulturbesitz.

HAAVARA-TRANSFER: W. Feilchenfeld, D. Michaelis, and L. Pinner. *Haavara-Transfer nach Palästina und Einwanderung deutscher Juden 1933–1939*. Tübingen, 1972.

HAMBURG 1941: "Ein Beitrag zur Geschichte der Deutsch-Israelitischen Gemeinde in Hamburg vom Herbst 1935 bis Mai 1941." YVA 08/76.

HAMBURG 1942: "Der jüdische Religionsverband Hamburg im Jahre 1942: Die Liquidation der jüdischen Stiftungen und Vereine in Hamburg." Wiener Library, W1c/K4b.

HANKE: P. Hanke. *Zur Geschichte der Juden in München zwischen 1933 und 1945*. Munich, 1967.

HERZFELD: E. Herzfeld. "Meine letzten Jahre in Deutschland 1933–1938." Manuscript in ALBI/NY and YVA, 01/8. Excerpts published in Ball-Kaduri and in Richarz, vol. 3, pp. 301–312.

HILBERG: R. Hilberg. *The Destruction of the European Jews*. Chicago, 1967.

HSTAA DÜSSELDORF: Rheinland-Westfälisches Hauptstaatsarchiv, Düsseldorf.

IFZ: Institut für Zeitgeschichte (Institute for Contemporary History), Munich.

IMT: *Internationaler Militärgerichtshof: Der Prozess gegen die Hauptkriegsverbrecher, Nürnberg 14.Nov.1945 bis 1.Okt.1946* (International Military Tribunal). 42 vols. Nuremberg, 1948.

JOINT 1936: American Joint Distribution Committee (JDC), European Executive Office, Paris. *Jewish Constructive Work in Germany During 1936*. Paris, 1937.

JOINT 1937: American Joint Distribution Committee. *Activities of the Zentralausschuss of the Reichsvertretung der Juden in Deutschland: January 1st to June 30th*. Paris, October 1937.

JÜDISCHE EMIGRATION: *Die jüdische Emigration aus Deutschland 1933–1941: Die Geschichte einer Austreibung*. Exhibition of the Deutsche Bibliothek, Frankfurt am Main, in cooperation with the Leo Baeck Institute. New York and Frankfurt am Main, 1985.

JWSP: *Jüdische Wohlfahrtspflege und Sozialpolitik*.

KAHN, "Einzelhandel": H. Kahn. "Umfang und Bedeutung der jüdischen Einzelhandelsbetriebe innerhalb des gesamten deutschen Einzelhandels: Hauptergebnisse einer wissenschaftlichen Untersuchung auf Grund einer Erhebung in 69 Grossgemeinden," Berlin, February 1934.

KAHN, "Handwerk": H. Kahn. "Das jüdische Handwerk in Deutschland: Eine Untersuchung auf Grund statistischer Unterlagen der Reichsvertretung der Juden in Deutschland." Berlin, 1936. Mimeo.

KAHN, "Schichtung": H. Kahn. "Die wirtschaftliche und soziale Schichtung der Juden in Deutschland." *JWSP* (1936): 5–22, 51–65.

KAPLAN: M. Kaplan. *The Jewish Feminist Movement in Germany: The Campaigns of the Jüdischer Frauenbund 1904–1938*. Westport, Conn., and London, 1979.

KNIPPING: U. Knipping. *Die Geschichte der Juden in Dortmund während der Zeit des Dritten Reichs*. Dortmund, 1977.

KOCHAN: L. Kochan. *Pogrom, 10. November 1938*. London, 1957.

KÖNIG: J. König (E. Ben Gershom). *David: Aufzeichnungen eines Überlebenden*. 1967. Reprint. Frankfurt am Main, 1979.

KRAUSNICK: H. Krausnick. "Judenverfolgung." In *Anatomie des SS-Staates*, edited by H. Buchheim et al. Vol. 2. Olten and Freiburg i.Br., 1965.

LAMM, "Entwicklung": H. Lamm. "Über die innere und äussere Entwicklung des deutschen Judentums im Dritten Reich." Diss., Erlangen, 1951.

LAMM, *Gedenkbuch:* H. Lamm. *Von Juden in München: Ein Gedenkbuch*. Munich, 1958.

LEIBFRIED: S. Leibfried. "Stationen der Abwehr. Berufsverbote für Ärzte im Deutschen Reich 1933–1938 und die Zerstörung des sozialen Asyls durch die organisierten Ärzteschaften des Auslands." *Bulletin des Leo Baeck Instituts* 62(1982): 3–39.

LESTSCHINSKY, *Schicksal:* J. Lestschinsky. *Das wirtschaftliche Schicksal des deutschen Judentums*. Berlin, 1932.

LESTSCHINSKY, *Zusammenbruch:* J. Lestschinsky. *Der wirtschaftliche Zusammenbruch der Juden in Deutschland und Polen*. Paris and Geneva, 1936.

LOWENSTEIN, "Modernisation": S. M. Lowenstein, "The Pace of Modernisation of German Jewry in the Nineteenth Century." *YLBI* 21(1976): 41–54.

LOWENSTEIN, "Rural Community": S. M. Lowenstein. "The Rural Community and the Urbanization of German Jewry." *Central European History* 13(1980): 218–236.

MARCUS, *Krise:* M. Marcus. *Die wirtschaftliche Krise der deutschen Juden*. Berlin, 1931.

MARCUS, "Lage": A Marcus. "Zur wirtschaftlichen Lage und Haltung der deutschen Juden." *Bulletin des Leo Baeck Instituts* 55(1979): 16–34. Originally written in 1933 as a festschrift for Leo Baeck that was not published.

MARGALIOTH, "Emigration": A. Margalioth. "Emigration—Planung und Wirklichkeit." In *Die Juden im nationalsozialistischen Deutschland 1933–1943,* edited by A. Paucker et al., 306–316. Tübingen, 1986.

MARGALIOTH, "Occupational Restructuring": A. Margalioth. "Sheelat ha-hasavah ha-miktsoit ve-ha-produktivizatsyah ke-moked dium be-kerev yehudei Germanyah bi-tehilat ha-reich ha-shlishi," *Yalkut moreshet* 29(1980): 99–120.

MARGALIOTH, "Reaction": A. Margalioth. "The Reaction of the Jewish Public in Germany to the Nuremberg Laws." *YVS* 12(1977): 75–107.

MARGALIOTH, "Rescue": A. Margalioth. "The Problem of the Rescue of German Jewry during the Years 1933–1939." In *Rescue Attempts during the Holocaust,* pp. 247–265. 2nd Yad Vashem International Historical Conferences, Jerusalem, 1977.

MARGALIOTH, "Tendencies": A. Margalioth. "Megamot u-derakhim be-maavak ha-kalkali shel yahadut Germanyah bi-tekufat ha-redifot ha-giziot." *Uma Vetoldothe'a* (Jerusalem), 1984, pp. 339–355.

MAURER: T. Maurer. "Ausländische Juden in Deutschland, 1933–1939." In *Die Juden im nationalsozialistischen Deutschland 1933–1943,* edited by A. Paucker et al. 189–210. Tübingen, 1986.

MARTIN: B. Martin. "Judenverfolgung und -vernichtung unter der nationalsozialistischen Diktatur." In *Die Juden als Minderhelt in der Geschichte,* edited by B. Martin and E. Schulin, 290–315. Munich, 1981.

MARTIN-SCHULIN: B. Martin and E. Schulin, eds. *Die Juden als Minderheit in der Geschichte*. Munich, 1981.

MOSES: S. Moses. "Salman Schocken—His Economic and Zionist Activities." *YLBI* 5(1960): 73–104.

MUELLERHEIM: M. Muellerheim. *Die gesetzlichen und aussergesetzlichen Massnahmen zur wirtschaftlichen Vernichtung der Juden in Deutschland.* Presented by the Jewish Trust Corporation for Germany, n.d.

NIEWYK, "Impact": D. L. Niewyk. "The Impact of Inflation and Depression on the German Jews." *YBLI* 28(1983): 19–36.

NIEWYK, *Weimar:* D. L. Niewyk. *The Jews in Weimar Germany.* Baton Rouge, La., and London, 1980.

PÄTZOLD, *Faschismus:* K. Pätzold. *Faschismus, Rassenwahn, Judenverfolgung, 1930–1935.* Berlin (DDR), 1975.

PÄTZOLD, *Verfolgung:* K. Pätzold. *Verfolgung, Vertreibung, Vernichtung: Dokumente des faschistischen Antisemitismus 1933 bis 1942.* Frankfurt am Main, 1984.

PHIEBIG 1936: A. J. Phiebig. "Die Bedeutung der Volkszählungsergebnisse von 1933 für die jüdische Sozialarbeit. *JWSP,* 1936, pp. 23–28.

PHIEBIG 1938: A. J. Phiebig. "Statistische Tabellen." In *Almanach des Schocken Verlag auf das Jahr 5699,* Berlin, 1938, p. 137ff.

PRINZ: A. Prinz. *Juden im deutschen Wirtschaftsleben 1815–1914,* edited by A. Barkai. Tübingen, 1984.

PROCHNIK: R. Prochnik. "Bericht über die organisatorischen und sonstigen Verhältnisse der jüdischen Bevölkerung in Berlin unter Berücksichtigung des gesamten Altreichs." Vienna, August 1941. Mimeographed manuscript in ALBI/Jm.

RICHARZ, vol. 3: M. Richarz, ed. *Jüdisches Leben in Deutschland: Selbstzeugnisse zur Sozialgeschichte 1918–1945.* Stuttgart, 1982.

ROSENBAUM: E. Rosenbaum. "M. M. Warburg & Co. Merchant Bankers of Hamburg: A Survey of the First 140 Years, 1798 to 1938." *YLBI* 7(1962): 121–149.

ROSENFELD: E. Behrend-Rosenfeld. *Ich stand nicht allein: Erlebnisse einer Jüdin in Deutschland 1933–1944.* 1949. Reprint. Frankfurt am Main, 1963.

ROSENSTOCK: W. Rosenstock. "Exodus 1933–1939: A Survey of Jewish Emigration from Germany." *YLBI* 1(1956): 373–390.

RV/ARB: *Reichsvertretung der Juden in Deutschland: Jahresbericht* (with corresponding year); until 1935: *Jahresberichte des Zentralausschusses für Hilfe und Ausbau bei der Reichsvertretung.*

RV/INF.: *Informationsblätter der Reichsvertretung der Juden in Deutschland.*

SCHAEFFER: Collection Hans Schaeffer, ALBI/NY.

SCHEFFLER: W. Scheffler. *Judenverfolgung im Dritten Reich.* Berlin, 1964.

SCHLEUNES: K. A. Schleunes. *The Twisted Road to Auschwitz: Nazi Policy toward German Jews 1933–1939.* Urbana, Ill., Chicago, and London, 1970.

SCHMELZ: U. O. Schmelz. "Die demographische Entwicklung der Juden in Deutschland von der Mitte des 19. Jahrhunderts bis 1933." *Zeitschrift für Bevölkerungswissenschaft* 8(1) (1982): 31–72.

SHERMAN: A. J. Sherman. "A Jewish Bank during the Schacht Era: M. M. Warburg & Co., 1933–1938." In *Die Juden im nationalsozialistischen Deutschland 1933–1943,* edited by A. Paucker et al., 167–172. Tübingen, 1986.

SILBERGLEIT: H. Silbergleit. *Die Bevölkerungs- und Berufsverhältnisse der Juden im Deutschen Reich: Vol. 1. Freistaat Preussen*. Berlin, 1930.

STA DUISBURG: Stadtarchiv Duisburg.

STAA MÜNSTER: Rheinland-Westfälisches Staatsarchiv Münster.

STRAUSS 1980, 1981: H. Strauss. "Jewish Emigration from Germany: Nazi Policies and Jewish Responses." Parts 1, 2, *YLBI* 25(1980): 313–358; 26(1981): 343–409.

SZANTO, "Economic Aid": A. Szanto. "Economic Aid in the Nazi Era: The Work of the Berlin Wirtschaftshilfe." *YLBI* 4(1959): 208–219.

SZANTO, *Erinnerungen:* A. Szanto. "Im Dienste der Gemeinde 1923–1939." Manuscript, ALBI/NY, Excerpts in Richarz, vol. 3, pp. 217–227.

TOURY, "Austreibungsbefehl": J. Toury. "Die Entstehungsgeschichte des Austriebungsbefehls gegen die Juden der Saarpfalz und Badens (22./23. Oktober 1940—Camp de Gurs)." *Jahrbuch des Instituts für deutsche Geschichte* (Tel Aviv) 15(1986): 431–464.

TOURY, *Geschichte:* J. Toury. *Soziale und politische Geschichte der Juden in Deutschland 1847–1871*. Düsseldorf, 1977.

TOURY, *Judenaustreibungen:* J. Toury. "Ein Auftakt zur 'Endlösung': Judenaustreibungen über nichtslawische Reichsgrenzen 1933–1939." In *Das Unrechtsregime: Festschrift für Werner Jochmann,* edited by U. Büttner, vol. 2, pp. 164–196. Hamburg, 1986.

TOURY, *Textilunternehmer.* J. Toury. *Jüdische Textilunternehmer in Baden-Württemberg 1683–1938*. Tübingen, 1984.

UHLIG: H. Uhlig. *Die Warenhäuser im Dritten Reich*. Düsseldorf, 1972.

URO: United Restitution Organization. *Die Ausnahmegesetzgebung gegen die Juden im Reich, den eingegliederten und besetzten Gebieten sowie den im Einflussgebiet liegenden abhängigen Ländern, unter besonderer Berücksichtigung der wirtschaftlichen Diskriminierung 1933–1945,* vol. 1. Frankfurt am Main, n.d.

VFZ: *Vierteljahreshefte für Zeitgeschichte*. Stuttgart.

WALK: J. Walk, ed. *Das Sonderrecht für die Juden im NS-Staat: Eine Sammlung der gesetzlichen Massnahmen und Richtlinien—Inhalt und Bedeutung*. Karlsruhe, 1981.

WOLLHEIM: N. Wollheim. Tape-recorded conversation with Dr. A. Margalioth. Collection of contemporary oral records, Institute of Contemporary Jewry, Hebrew University Jerusalem, no. 2098 a + b.

WORLD JEWISH CONGRESS 1937: *Der wirtschaftliche Vernichtungskampf gegen die Juden im Dritten Reich,* Jüdischer Weltkongress (World Jewish Congress). Paris, Geneva, and New York, 1937.

WORLD JEWISH CONGRESS 1943: Institute of Jewish Affairs of the American Jewish Congress and World Jewish Congress. *Hitler's Ten-Year War on the Jews*. New York, 1943.

YLBI: *Yearbook of the Leo Baeck Institute*. Jerusalem.

YVA: Yad Vashem Archive, Jerusalem.

YVS: *Yad Vashem Studies*.

INDEX